A Manner of Correspondence
A Study of the Scriblerus Club

A Manner of Correspondence examines one of the most interesting of literary clubs – the Scriblerus Club – whose members were Jonathan Swift, Alexander Pope, John Gay, John Arbuthnot, Thomas Parnell, and Robert Harley, Earl of Oxford. Patricia Brückmann shows that the Scriblerians were bound by correspondent values, complementary talents, and a united satiric program.

Tracing their shared vision in such works as *Memoirs of Scriblerus, Travels into Several Remote Nations of the World, The Beggar's Opera*, and *The Dunciad*, Brückmann identifies the pastoral as their common ideal and analyses their shared hostilities and anxieties regarding the erosion of that ideal in an age they saw as grotesquely degenerate. She points out that in many ways the group was out of step with its own time and much more attuned to ancient and traditional images of felicity and to ancient authors who subscribed to these values. The influence of Erasmus and Sir Thomas More, who both figure as icons in the Scriblerians' work, as well as such authors as Seneca, Lucian, Lucius Apuleius, and François Rabelais is explored in detail.

Brückmann highlights the Scriblerian influence on writers such as Henry Fielding, Lawrence Sterne, Vladimir Nabokov, John Barth, Robert Coover, and James Joyce, offering a place for dialogue between modern humanists and their eighteenth-century forebears.

PATRICIA C. BRÜCKMANN is professor of English, University of Toronto.

A Manner of Correspondence

A Study of the Scriblerus Club

PATRICIA CARR BRÜCKMANN

McGill-Queen's University Press
Montreal & Kingston · London · Buffalo

© McGill-Queen's University Press 1997
ISBN 0-7735-1546-1

Legal deposit second quarter 1997
Bibliothèque nationale du Québec

Printed in the United States on acid-free paper

This book has been published with the help of a grant from the Humanities and Social Sciences Federation of Canada, using funds provided by the Social Sciences and Humanities Research Council of Canada.

Canadian Cataloguing in Publication Data

Brückmann, Patricia Carr, 1932–
   A manner of correspondence : a study of the Scriblerus Club
   Includes bibliographical references and index.
   ISBN 0-7735-1546-1
   1. Scriblerus Club. 2. Satire, English – History and criticism.
3. English literature – 18th century – History and criticism.
1. Title.
PR441.B78 1997   827'.509   C97-900143-9

Typeset in Adobe Garamond 11/13
by Caractéra inc., Quebec City

To Peter and Elisabeth Brückmann

Contents

Acknowledgments ix

Works Frequently Cited xi

Preamble 3

1 The Province of the Friend 7
2 Gardens and Parks 19
3 Monsters and Metropolis 59
4 Scriblerian Fictions 99

Notes 137

Bibliography 151

Index 179

Acknowledgments

I owe two large debts, to my students and to my own teachers. Among the former group, who were part of the graduate seminars I taught on Pope, on the Scriblerus Club, and on the eighteenth-century novel are Ian Alexander, Reginald Berry, Martha Bowden, Brian Boyd, Kristin Brady, Nanette Clinch, David Dowling, Christopher Fanning, Marjorie Garson, Alan Hertz, Gerald Hopson, Joe Jones, Vanessa Kelly, Anne McWhir, David Oakleaf, Carl Palm, Diana Patterson, Janōs Svilpis, Kathryn Walls, Ava Weinberger, and David Wright.

Among the latter is my tutor at Trinity College, Washington DC, Margaret Giovaninni. For my special interest in the eighteenth century I am indebted beyond account to Kenneth MacLean, who, in his 1936 study of Locke, first described the Age of Reason as the Age of Passion. His seminar introduced me to an eighteenth century I did not know and made me wish to make it my own. Marshall McLuhan, almost unknowingly, gave help in long conversations. I should not have been surprised to discover how influential he had been in new perspectives on the eighteenth century. One day his unpublished Cambridge dissertation will, I hope, be in print and show how extensively he knew the period and how vividly he responded to it in days when reading the eighteenth century was not yet fashionable. My largest intellectual debt is to Arthur Edward Barker. I suppose that the notion of seeing the Scriblerians as a group emerged from his graduate seminar in Renaissance English Humanism, where we read More, Erasmus, and their friends, individually and in concert. I cannot adequately record my obligation to our letters and familiar colloquies; there was and is a manner of correspondence between us, wherever we are.

John Brückmann, George Falle, Roma Januszewska, James A. Philip, and Harriet White listened to me talk about the Scriblerus Club and were almost always helpful. Jocelyn Harris invited me to the Seventh Nichol Smith Seminar at the University of Otago in 1986 to give a paper on Scriblerus. I am grateful to the members of her seminar for turning some of my darkness into light and for lending, in their papers, particular light of their own, especially W.B. Carnochan, Margaret Anne Doody, Michael Neill, and Howard D. Weinbrot. Robert P. Maccubbin read and patiently edited the manuscript of my Nichol Smith paper for *Eighteenth-Century Life*.

I am particularly grateful to those who read the text of this book – Brian Corman, Frederick T. Flahiff, and Milton Wilson. Peter Walmsley read it more times than a generous friend should ever offer to do, always giving tactful improvement, especially, but not exclusively, for presentation. Readers for the Canadian Federation for the Humanities gave very helpful commentary and many suggestions for improvement of the text. Susan Kent Davidson copy-edited with exceptional care. The Social Sciences and Humanities Research Council of Canada generously funded research time, as has the Office of Research Administration at the University of Toronto. Trinity College provided funds for travel abroad and for two research assistants over summers. These are Neil Guthrie and Karen Bamford. Elisabeth Brückmann acted as assistant and editor for a summer, later checked bibliographical references, and provided fierce encouragement. Peter Brückmann gave support of an intangible but quite indispensable kind.

Trinity College, Toronto
October 1996

Works Frequently Cited

Arbuthnot, John. *The History of John Bull.* Ed. A.W. Bower and R.E. Erickson. Oxford: Clarendon Press 1976. *Cited by page.*
– *Miscellaneous Works of the late Dr. Arbuthnot.* 2 vols. London 1770. *Cited by volume and page.*
Bolingbroke, Henry St John. *The Works of Lord Bolingbroke.* 4 vols. Philadelphia: Carey and Hart 1841. *Cited by volume and page.*
Dryden, John. *The Poems of John Dryden.* Ed. James Kinsley. 4 vols. Oxford: Clarendon Press 1958. *Cited by volume and page.*
Fielding, Henry. *The History of Joseph Andrews.* Ed. Martin C. Battestin. The Wesleyan Edition. Oxford: Clarendon Press 1967. *Cited by book, chapter, and page.*
– *The History of Tom Jones, A Foundling.* Ed. Fredson Bowers, with introduction and commentary by Martin C. Battestin. The Wesleyan Edition. 2 vols. Oxford: Clarendon Press 1974. *Cited by book, chapter, and page.*
Gay, John. *Dramatic Works.* Ed. John Fuller. 2 vols. Oxford: Oxford University Press 1983. *Plays cited by act, scene, and line, prefaces by volume and page.*
– *The Letters.* Ed. C.F. Burgess. Oxford: Clarendon Press 1966. *Cited by page.*
– *Poetry and Prose.* Ed. Vinton A. Dearing, with the assistance of Charles E. Beckwith. 2 vols. Oxford: Clarendon Press 1974. *Cited by volume and line or page.*

The Memoirs of the Extraordinary Life, Works, and Discoveries of Martinus Scriblerus. Ed. Charles Kerby-Miller. New Haven, Conn.: Yale University Press 1950, 1966. *Cited by page.*

Parnell, Thomas. *Collected Poems of Thomas Parnell*. Ed. Claude Rawson and F.P. Lock. Newark: University of Delaware Press 1987. *Cited by line and page.*

Pope, Alexander. *The Correspondence of Alexander Pope.* 5 vols. Ed. George Sherburn. Oxford: Clarendon Press 1956. *Cited by volume and page.*

– *The Prose Works of Alexander Pope.* 1. *The Earlier Works, 1711–1720.* Ed. Norman Ault. Oxford: Blackwell 1936. 2. *The Major Works, 1725–1744.* Ed. Rosemary Cowler. Hamden, Conn.: Archon 1986. *Cited by volume and page.*

– *The Twickenham Edition of the Poems of Alexander Pope.* Ed. John Butt *et al.* 11 vols. in 12. London: Methuen, and New Haven: Yale University Press 1939–69. *Cited by volume and line or page.*

Spectator. Ed. Donald F. Bond. 5 vols. Oxford: Clarendon Press 1965. *Cited by volume, number, and page.*

Spence, Joseph. *Observations, Anecdotes and Characters of Books and Men.* Ed. James M. Osborn. 2 vols. Oxford: Clarendon Press 1966. *Cited by volume and page.*

Sterne, Laurence. *The Life and Opinions of Tristram Shandy, Gentleman.* Ed. Melvyn New and Joan New. 3 vols. Gainesville: University Presses of Florida 1978. *Cited by volume, chapter, and page.*

Swift, Jonathan. *The Correspondence of Jonathan Swift.* Ed. Harold Williams. 5 vols. Oxford: Clarendon Press 1963–65. *Cited by volume and page.*

– *The Poems.* 3 vols. Ed. Harold Williams. Oxford: Clarendon Press 1958. *Cited by volume and line.*

– *Prose Writings.* Ed. Herbert Davis. 14 vols. Oxford: Blackwell 1939–68. *Cited by volume and page.*

– *A Tale of a Tub, to which is added The Battle of the Books and the Mechanical Operation of the Spirit.* Ed. A.C. Guthkelch and D. Nichol Smith. 2nd ed. Oxford: Clarendon Press 1958. All references to *A Tale* are from this edition and are *cited by page.*

The use of double-year dates for days from 1 January to 24 March was standard practice before 1751. The correspondence of Gay, Pope, and Swift cited here follows the scholarly editions in this practice.

A Manner of Correspondence

Preamble

This book has grown from a reading of Pope, Swift, Gay, Arbuthnot, and Parnell as a group – as members of the Club called Scriblerus. Charles Kerby-Miller's learned edition of *The Memoirs of Martinus Scriblerus*, their principal project as a group, gives an account of the background of the Club (1–22). Swift is perhaps most properly described as the founder, at least in so far as the group that finally emerged in 1714 came from his desire for a congenial society of friends with common and preferably literary interests. His first attempt at such a society, the Saturday Club, with himself, Harcourt, Harley, and Bolingbroke as members, lasted only briefly. Its successor, the Brothers Club, where he hoped to launch an Academy, had a distinguished membership but was too large for conviviality. At this point Pope entered the scene with a project for a publication of the works of the unlearned, as a parody of the monthly *Works of the Learned*, an abstract of scholarly contribution. With the addition of Arbuthnot and Parnell, Swift's contemporaries, and Gay, like Pope, from a younger generation, the number was about right and the end specifically literary, although literary concerns in the eighteenth century were always intertwined with political and religious matters. Although his talents as an author were slight, Harley's presence kept the group anchored in the political world.

The Scriblerians met for only a short period in 1714, in Arbuthnot's rooms at St James's Palace, before Queen Anne's death brought down the Tory ministry and dispersed the group. Its members, however, stayed in touch, principally through letters, for the rest of their lives. Given their contentious and rivalrous personalities, it is just possible that a continuation of real meetings might have split them apart, but that can only be conjecture. Their "great work" as a group was to be the memoirs of a universal pedant, corrupted by mechanical education and dedicated to curiosity rather than to wisdom. Martinus Scriblerus would not have been out of place in a document like Erasmus's *Praise of Folly*, a text the Scriblerians knew well. Few read the wildly funny *Memoirs*, but its spin-offs, *The Dunciad*, the *Beggar's Opera*, and the work miscalled *Gulliver's Travels*, are central eighteenth-century satiric texts.

The first question to be asked about the Club is what sort of common spirit brought its members together and kept them so for the rest of their lives? The group was in many ways out of step with its own time and much more attuned to ancient and traditional images of felicity and to ancient authors who subscribed to these values, as well as to a satiric spirit and method to be displayed when these values were menaced. I have alluded to Erasmus. In many ways Scriblerus resembles, both as a group and in some of its ideals, the conversations and projects of Erasmus and More, both of whom figure as icons in their works. All looked back to authors like Seneca, Lucian and Apuleius, and Rabelais. If the spirit of Erasmus helped to form the genius of Cervantes, it came in part to the Scriblerians through the author of *Don Quixote*.

The Scriblerian ideal most often takes the form of some version of pastoral. By pastoral I do not mean the poems Samuel Johnson later described as easy, vulgar, and therefore disgusting but rather a vision of civilized harmony, often rendered in the imagery of garden. This positive image was, they thought, perpetually threatened by the monstrous corruption of uncivilized cities and the consequent threat of ruination or loss of a possible earthly paradise. It was important that this ideal be articulated and sustained in the world, for it seems clear, to me at least, if not always to others who write about individual authors in the group, that the members of the Scriblerus Club, even those in holy orders, were by no means persuaded that they would find a paradise elsewhere. Their sensibilities are in every way secular.

Scriblerian writing, precisely as a consequence of Scriblerian distress and desperation, never fully realizes a fictional world. Their work is typically fragmentary and, as such, possibly distressing in its own way to readers in search of clearly articulate wholes. It is often reminiscent, overtly or covertly, of other earlier traditions of learned wit and comedy, of Seneca's *Apokolokyntosis*, Lucian's *True History*, *Gargantua and Pantagruel*, *Don Quixote*, *The Praise of Folly*, the *Utopia*. Later writers in their own century who are also in some sense Scriblerian, and hence helpful in reading them, are Fielding – in his novels as well as in the plays he signed, wishing to be counted among writers he recognized as cousins german, as Scriblerus Secundus – and Sterne, whose *Tristram Shandy* was recognized by at least one early writer as close in subject and tone to *The Memoirs of Martinus Scriblerus*. Fielding, of course, was not really Scriblerian in the ways in which I should describe their sensibility, notably after he moved from the stage to the novel. And Sterne is probably too cheerful. Shandeism, zany as it is, is not the same as the extravagant conceptions and deceptions of Scriblerus at his best. But the two styles have something in common that can be helpful in establishing what the creators of Martinus did. Their appeal, like the appeal of all literature that demands active participation from readers, has obvious limitations. It is unabashedly elitist, often offensive in tone, and perpetually insistent that readers pay attention, not to a plot, because mainly there are no plots, but rather to every kind of detail within the main text and to apparently ancillary materials around the text – glosses, mock notes, and even apparently gratuitous indexes. My study tries to describe Scriblerian ideals and Scriblerian anxieties, to trace out some parallels and influences, and finally to suggest how these ideals and anxieties shaped their writing.

Characters who frequented Button's coffeehouse, c. 1720. Engraving by William Hogarth

1 The Province of the Friend

No one currently working on individual members of the Scriblerus Club can complain of inadequate editorial and critical work for their subject. The Twickenham edition of Pope is now well over thirty years old, as is Sherburn's edition of the correspondence. The Oxford Swift is nearly as old and is supplemented by the five volumes of letters. A scholarly edition of Gay's plays appeared in 1983. Burgess provided the letters long ago, and in 1974 Beckwith and Dearing gave all the rest. Partially because of the pioneering work of Patricia Köster in the fifties, Erickson and Bower have been able to produce an elaborately annotated edition of *The History of John Bull*. Köster has continued to bring out some of Arbuthnot's shorter pieces in places like the Augustan Reprint Society. The esteem in which Arbuthnot was held by his contemporaries, as well as by his brothers in Scriblerus, ought to argue for a reissue of his less well-known works, like the *Argument for Providence* and the sensible essays on diet and health. Claude J. Rawson's edition of Parnell, co-edited by F.P. Lock, now makes the least-known member of the group available. While Gay needs a biographer to update W.H. Irving, Ehrenpreis on Swift will continue to be standard, although modified in perception by the more recent work of David Nokes. We have had Maynard Mack on Pope since 1985.

And there are critical studies of every kind, from those that pursue the whole man in his work, through themes and style, to articles in interpretation and annotation. All this has been immeasurably helped by the renaissance of interest in both the English eighteenth century and in the Enlightenment more generally, so that the creators of the classics of our prose, those cousins who would never be poets, have been increasingly found exciting writers on their own, masters of the formal rhetoric of whose turns we are now able to speak with some precision. Far from sitting tenants in a world of sweet reason, these are now more often perceived as dwellers in a universe where the shades of Bedlam fell across the enlightened, casting a double darkness across an age when the new philosophy had long since called all in doubt and no comfortable new theology had come to replace it.

This is a world hospitable to the newest criticism too, for the language of madness works easily with the language of carnival, and the uncertainties about language with a sense of a text working on its own. The perceptions of writers like Donald Greene, Kenneth MacLean, Jean Hagstrum, Martin Price, Maynard Mack, Claude J. Rawson, Howard D. Weinbrot, and W.K. Wimsatt, Jr, to add only a few to those who edit and write biography, have made Pope, Swift, Gay, Arbuthnot, and Parnell accessible to twentieth-century readers as they were not some years ago. Because of their tracks, there will be many others to follow, to extend our sense of the text, its context, even perhaps its intertexuality. The moderns meet the ancients when we discover Jacques Derrida's "Scribble" and his fascination with *The Divine Legation of Moses*, that long work in part about language that Warburton wrote in Somerset at Prior Park while Pope worked there on the fourth book of *The Dunciad*.[1]

Although it would be foolish to argue that one cannot read one of these authors without the others, it is true that they saw themselves as a group. Those works for which they are most recalled by the common reader – *Travels into Several Remote Nations of the World*, *The Dunciad*, and *The Beggar's Opera* – are works that come from the group, fragments of their grand design, the hilarious and almost totally neglected *Memoirs of Martinus Scriblerus*. Indeed the common reader would have no difficulty in recognizing the validity of Swift's sense that these three works were in a real way not simply from the group but representative of a competition within it, an example of what Howard D. Weinbrot has described as a central feature of eighteenth-century aesthetics, an emulation to excel. On 28 March 1728 Swift writes to Gay to say that "The Beggers Opera hath knockt down Gulliver" and that he hopes "to see Popes Dullness knock down the Beggers Opera" (3.278).[2] Legend has it, of course, that the *Opera* itself came from Swift's hint that Gay might try a "Newgate pastoral," having already written (in 1714) his *Shepherd's Week* as a contribution to the pastoral war being waged between Pope and Ambrose Philips, or, more accurately, between Pope and Addison's wits of the Little Senate. This skirmish in itself was a continuation, in familiar dress, of the *Battle of the Books*, part of Swift's contribution to the war of the Ancients and the Moderns.

But there was more friendship than competition. Having already dedicated *Rural Sports* to Pope, Gay dedicated *The Shepherd's Week* to Henry St John. Bolingbroke was never a formal member of the Club but was, perhaps, as Isaac Kramnick argued in 1967, its ideological centre. His presence shapes *An Essay on Man*, although not, I think, quite in the philosophical ways in which this influence is usually described. Bolingbroke set Pope to imitate Horace; Pope dedicates *The Dunciad* to Swift. Writing to Swift on 9 October 1729 (3.57), Pope said that his "principal aim in the entire work [is] to perpetuate the friendship between us, and to shew that the friends or the enemies of one were the friends or enemies of the other: If in any particular, any thing be stated or mention'd in a different manner from what you like, pray tell me freely, that the new Editions now coming out here, may have it rectify'd." Later, in 1737 (31 May, 5.41), Swift complains to Pope that he has "a pretence to quarrel with you, because I am not at the head of any one of your Epistles." In a letter to Charles Ford (6 Jan. 1718/ 19, 2.310) Swift remarks, after the death of the Dean of Clogher, that Pope now "should bestow a few Verses on his friend Parnels memory." Pope dedicated the *Iliad* translation to Congreve, as "a Memorial of ... Friendship" (*Iliad*, 8.578), but he pays tribute to Parnell, as his labours warranted, by thanking the late archdeacon for his essay on Homer, adding: "How very much that Gentleman's Friendship prevail'd over his Genius, in detaining a Writer of his Spirit in the Drudgery of removing the Rubbish of past Pedants, will soon appear to the World, when they shall see those beautiful Pieces of Poetry the Publication of which he left to my Charge, almost with his dying Breath" (8.578).

Pope's editorial choices in the *Poems on Several Occasions* (1722), to which he here alludes, give his personal view of his friend's work. He does not print the scriptural paraphrases and other solemnities.[3] What emerges in Pope's edition is a poet closer to the comic world of the Scriblerians. Even as he fashioned his public self, in verse and in the images he presented to painters, Pope also had an image of what he wanted Scriblerus and its members to be.

Swift's sense of the group and its obligations, one to another, was particularly strong, precisely because he found in it the intense associations and resonances of thought that he had not found in the earlier societies to which he belonged before Scriblerus was founded.[4] Swift's correspondence with Lord Oxford in 1724 (9 July 1724, 3.8–19), Oxford's reply (2 Nov. 1724, 3.38–9), and Swift's response (27 Nov. 1724, 3.39–41) are perhaps the most vivid demonstrations of his nearly desperate reliance on the group. Oxford had not sent his portrait of himself to Swift, whose letters make heavy weather of the omission. In addition to wishing for verses on Parnell from Pope, Swift himself worked to advance Parnell's cause, as in his letter to Archbishop King six years before Parnell's death. He speaks of Parnell's "Merits; by which he hath distinguished himself so much, that he is in great Esteem with the Ministry, and others of the most valuable Persons in this Town" (30 Apr. 1713, 1.344–5). In "*To Mr POPE*" Parnell complains that fortune has placed him in "unfertile ground. / Far from the joys that with my soul agree, / From wit, from learning, – very far from thee" (78–80). Parnell dedicated his *Essay on the Different Styles of Poetry* (1713) to Bolingbroke.

When Swift heard of Arbuthnot's illness, he said that if there were a "dozen Arbuthnetts" he would "burn [his] Travells" (29 Sept. 1725, 3.104). What is not usually recalled is the next part of the letter. "However," Swift says, "he is not without Fault." The fault is Arbuthnot's "sort of Slouch in his Walk." Swift compares his comment on his friend to Bede on the Irish: much praise, all altered by their keeping Easter on the wrong date. The observation is double-edged and as tinged as most Scriblerian observations, especially Swift's, with sharp irony. Not all know Pope's poems on the *Travels*, the Lilliputian ode in dimeters, the lament of Glumdalclitch and the shrewdly interpretive complaint of Mrs Mary upon Lemuel's return from the land of the Houyhnhnms, when he spends his time in the stable with the sorrel mare (6.266–81). As these poems suggest, the Scriblerians responded to each other's work in a way that gave their productions a nearly independent life. They existed, to some extent, in a fictional universe of their own creation, one that was perceived as such by other readers. Bolingbroke writes via Swift (23 July 1726, 3.146–7) with the superscription: "Viscount Bolingbroke to the three Yahoos of Twickenham." "I have writ," says Gay to Parnell on 29 January 1714/15, "one book of the walking the streets

[*Trivia*]"; in an allusion to *The What D'ye Call It* he adds "& *among us we have just finish'd a Farce in Rhime, of one Act, which is now ready for the Stage*" (17). In 1728, before citing the theme of *The Dunciad* as the celebration of their friendship, Pope writes to Swift about the ancillary material in the poem, especially about the Notes Variorum (28 June 1728, 2.503): "As to the latter, I desire you to read over the Text, and make a few [notes] in any way you like best, whether dry raillery, upon the stile and way of commenting of trivial Critics; or humorous, upon the authors in the poem; or historical, of persons, places, times; or explanatory, or collecting the parallel passages of the Ancients." He is evidently pleased that the "Dunciad is going to be printed with all pomp," but "the inscription … makes me proudest."

In 1732 Swift wrote to Charles Wogan (July–Aug., 4.53): "and therefore I had reason to put Mr. *Pope* on writing the Poem, called the *Dunciad*, and to hale those Scoundrels out of their Obscurity by telling their Names at length, their Works, their Adventures, sometimes their Lodgings, and their Lineage; not with *A—'s* and *B—'s* according to the old Way, which would be unknown in a few Years." This is an expansion of his letter to Pope on 16 July 1728 (3.293), in which he urges Pope to "have your Asterisks filled up with some real names of real Dunces." The crucial aspect of the later observation is Swift's claim to have launched the poem. Pope's request is his invitation to participate.

The group was perceived as one, not just in pieces like Cibber's *Refusal* and in the hostile activity around *Three Hours after Marriage*, explicitly a group production, but in events like Rich's conversion of parts of the *Beggar's Opera* into a piece acted by a "sett of Lilliputian Comedians."[5] Scriblerian works were thought to reflect each other. Among contemporary works that saw the group together, and attacked them this way, one of the more amusing is *Gulliver decypher'd*.[6] The author's animosity towards Gay in the *What D'Ye Call It* is most strongly expressed (45), but he sees the whole group ironically as a menace. We are told in the prefatory remarks (13) that there are proposals "for printing by Subscription the *Secret* History of the Life and Action of SCRIBLERUS or the witty D—n set forth: With an Account so far as can be gathered from authentick Records of his Writings, their best Editions, Prices *&c*. Translated into *French* from the original *Persian*, by the *Abbé de St. Pierre*, of the Royal Academy of Sciences at *Paris*, and now faithfully render'd into *English* by Dr. *Sw—t*. The Title of it in *English* is the *Life of Scriblerus*, which tho' for some reasons has never been made publick" (31). Pope, Swift, and Arbuthnot are decoded as Peter, Martin, and John (29), and later (45) described as "the *Triumvirate, Martin, Peter,* and *Johnny.*"

Even the later editorial quarrels about the authorship of *John Bull* document the public perception of the group as a force working collectively. Although they met formally only in that single year, their own sense of the Club's continuing is suggested by Arbuthnot's letter to Swift on 19 March 1728/29 (Swift, *Corr.,* 3.326): "As to the condition of your little club, it is not quite so desperate as you might imagine, for Mr. Pope is as high in favour as I am affraid the rest are out of it." We are always aware of the group reading and responding to each other's works, long after the death of Anne brought an end to the meetings at the palace convened by the comic invitations in verse. Considerable distress must often have led to these meetings. The comedy in the invitations is in some ways a nervous response to this distress and the possibility of meeting a consoling balance.

The Club also wrote, in a very real way, under each other's direction. According to W.H. Irving, Faulkner said that Swift sent Gay off to write acts for a play with a title of *The Rehearsal at Goatham* – another challenge from within the group.[7] There are sometimes echoes between their works – like the weeping lovers in Gay's *Zerbin and Isabella* and Pope's *Eloisa to Abelard* (325ff, 343ff). Dennis Hoilman's study of Pope's revision of *An Essay on Man* shows Swiftian imagery from the *Tale* in the earlier version, especially in two brothers, one fluttering in rags, the other in brocade.[8] As Pat Rogers has pointed out in his study of Gay's poem "Mr Pope's Welcome from Greece," a celebration of the end of the Homer translation, Gay manages, in a style Pope himself employed when he wrote of George Augustus, to turn the occasion of a poem celebrating the achievement of a friend to a second purpose, so that praise becomes satiric comment upon the accession of the monarch.[9] On this occasion another member of the group becomes part of the procession:

> *Arbuthnot* there I see in *Physicks* art
>   As *Galen* learned or famed *Hippocrate*
> Whose company drives Sorrow from the Heart,
>   As all Disease his Medecines dissipate.   (1.121–4)

Swift is recalled in Gay's *Newgate's Garland,* in an allusion to all the "Pother ... with *Wood* and his Brass" (1.53). One of the lighter touches comes in Parnell's "The Book-Worm." He complains that

Thy rabid Teeth have half destroy'd
The Work of Love in *Biddy Floyd*
They rent *Belinda*'s Locks away,
And spoil'd the *Blouzelind* of *Gay*.   (35–8)

As Mack's list of Pope's books shows, there was constant commerce among the group in book giving, like the Maittaire folios and Homer's *Battle of the Frogs and Mice* from Parnell, *Les Aventures de Télémaque* from Gay, Erasmus's New Testament from Swift, and Pope's own gift of the *Epistolae Obscurorum Virorum* to Swift.[10]

The project of the *Memoirs* was more important than the later readership of it may suggest. On 28 June 1714 Pope writes to Swift: "Dr. Arbuthnot is singular in his opinion, and imagines your only design is to attend at full leisure to the life and adventures of Scriblerus. This indeed must be granted of greater importance than all the rest; and I wish I could promise so well of you. The top of my own ambition is to contribute to that great work, and I shall translate Homer by the by" (1.231). This is not Pope in an extravagant mood. Scriblerus was perhaps best noted in his own time for aggressive action, like the representation of Cibber in *Three Hours after Marriage*, Gay's dedication of *The Mohocks* to Dennis, and his derogation of Sir Tremendous Longinus in *The Distress'd Wife*, but many of these, like the allusion in *Trivia*, were the support of one beleaguered friend for another. Friendship is the central motif in Scriblerian observations about their relationships with each other and, in subtle ways, in the strengths and limitations of their work. Swift's most famous remark in this vein is well known: "I have often endeavoured to establish a Friendship among all Men of Genius, and would fain have it done. They are seldom above three or four Cotemporaries and if they could be united would drive the World before them" (20 Sept. 1723, 2.465).

This passage, sometimes thought affirmatively cheerful, comes in fact from a very bitter letter to Pope where Swift complains of Pope and Bolingbroke as "pretenders to retirement" (464), not just reasonably resenting the tones of part of the letter from Twickenham and especially from Dawley Farm but also deeply resenting his own isolation. In 1730 he writes to Gay: "different circumstances of life have always separated those whom friendship would joyn, God hath taken care – of that to prevent any progress towards real happyness here, which would make life more desirable & death too dreadful" (10 Nov., 3.417–18).

"Real happyness here," then, was the friendship of the group. To the Rev. James Stopford, on 20 July 1726 (3.145), Swift writes of Stella's impending death: "believe me that violent friendship is much more lasting, and as much engaging, as violent love." His tones are worth noting – the bitterness of the disappointed letter, the sense that real happiness is not part of the worldly condition because friendship cannot last, and especially the notion of *violent* friendship. The adjective is right for collected Scriblerian activity. In a note on Achilles mourning Patroclus in the twenty-fourth book of the *Iliad*, Pope says: "there is something very instructive in this whole Representation, it shews us the Power of a sincere Friendship, and softens and recommends the Character of *Achilles*; the Violence he us'd towards his Enemy is alleviated by the Sincerity he expresses towards his Friend; he is a terrible Enemy, but an amiable Friend" (8.535).

Violence and the terrible – sharply opposed to amiability, a word whose meaning was much stronger in the period. It was a condition, for the Scriblerians, only rarely achieved, and in Scriblerus the only persons truly amiable were friends dependent upon each other, for books, talk, support, society. They are not diminished if we reflect that this dependence also shows them, as C.S. Lewis long ago perceived, persons of deep melancholy and, in the rest of his fine observation, persons who were not often serious.[11] Lewis compares Addison's careful balance to Tory gloom and finds the former wanting in attractiveness. But we might also look to the unserious, most vividly embodied in Swift's desire that the bagatelle might live long and in those episodes in Pope's career that troubled George Sherburn – the imagined and literal attacks upon the body of Mr Edmund Curll, the delight the group took in the response of the dunces and then in incorporating their foolish replies into *The Dunciad*.[12] This aspect of Scriblerian activity is well described in Rawson's study of Fielding, who signed himself Scriblerus Secundus, as the penchant among the group for schoolboy jokes as well as for sophisticated verse and prose.[13] There is a child element in any friendship and a very strong one in a friendship whose members see themselves so exclusively in a union founded not simply upon likeness but also on some kind of revolt against forces perceived to be inimical to them. Satire is motivated in part by defensive paranoia. It is hard to think of the author of *Tristram Shandy* masquerading up and down the sands near Hall-Stevenson's Crazy Castle[14] until we reflect on the child-world of the novel and of its author – neurotic, dependent upon praise, painfully insecure in the midst of brilliance and making the Shandy world from this insecurity. Writing in a note on the opening of the seventeenth book of the *Iliad* of the relationship between Patroclus and Achilles, Pope says: "The Dissimilitude of Manners between these two Friends, *Achilles* and *Patroclus*, is very observable: such Friendships are not uncommon, and I have often assign'd this Reason for them, that it is natural for Men to seek the Assistance of those Qualities in others, which they want themselves. That is still better if apply'd to Providence, which associates Men of different and contrary Qualities, in order to make a more perfect System" (8.287–8, n 5). The differences between Swift, Gay, Pope, Arbuthnot, and Parnell were resolved, at least for the brief time of their actual meetings in the palace, and made the group nearly as much as the similarities that brought and kept them together. These differences, of course, were acceptable, unlike their variations from the subjects they attacked.

The Scriblerian sense of the Club as a driving force, out to reform, gave a power to their rhetoric and certain kinds of predictable limits. The most obvious, apart from a necessary and mainly justifiable superiority, is a restriction in audience. Men in groups speak a special language, one that runs the risk of exclusiveness. The consciousness of a task to be done, with particular goals, can mar the grandeur of generality in tones not found in other muses, those with less of the oddness that sometimes does not last.

Arbuthnot, the scientist of the group, was interested in the theory of games that *"may be supposed to be a Trial of Wit as well as Fortune, and every Man, when he enters the Lists with another, unless out of Complaisance, takes it for granted, his Fortune and Judgment are, at least, equal to those of his Play-Fellow; but this I am sure of, that false Dice, Tricks of Leger-de-Main, &c. are inexcusable, for the Question in gaming is not, Who is the best Jugler."*[15]

Readers of Scriblerian literature, now as then, are expected to enter a universe of game, to seek for meaning, to find the author, to prove intellectual liveliness in the "Trial of Wit." While we are told ironically in the *Tale* that the seven scholars from seven kingdoms are locked up to find out meanings and that we are meant to find this activity ridiculous, we are in fact nearly always in a verbal universe that takes us to annotation and often to puzzlement. These nearly opposing positions are dictated by the value-system the Scriblerians shared, their conviction that this system was increasingly assaulted and that they personally carried on the tradition under assault. The oppositions, tensions, and problems of group satirical writing affect and effect individual styles and the group style as well — as happy families develop an inner language that affirms their happiness and excludes others who might threaten it.

Twelve days after the death of the queen, Arbuthnot, the most secure of all the group and perhaps the least devoted to driving the world before him, attempts to compose Swift in a moving letter:

Dear Freind the last sentence of your letter quite kills me: never repeat that melancholy tender word that you will endeavour to forgett me. I am sure I never can forgett yow, till I meett with, (what is impossible) another whose conversation I can so much delight in as Dr Swifts & yet that is the smallest thing I ought to value you for. That hearty sincere freindship That plain & open ingenuity in all your commerce, is what I am sure I never can find in another alas. I shall want often, a faithfull monitor one that would vindicate me behind my back & tell me my faults to my face. god knows I write this with tears in my eyes. yet do not be obstinate, but come up for a little time to London, & if you must needs go, we may concert a manner of Correspondence wherever we are.   (Swift, *Corr.*, 12 Aug. 1714, 2.122)

That in effect is what happened, not simply in the letters between members of the group but in that correspondence that dictates the commonality of theme and style to which the essays in this book are addressed. The first is concerned with Scriblerian preoccupation with pastoral, not simply or even primarily as a poetic form, although that is how Pope began, but as a state of mind, articulate not only in a view of country as opposed to city but also as an ideal, a complicated oasis, the *locus amoenus* of which Renato Poggioli and others have written.[16]

I have begun that essay with a famous pastoral place in *Tom Jones* to give the pastoral topos an articulate habitation and a name. Although much taken by country, the Scriblerians had no quarrel with the city, only with its unreality. It is to that unreality and grotesquerie that the second essay is addressed. To both these themes the Scriblerians brought known traditions; they saw themselves as the heirs of earlier coteries that had engaged in similar programs and performances. It is not fortuitous that the motto for *Three Hours after Marriage* (from Martial) is also the last motto in Jonson's *Poetaster*, a play about the issue central to the later play, the war of wit and words and the relevance of this war to the fabric of human relations. Pope wanted to write Erasmus's life and left his eleven volumes of Erasmus to Bolingbroke. Thomas More is the only modern figure among the persons of virtue cited in the third book of the *Travels*. Rabelais and Cervantes are everywhere, and the background echoes with Seneca, Lucian, and Apuleius. I have begun the third chapter with *Tristram Shandy*. While to be Shandeian is not quite the same as being Scriblerian, John Ferriar, an early reader of Sterne, saw a similarity, at least in stylistic matters, to the *Memoirs of Martinus Scriblerus*. Sterne's way of carrying on the tradition of learned wit is reminiscent of the Scriblerian recommendation of looking to the ways that are past. Their kind of reading, with the special sense of the world against which it was played, made Scriblerian style, the subject of the last essay, the oddly rich, resonant, and fragmented rhetoric it was – some of the best of its kind ever heard.

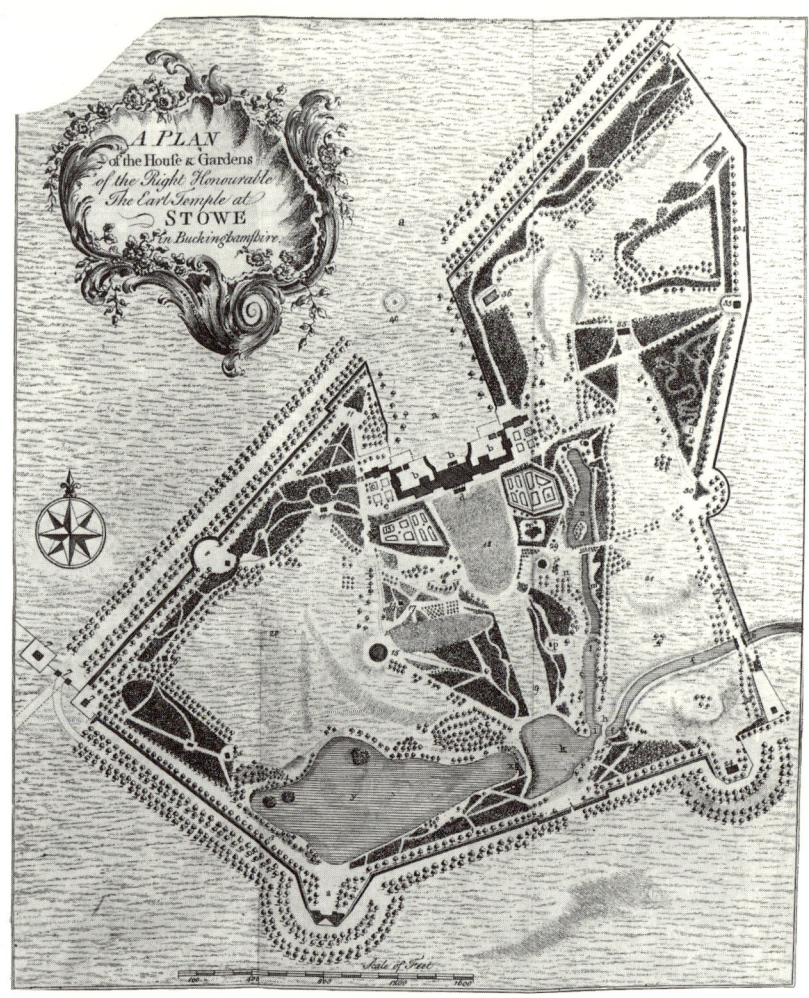

A plan of the house and gardens of the Right Honourable The Earl Temple at Stowe. Courtesy Thomas Fisher Rare Book Library, University of Toronto

2 Gardens and Parks

Nearly half the fourth chapter of the first book of *Tom Jones* is given to a description of Mr Allworthy's house and its natural setting. Both house and grounds incorporate every feature thought essential in houses and landscapes of the period – essential because they embodied a complete and harmonious world: "The *Gothick* stile of Building could produce nothing nobler than Mr. *Allworthy*'s House. There was an Air of Grandeur in it, that struck you with Awe, and rival'd the Beauties of the best *Grecian* Architecture; and it was as commodious within, as venerable without" (1.4.42). This balance of styles, in actuality or implication, is echoed in the rest of the description. The house is on a hill, but "nearer the Bottom than the Top … yet high enough to enjoy a most charming Prospect of the Valley beneath." The lawn, the spring, "tumbling in a natural Fall," ends in a lake. The river issuing out of this meanders "through an amazing Variety of Meadows and Woods." The prospect ends in a sea and an island.

What is seen from the house is a landscape painting.[1] But the other details in the scene are important too. The next valley has "an old ruined Abbey,"[2] and "The left Hand Scene presented the View of a fine Park, composed of very unequal Ground, and agreeably varied with all the Diversity that Hills, Lawns, Wood and Water, laid out with admirable Taste, but owing less to Art than to Nature, could give. Beyond this the Country gradually rose into a Ridge of wild Mountains, the Tops of which were above the Clouds."(43)[3] The eye moves through the beautiful to the sublime.[4] No readers of the novel then, should be surprised to find (especially with all the echoes of Milton) that the name of the house is Paradise Hall, as was Sir John Stanley's villa at Fulham.[5] Tom, of course, knowing "no more than *Adam*" (8.2.331) where he can go after his expulsion, will have to work his way back to this place through deeds answerable. He will perhaps not have found a paradise within, happier far, in this new age of social action. But he will have learned through other scenes on his progress, not least those in London,[6] enough to inherit his godfather's estate, to prove himself worthy of it, and even to make more of it in Milton's deeds answerable than in the withdrawn behaviour of Mr Allworthy.[7] His return to Somerset will demand further work on houses and parks, for, through his marriage to Sophia and the departure of her father to a kind of wilderness, he is able to take over the Western estate, to extend Eden where the Edenic is badly needed.

Tom's vigour is essential at this stage in the history of Paradise Hall. Mr Allworthy's wife is dead and so are his three children. While he has not become a wholly soured Man of the Hill, Allworthy shares, with the chief figure of that later resonant encounter, an understandable pull to solitude and melancholy, as well as a considerable trust in his own powers of judgment and analysis. The heading of the house and garden chapter hints comically and instructively that the reader's neck may be brought into danger, and this hint is repeated in the chapter (1.4.43). We are only at the beginning of Tom's story. The tops of the mountains are hidden behind the clouds. Mr Allworthy appears in the sublime style, "replete with Benevolence" (43). The adjective is out of place for the noun, so that we sense something amiss about him, long before we have, risking our necks rhetorically, slid down the hill into the breakfast room and watched him vanish, at the very end of the chapter, into his study.[8] Owner of a "shining palace" that is an obvious heir to those of which James Yoch has spoken,[9] presumably with the clear air and cleanliness to which John Arbuthnot was dedicated,[10] Mr Allworthy is no longer able to act the part such owners were expected to play in their secular roles as inheritors of ancient traditions of the prince, creators on earth of a mirror of heavenly harmony.[11] But the positive pastoral ideal, cut across with Fielding's irony and his acute perception of Allworthy's limits, for all his evident virtue, is set down early in the novel. This is the style of life to which Tom will come after his moral education for that shepherd world of which Paul Alpers has written.[12]

Later in the novel we have another pastoral scene, very clearly presented as a *locus amoenus*. Just before Tom enters London, that "bad Place"[13] of which Joseph Andrews speaks in his letter back to the country, he meets the gypsies, in an episode that used, with the Man of the Hill, to be thought a puzzling digression.[14] It is certainly digressive, but like most epic and romantic divergences it serves to define the nature of the action and the issues at a critical place in the narrative. Tom and Partridge discover "a Light at some Distance" (12.12.663). Their ambiguous response to this light, a sharp contrast to the unwelcoming dark scene of the Man of the Hill, is increased when they hear "a confused Sound of Human Voices; of singing, laughing, and hallowing, together with a strange Noise that seemed to proceed from some Instruments; but could hardly be allowed the Name of Music" (664). These lines introduce us, not to another Paradise Hall, where we can imagine the harpsichord (although not one punctuated, as in Western's house, with the barking of dogs), but certainly to what is in its own way an Eden, even if one of a primitive kind, a nearly alternate society, as Fielding's observations about confusion in voice and instrument suggest. The gypsies are, appropriately, celebrating a wedding with "utmost Mirth" yet not in a style "totally void of all Order and Decorum" (667).

The scene, formalized a little, might come from Pope's account of Lord Burlington in the fourth of the *Epistles to Several Persons* (4.41–6); certainly, although it is rustic, it has warm hospitality and responsibility, qualities that were supposed to inform properly run country houses with their gardens and parks, reflective in their own way of the friendly scenes in the meetings of Scriblerus.[15] After his image of nature triumphing over a false builder, Pope says:

Who then shall grace, or who improve the Soil?
Who plants like Bathurst, or who builds like Boyle.
'Tis Use alone that sanctifies Expence,
And Splendour borrows all her rays from Sense.
His Father's Acres who enjoys in peace,
Or makes his Neighbours glad, if he encrease;
Whose chearful Tenants bless their yearly toil,
Yet to their Lord owe more than to the soil;
Whose ample Lawns are not asham'd to feed
The milky heifer and deserving steed;
Whose rising Forests, not for pride or show,

But future Buildings, future Navies grow:
Let his plantations stretch from down to down,
First shade a Country, and then raise a Town.   (4.177–90)

The basis of Burlington's moral power lies in his instinct for appropriate pastoral, in the "Good Sense, which only is the gift of Heav'n" (43). That allows him to "build, to plant, whatever you intend" (47). It is the "Light, which in yourself you must perceive," for "Jones and Le Nôtre have it not to give."

The centre of the action in the gypsy episode in *Tom Jones*, which begins with its own generous light, is the gypsy king: "He was very little distinguished in Dress from his Subjects, nor had he any Regalia of Majesty to support his Dignity; and yet there seemed … to be somewhat in his Air which denoted Authority, and inspired the Beholders with an Idea of Awe and Respect" (12.12.667). The king operates simply, more as a father to his people. He has often wished, we are told, to return to private life. In an important aside Fielding comments on the polity of the gypsies:

And here we will make a Concession, which would not perhaps have been expected from us, That no limited Form of Government is capable of rising to the same Degree of Perfection, or of producing the same Benefits to Society with this. Mankind have never been so happy, as when the greatest Part of the then known World was under the Dominion of a single Master; and this State of their Felicity continued during the Reigns of five successive Princes. This was the true Aera of the Golden Age, and the only Golden Age which ever had any Existence, unless in the warm Imaginations of the Poets, from the Expulsion of *Eden* down to this Day.   (12.12.671–2)[16]

Ideally, he then goes on to say, this would prevail. In reality, it is impossible. Fielding shared the Scriblerian ideal of an age in which men might be governed by an absolute monarch who would not be a tyrant but a man of sufficient moderation, wisdom, and goodness that he could put others before himself. The Prince of Darkness has not, however, been entirely banished from this pastoral oasis. The presence of laws in the polity, even as those in Thomas More's apparently ideal state of Utopia, argues for aberrant conditions for which laws have had to be made.

Fielding's sense of the real cause for the failure fully to articulate the Golden Age is illustrated by the parley between a young female in the group and Partridge in the gypsy digression. The seduction is clearly initiated by the woman, who is "more remarkable for her Wit than her Beauty" (13.12.670). "Wit oblique" breaks the "steddy light" afforded by Nature. These words come from Pope's articulation of a pastoral place in *An Essay on Man* (3.231). The gypsies are nearly primitives, and as such they resort to an attractively literal and primitive form of punishment in the wearing of horns, a public emblem of shame, by the witty gypsy's husband. At the end of the chapter, which is also the end of the discussion of the possible virtues and vices of absolute monarchy, provided that this be the province of a man who is moderate, wise, and good, Fielding says that he cannot urge the politics and social example of the gypsies on our society's vain and shameless citizens. The gypsies "have no false Honours among them; and ... they look on Shame as the most grievous Punishment in the World" (673). Shame speaks only to those motivated by inner virtue. For such persons, laws need not be elaborate and hence susceptible to twist and turn. They will be built on simple principles and open modes of revelation of crime, like the *literal* rendition of shame for the husband in real horns, a sign that needs no verbal commentary. This literalism is not carried quite so far as is Swift's pastoral world in the fourth voyage of his *Travels into Several Remote Nations of the World*. Fielding's gypsies lament things as they are and do not say that "they are not," but in their simplicity they remind us of Swift's faraway land in another important way. As well as calling their music strange, Fielding also gives them, a little awkwardly, a dialect, a difference in speech, although one not quite so radically different as the language of the Houyhnhnms. They are deliberately placed outside English experience, even as their government is outside English custom. They are outlaws, but as such free from that "bottomless Pit" in which Arbuthnot's John Bull is ensnared, his life brought into jeopardy, as is Tristram Shandy's, by the tyranny of words. *Tom Jones*, then, presents us with two versions of pastoral. There is the potentially shining house of virtue in Somerset; with a sociably welcoming light that contrasts so sharply with the darkness in the misogynist and melancholy Man of the Hill, there is the Society of the Egyptians, not really beggars and thieves, as they are conventionally perceived to be (and very probably were), but spontaneous moralists, persons for whom, say, Shaftesbury, would have nothing but praise.

Now Fielding came slowly to *Tom Jones*, through *Joseph Andrews* and *Shamela* from the stage and a variety of plays. He signed himself H. Scriblerus Secundus in the preface to *Tom Thumb*, a work reminiscent of the earlier Tory satirists in its method and orientation, although

Fielding is nearly always more positive than the Club. I have used him quite deliberately to open a consideration of Scriblerian ideals and to lend a habitation as well as a name to this discussion of the Scriblerian sense of the rhetorical and physical places likely to generate that ideal. Paul Alpers takes issue with those who describe the chief impulse of pastoral (and he uses the term in a wider sense) as an escape from city to country, so that the principal value is the physical matter of scene: "The presence, emergence, and history of pastoral landscape is not a matter of nature poetry or of visionary or psychological projection but rather an interpretation, a selective emphasis determined by individual or cultural motives, of the central fiction that the shepherds' lives represent human lives ... landscapes are pastoral when they are conceived as fit habitations for shepherds or their equivalents" ("What Is Pastoral?" 459). "Shepherds' lives, not landscape, are at the heart of pastoral," he says. Pastoral "is a sophisticated form ... of the country, but by and for the court or city" (457). The informing principle is clear enough: "Pastoral poets have always been concerned with the extent to which pleasurable song can confront and, if not transform and celebrate, then reconcile man to the stresses and realities of his situation" (458). At the beginning of his study Alpers presents René Rapin as the first important commentator on the pastoral as a form. Rapin provides what Alpers calls "a representative anecdote" (443), a representation of shepherd life. An account of each of the Scriblerians' versions of pastoral will set out their view of garden and park.

Pope began his own poetic career with Rapin and Fontenelle, or, more accurately, provided a gloss on these in the pastorals he wrote in 1709. This neglected gloss is his preface of 1715, revised in 1717, a document designed to explain his own pastoral procedures. The preface comments on the pastoral form in a way that reflects Pope's considerable study of early writers on pastoral and his own reading in what he took to be the principal practitioners of the art. In 1705 he writes to Wycherley, whose later poems he had been asked to edit: "As for my green Essays, if you find any pleasure in 'em, it must be such as a Man naturally takes in observing the first Shoots and Buddings of a Tree which he has rais'd himself: and 'tis impossible they should be esteem'd any otherwise, than as we value Fruits for being early, which nevertheless are the most insipid, and the worst of the Year" (25 Mar. 1705, 1.5). Just a month later Walsh sent an enthusiastic letter to Wycherley in praise of the poems; he also commends the *Discourse* as "very judicious and very learned" (10 Apr., 1.7).

As we know, the battle between the Ancients and the Moderns in England was in part touched off by a quarrel about the apparently opposing views of Rapin and Fontenelle. The opening paragraph of Pope's *Discourse* shows him aware of the controversy:

There are not, I believe, a greater number of any sort of verses than of those which are called Pastorals, nor a smaller, than of those which are truly so. It therefore seems necessary to give some account of this Kind of Poem and it is my design to comprize in this short paper the substance of those numerous dissertations the Criticks have made on the subject, without omitting any of their Rules in my own favour. You will also find some points reconciled, about which they seem to differ, and a few remarks which I think have escaped their observation.[17] (1.23)

Pope's sense of what is critical about the pastoral as a form is instantly clear: "we are not to describe our shepherds as shepherds at this day really are, but as they may conceiv'd then to have been: when a notion of quality was annex'd to that name, and the best of men follow'd the employment" (1.25). The manners are, as Rapin had said, based on "unstain'd, uncorrupted Nature" and neither "too Clownish nor too Courtly" (1.24n). The expression, Pope says, following Rapin, will be as pure as the language can afford, delicately balanced between the completely plain and the florid, easy yet lively. This kind of emphasis is only reinforced by Fontenelle's discussion of the form. Like Rapin, he does not advocate a naturalistic representation of country life but a complex poetic exercise using country image as convention. Fontenelle's representation of a ribboned shepherdess underscores the notion of the pastoral as a representation of a *rhetorical* universe, a fit place for what Alpers sees as the "shepherds' lives" (457).

Pope's silent adoption of Fontenelle's position that love is the presiding emotion of pastoral further circumscribes the form so that it becomes a poetical study of an elemental human passion. His search for the place that will perhaps be no place is emphasized by a crucial emendation of Rapin, who had said that the pastoral is "*the imitation of the Action of a Sheapard or of one taken under that Character.*"[18] Pope sets down this qualification almost exactly but omits Rapin's alternative, thus ruling out allegorical pastoral. He makes the same kind of change when he lists the varieties of pastoral. Rapin says: "*the Character of* Bucolicks *is a mixture of all sorts of Characters, Dramatick, Narrative,* or mixt: from all which tis very manifest that the manner of *Imitation* which is proper to *Pastorals* is the mixt" (29). Pope says that "the form of this imitation is dramatic or narrative or mix'd of both" (1.24), deleting Rapin's assertion that the mixed is the appropriate mode. Anything that adds to "design'd scene or prospect" (1.28) to shape the form is welcomed. Spenser's calendar "is very beautiful: since by this, besides the general moral of innocence and simplicity, which is common to other authors of pastoral, he has one peculiar to himself; he compares human Life to the several Seasons, and at once exposes to his readers a view of the great and little worlds, in their various changes and aspects" (1.32). This passage comes from the first version of the *Discourse*, where Pope's praise of Spenser is hyperbolic. When he revises in 1717 he worries about Spenser's length, his allegory, and "the old English and country phrases."

The *Pastorals* themselves, mainly neglected by modern readers (although admired by Johnson for their numbers),[19] are pre-Scriblerian, but they are important texts, with the *Discourse*, for their articulation of the theme of *locus amoenus*, that place to which the Club aspired. They also support Alpers' argument that the pastoral presents a mode of reconciliation. They give four anecdotes of life, from the innocence of the singing contest of "Spring" to the complications of love in the monologue of "Summer," to the losses of "Autumn," antiphonally sung by two discernably older figures, to the reconciliation to love lost to death in "Winter." At the end of this pastoral, love is put aside, with an important change in the Virgilian lines. "Amor vincit omnia et nos cedamus amori" becomes in Pope "Time conquers All and We must Time obey" (1.95). The little world becomes or mirrors the greater, not only in the orchestrated shift of seasons but in the change of scene and time and employment and age, so that we conclude at midnight in "Winter" with a prospect over all scenes, times, places, and experiences.

The formal resolution and patterning of Pope's pastoral world separates him sharply from all the earlier ancient and modern authors from whom he creatively steals. Yet the sense that the country is for the use of the city is conveyed with special force, even though the revisions Pope made later often omit references that tied language to the specifics of time and space.[20] Pope addresses the final poem to Mrs Tempest, earlier memorialized by Walsh, Pope's first teacher in verse. Walsh died the year before the poems were published. "Spring" is dedicated to Trumbull, who is also the subject of its opening lines. "Spring" is, then, a poem of youth given to a statesman retired in old age. Given the same kind of proems, Garth and Wycherley preside over the next two poems, the first as physician, the other as satirist. The death of Mrs Tempest, presiding genius of "Winter," resolves the complications of contests and failures in love as the action is translated to "Fields ever fresh and Groves for ever green!" (1.94). This is a prospect even more ideal than Fielding's picture of Paradise Hall and environs in *Tom Jones*. It is, however, the same ideal in a more compressed style. The real persons who come from outside the ideal landscape of Strephon, Lycidas, and so on tell us (at least in these early days) that the ideal landscape *is* possible to realize in the real world. In this way the *Pastorals* are important early studies for and, in their inclusion of actual contemporary figures, important predecessors of the later *Epistles to Several Persons*, where three owners of landed estates in effect act out the lives of shepherds.

The *Pastorals* themselves became a subject of controversy and comic Scriblerian activity when Pope responded to Theobald's ranking of pastoral authors by putting Gay up to *The Shepherd's Week* and writing his own fortieth paper for the *Guardian*.[21] And Pope carried the pastoral theme on to *Windsor-Forest*, whose last line, in imitation of Virgil, is from the *Georgics*, that extension of pastoral vision into the real world of action. This line is also the first line of the *Pastorals*. The point is obvious: the *Pastorals* define a world in their anecdotes of the lives of shepherds, in the most intense moments of rural experience. They establish, in literal pastoral poems, the values for virtuous experience that carry on the pastoral world in larger places. In *Windsor-Forest*, by rhetorical cue, that ideal moves from psychological to political and nationalistic space. The Forest establishes a royal centre from which the vision of the pastorals can be realized in England and radiate from her shores to the rest of the world. The connection of the private world of pastoral with the public in *Windsor-Forest*, even here, where the move to the public is clear, is made at the beginning by the same gesture of dedication, this time to Lansdown. The forests of Windsor are at once "the Monarch's and the Muse's Seats" (1.148.2). Here, as in *An Essay on Man* and in the varied epistles over whom secular heroes will later preside, poet and patriot, as in Fielding's doubting political gloss on the episode of the gypsies, are linked together in pastoral, in parks, and in shining palaces. Here, as there, the imagery of Milton's Eden and of Isaiah are strongly felt as the background of that new paradise of peace and plenty that can be realized because a particular monarch reigns.

The theme of *translatio studii*, of which Marshall McLuhan wrote,[22] is rehearsed in *An Essay on Criticism*, where England is projected as the new paradise in letters. Here paradise comes in literary dress, as "the

Groves of *Eden* vanish'd now so long" (1.7) are restored not just in Eden and Olympus but in English places like *Cooper's Hill.* All pastoral values centre in this "Mansion of our earthly Gods"(1.230), so that the happy man may retire, like Scipio and Atticus in classical times and Trumbull, Lansdown, Cobham, Bathurst, and Burlington in the present. In *Windsor-Forest* English history advances from troubled days to a new visionary scene where (with some stretch of the imagination) "great *ANNA*" reaches, in an echo of that phrase the century found the prime sublime, in "Let Discord cease, / She said, the World obey'd, and all was *Peace!*" (1.327–8). The next appearance of this Longinian allusion will be in *The Rape of the Lock*, when "Let there be light" is comically turned upside down in the famous lines about black Spades and Trumps. But here Pope is completely celebratory, as Arbuthnot was in his Mercat Cross sermon of 1707 when he pleads for a positive response from the Scots to the Union. England is "a Nation whose Laws are more Just, whose Government is more Mild, whose People are more Free, Easie and Happy, than any other in *Europe.*"[23] The Scots are to

> consider ... the happy Condition of [their] ... Neighbouring Nation; Survey their verdant Fields, beautiful Plantations, and sumptuous Gardens, where Culture, Art and Expences reign; the populous and flourishing Cities: View the Magnificence of their Publick Structures; the Neatness, Cleanliness, Conveniency and costly Furniture of the Private Houses: Consider the Liberty and Plenty of their meanest Commons; the comfortable Estates which even the basest of their Tradesmen leave to their Families; the immense Riches of their Merchants; the Grandure [sic] and Magnificence of their Learned Societies; the prodigious Stocks of their Trading Companies; the unconquerable Force of their Fleets and Armies; the Justice and exact Execution of their Laws; and the wise Administration of their Government. (*Mercat-Cross*, 16)

What should be emphasized in Arbuthnot's commendation (John Bull's tangled adventures are still in the distance) is not simply the plantations and gardens and those other English devices of country life but his observations on "the populous and flourishing Cities." While in his treatise upon clean air he says that "the good air ... the chief Instrument of Health ... / justly ... reckon'd amongst the greatest natural Blessings" (205) is not often found in the city ("for it is replete with Sulphureous Steams of Fuel, and the perspirable Matter of Animals"), he does not rule out cities but advises temperately that physicians observe "the Situation, Air and Water of a City, in order to come at the Knowledge of their popular Diseases, and their Seasons" (120–1).²⁴ Like Gay in the midst of *Trivia* and its mainly seedy account of London, he can see the possibility of a shining palace like Burlington House.²⁵

When Pope translates his own pastorals into the national scene in *Windsor-Forest*, he allows, even as he does in *An Essay on Man*, for a city, as well as for the country, and his shepherds are, if not urban, certainly urbane. The city, at least in the form of the shining palace, is vividly present in the *Homer*. In his "Collection of the most remarkable [images] throughout the Poem" (*Iliad*, 8.598), Pope gives book and line references that send his readers to the "starry Mansion" of Jove (1.689) and, later, to his "eternal Adamantine Dome" (20.10). The unfavourable view of Paris is to some extent modified by the Prince's possession of "several polite Accomplishments." Among these, and highlighted, is the fact that he has "assembled the most skilful Builders from all Parts of the Country, to render his Palace a compleat Piece of Architecture" (6.390n).²⁶ The *concordia discors* of the Forest scene is resolved finally into latter-day palaces and cities.²⁷ The "ascending *Villa's* ... Project long Shadows o'er the Chrystal Tyde" (1.375–6) and "two fair Cities bend / Their ample Bow"(378). "Temples rise, the beauteous Works of Peace" – the garden as city, the city as garden. These temples, the fifty new churches, are the works of peace and part of the architectural view of the restored London. They are, it should be noted, *buildings*, not essentially places of worship. As Renato Poggioli notes, the pastoral in its clearest form is secular and so is Pope's Pisgah sight of the urban and urbane pastoral to be wrought by Windsor and the royal power of which it is a metaphor.²⁸

Pope's versions of pastoral were sustained past 1713, the year of *Windsor-Forest*, and even past the first of August in 1714, when the reigning sovereign, source of peace, plenty, and the rooms at St James's for the Club, gave way to the Hanoverians. The Twickenham house and garden mark in many ways his positive response to the collapse of Tory pastoral. These became, if not Paradise Hall, certainly a miniature image of what that hall was supposed to be, from the pictures of friends in the dining room, *topoi* when they could not be there for apt and cheerful conversation, to the grotto below, constantly laboured as that piece of *ars poetica*, with the other "tramgrams," as Swift called them when he recommended other creations for a time when Pope was melancholy (20 Apr. 1731, 3.457). The accounts of Pope's rambles, recorded in Sherburn's index to the *Correspondence* (5.180), are often accounts of his advice to others as they built and planted, reclaiming the landscape, making gardens and parks. Certainly the meetings at Stowe, with its temples and icons of ancient liberty in visualized criticisms of modern virtue, were meant to deal with and to transform the city. The so-called *Moral Essays* were badly renamed. The particular persons to whom these epistles are addressed, Cobham, Bathurst, and Burlington, are all in varying ways pastoral people, deep in country estate and in gardening. It is not usual to read *An Essay on Man* as a pastoral poem, but (and not least because of its evocation of Milton or its physical setting in a conversation between Pope and Bolingbroke in their country landscape) it is perhaps most fruitfully read in these terms, especially because of Bolingbroke's place, not only in Pope's world but in the Scriblerian world at large. In a special way, Bolingbroke's fall and exile marked the end of their golden dreams.

Bolingbroke was not a member of the Club, but all the Scriblerians praise him and his views are absolutely central to the pastoral vision that informed their most positive moments, their most hopeful dreams. Although Swift was impatient with St John's later preference, as he himself puts it in a letter to Swift, for "an uninterrupted tenor of philosophical Quiet" (2 Aug. 1731, 3.490) and complained with bitterness of this tenor as it was reflected in the Pope-Bolingbroke relationship after St John returned from exile, his view of Bolingbroke was fundamentally admiring. A lover of horses, Swift named one of his own after his friend.[29] In his *Enquiry into the Behaviour of the Queen's last Ministry*, there is an elaborate encomium of St. John and Oxford, with a note that "Men of great Genius are superiour to common Rules" (8.152).[30] In an observation in the *Four Last Years of the Queen* on "that superior universal Genius," Swift describes St John as one who through "the force of an extraordinary Genius, and Application to Publick Affairs, joined with an invincible Eloquence; laid open ... the whole Course of the War" (7.98). These positive comments far outweigh the negatives.[31] Gay's dedication of *The Shepherd's Week* to Bolingbroke was a dangerous gesture, given the date, for St John was already under attainder. Swift later writes: "Tell me, are you not under originall Sin by the Dedication to your Eclogues" (8 Jan. 1722/23, 2.443). In the year before the Queen's death Parnell dedicated his *Essay on the Different Stiles of Poetry* to Bolingbroke, who, he imagines, "descends to hear [him] sing" (49.4). Had his eloquence not brought him to "still the Tumults of the World below," he might also have had a place in the shining palace of poetry, with poems written from a "Soul so wonderfully wrought / For ev'ry depth and turn of curious Thought" (449–

50.60). In his "On Queen Anne's Peace" Parnell writes that he flies "with speed / To sing such lines as BOLINGBROKE may read" (299.11–12), and, in a later place:

> These toils the graceful Bolingbroke attends,
> A Genius fashion'd for the greatest ends,
> Whose strong perception takes the swiftest flight,
> And yet its swiftness ne'er obscures its sight:
> When schemes are fix'd and each assign'd a part,
> None serves his country with a nobler heart.   (91–6.301)

Bolingbroke held a central place in Scriblerian ideology, as he did later in the gardens and parks of pastoral Virginia for Jefferson, who reread him, recommended him to his grandson, and praised his moral values and his style: "You ask my opinion of Ld. Bolingbroke and Thomas Paine. They were alike in making bitter enemies of the priests and Pharisees of their day. Both were honest men; both advocates for human liberty ... These two persons differed remarkably in the style of their writing, each leaving a model of what is most perfect in both extremes of the simple and the sublime."[32]

St John's concern for the "simple and the sublime" in government is best shown in his treatise on kingship, an essay whose issues and central themes are essentially pastoral, like the vision of ideal monarchy Fielding describes in the gypsies' episode in *Tom Jones*, like Pope's *Essay*, like the *Epistles to Several Persons*, and like the implied landscape for the Horatian imitations. The *Idea of a Patriot King* belongs to a very old tradition, the speculum for princes.[33] Nearly every ancient and modern rhetorician wrote about the good prince because only good princes can be centres for encouraging good rhetoric. Bolingbroke cites none of these earlier mirrors for magistrates, not even the *Enchiridion Militis Christiani*, although Erasmus was a favourite author.[34] His source is, perhaps predictably, Machiavelli's *The Prince* and *The Discourses*. His monarch, unlike those of whom Kantorowicz speaks, has only one body. The full title of the treatise is itself suggestive. "Idea" is not, as Jeffrey Hart argues, used in quite the same way as it is in earlier manuals.[35] Bolingbroke's Platonism is more extreme than that of the earlier *specula principorum*. It seems possible, for example, to imagine a real king emerging from, say, Aquinas or Machiavelli, the one possibly a good man, anointed and given special power, the other a lion and a fox. The peroration of the *Patriot King* sounds like an epic apotheosis. In this way it strongly resembles Pope's ending of the *Pastorals*, in the epic ascent in "Winter" and especially in the imitation of Virgil's *Pollio*.[36] Bolingbroke's essay oscillates between bare "scientific" analysis to an effort to create and sustain a kind of dramatic imagery and allusion and to generate convincing energy from these.

We are told in many places in the *Patriot King* what kings are not. Bolingbroke is not "one of those oriental slaves who deem it unlawful to look their kings in the face" (2.372). Oriental despotism, seen in England as the Stuart and Jacobite assumptions about the divine right of kings, is ridiculed as "the chimeras of madmen" (379) and associated with those "labyrinths of disputation" (376) typical of the "sons of Loyola" (409) and with that "turn of imagination, often as violent and as sudden as a gust of wind" (410) that breeds "madness and folly" as wild as the projections of a "conscientious fifth monarchy man." As in letters 19–23 of his *Remarks on the History of England*,[37] James I is Bolingbroke's villain, a fool about divine power and a fool in language and behaviour "commonly suited to such foolish pretensions" (425). Those who try to construct a royalist myth in this mode are made to sound like the creators of crude pantomime. The Patriot King can have no part in this activity for – in an oddly jarring biblical allusion – "the royal mantle will not convey the spirit of patriotism into another king, as the mantle of Elijah did the gift of prophecy into another prophet" (397). The Patriot King will not extend the reign of what are derisively called, in tones like the voice in the *Praise of Folly* or in Seneca's *Apokolocyntosis* (a text cited early in the *Patriot King*), "burlesque Jupiters" (383). "Majesty," Bolingbroke says, "is not an inherent but a reflected light."

This sentence is the last in a paragraph beginning with an account of the legal reverence due the king. The "spring [for this reverence] ... is national, not personal." "As well," he continues, "might we say that a ship is built, and loaded, and manned, for the sake of any particular pilot, instead of acknowledging that the pilot is made for the sake of the ship, her lading, and her crew, who are always the owners in the political vessel; as to say that kingdoms were instituted for kings, not kings for kingdoms" (380). Spelling out the metaphor is a problem. No medieval or Renaissance writer describing the ship of state would dissect in this way. Bolingbroke silently rewrites the old imagery of the sun as it represents the king: "As men are apt to make themselves the measure of all being, so they make themselves the final cause of all creation. Thus the reputed orthodox philosophers in all ages have taught, that the world was made for man, the earth for him to inhabit, and all the luminous bodies in the immense expanse around us, for him to gaze at. Kings do no more, no, not so much, when they imagine themselves the final cause for which societies were formed, and governments instituted" (385).

If this modified imagery and ridicule wash the balm from anointed kings, one wonders what might come to replace them. Some pageantry is to be maintained (381, 399), although it is "like many other despicable things" (399): "We must tell ourselves once for all, that perfect schemes are not adapted to our imperfect state; that Stoical morals and Platonic politics are nothing better than amusements for those who have had little experience in the affairs of the world, and who have much leisure, "verba otiosorum senum ad imperitos juvenes"; which was the censure, and a just one too, that Dionysius passed on some of the doctrines of the father of the academy" (381). This is a doctrine of accommodation. It is extended in an odd quotation, a little mixed, from Terence: *Insanire cum ratione* (to be rationally mad), "which appears on many occasions not to be the paradox it has been thought" (381). Bolingbroke argues by implication that the king will be perceived to be rationally mad. This is not a paradox but an emphasis on the king as no ordinary man. This substitute for the burlesque Jupiter is not to be left with "at most a few tattered rags to clothe ... majesty" (383), but it is hard to find an image to describe exactly *what* he is, although the usual phrases from the kingship manuals about the patriarchal family appear. Even God seems to be a limited monarch. The Patriot King is an enlightened eighteenth-century gentleman, transforming the landscape, probably creating gardens and parks. This image of the monarch is particularly strong near the end of Bolingbroke's treatise, when the king is sketched as a man. "By never saying what is unfit for him to say, he will never hear what is unfit for him to hear. By never doing what is unfit for him to do, he will never see what is unfit for him to see. Decency and propriety of manners are so far from lessening the pleasures of life, that they refine them, and give them a higher taste: they are so far from restraining the free and easy commerce of social life, that they banish the bane of it, licentiousness of behaviour" (426).

The balance of the rhetoric, like that of a heroic couplet in prose, reflects the moral balance. St John is, however, by no means optimistic. That "certain 'species liberalis,'" that "certain propriety of words and actions, that results from their conformity to nature and character" (419) will be able to "render ... the proceedings more orderly and more deliberately" (403), in a kingdom whose tenor is one of Senecan tranquillity. "I am not wild enough," he says, "to suppose that a Patriot King can change human nature. But I am reasonable enough to suppose, that, without altering human nature, he may give a check to this course of human affairs" (412). The word that stands out is "easy"; it comes again and again: given this situation, given that, it will be easy to do as follows, to translate the balance of this monarch to every crisis.

This aura of possibility conflicts with the other pull of the treatise. Bolingbroke's is an age of betrayal, marked by a minister who "preaches corruption aloud and constantly, like an impudent missionary of vice" (374). How can a Patriot King deal with "the uncertain and irregular motions of the human mind, agitated by various passions, allured by various temptations, inclining sometimes towards a state of moral perfection, and oftener, even in the best, towards a state of moral depravation"? (393) Bolingbroke uses *enumeratio*, that favourite reductive device of the satirist, as he views a world that renders all the "most incapable, awkward, ungracious, shocking, profligate and timorous wretches, invested with power, and masters of the purse" (394).[38] "All the prostitutes who set them selves to sale, all the locusts who devour the land, with crowds of spies, parasites, and sycophants, will surround the throne under the patronage of such ministers; and whole swarms of little, noisome, nameless insects will hum and buzz in every corner of the court" (398). If we compare this passage with the persistent imagery of the wild turns of the Stuarts, it is no wonder that the nation no longer makes her "proper figure" (417) and is no longer new Rome.

Given Bolingbroke's view of James I, it is no wonder that he reaches back to Elizabeth I as a suitable icon for monarchy. But this is a reimagined Elizabeth whose chief power was to sort out factions and, most critically, to make England consequential as chief in trade and in commerce. She could come from the end of *Windsor-Forest*. She is also a consummate creator of appearance. Kramnick suggests that this "theatrical image of politics" is central in an essay that ends (partially) "by invoking that greatest and most dazzling of all political actors – Elizabeth" (168). A variety of passages in the treatise represent pageantry as accommodation to a flawed human nature that cannot cope with much reality without the benign paternalism of a monarch who knows what is good for his subjects and uses whatever means he can to work out his polity. He is neither a lion nor a fox but, in a very real sense, a shepherd or a regal gypsy. His destiny is potentially noble:

35 Gardens and Parks

A corrupt commonwealth remains without remedy, though all the orders and forms of it subsist: a free monarchical government cannot remain absolutely so, as long as the orders and forms of the constitution subsist. These, alone, are indeed nothing more than the dead letter of freedom, or masks of liberty. In the first character they serve to no good purpose whatsoever: in the second they serve to a bad one; because tyranny, or government by will, becomes more severe, and more secure, under their disguise, than it would if it was barefaced and avowed. But a king can, easily to himself and without violence to his people, renew the spirit of liberty in their minds, quicken this dead letter, and pull off this mask.   (396)

With *fiats* implicit and stated in passages that react to the agitated human mind ("We must choose"; "We must determine"; "we must not proceed" [393]), this paragraph represents the king not just as father but as corrector of a rebellious nation, somewhat like the Israelites of old, although all the biblical tones are muted. Soon the passage rises to a crescendo:

Men decline easily from virtue; for there is a devil too in the political system, a constant tempter at hand: a Patriot King will want neither power nor inclination to cast out this devil, to make the temptation cease, and to deliver his subjects, if not from the guilt, yet from the consequence, of their fall. Under him they will not only cease to do evil, but learn to do well; for, by rendering public virtue and real capacity the sole means of acquiring any degree of power or profit in the state, he will set the passions of their hearts on the side of liberty and good government. A Patriot King is the most powerful of all reformers; for he is himself a sort of standing miracle, so rarely seen and so little understood, that the sure effects of his appearance will be admiration and love in every honest breast, confusion and terror to every guilty conscience, but submission and resignation in all. A new people will seem to arise with a new king. Innumerable metamorphoses, like those which poets feign, will happen in every deed: and while men are conscious that they are the same individuals, the difference of their sentiments will almost persuade them that they are changed into different beings.   (396–7)

While the "sort of" considerably mutes the edge of the standing miracle (the phrase is odd and is used earlier for the "sort of engagement" the Patriot King has with his people), the rhetoric of this passage is the positive side of the oratory that speaks of "burlesque Jupiters." It is, in another way, a form of speaking that would not discredit a Fifth Monarchy man in its talk of miracles and metamorphoses (like those that poets feign) and in its recollection of other castings out of devils. The good shepherd chastises his sheep, like the gypsy king.

Pope's *Pastorals* look at individual human states of mind, but *Windsor-Forest*, in its translation of these ideals to the world of the court, takes a sterner view, one that anticipates the voice of the later satires and is at one with this voice. St John's idea of a new people rising with a new king is embodied in the language of epic apotheosis. Virgil presides over his final view of "the greatest and most glorious of human beings, a Patriot King" (1.428):

let the imagination range through the whole glorious scene of a patriot reign: the beauty of the idea will inspire those transports, which Plato imagined the vision of virtue would inspire, if virtue could be seen ... What spectacle can be presented to the view of the mind so rare, so nearly divine, as a king possessed of absolute power, neither usurped by fraud, nor maintained by force, but the genuine effect of esteem, of confidence, and affection; the free gift of liberty, who finds her greatest security in this power, and would desire no other if the prince on the throne could be, what his people wish him to be, immortal? of such a prince, and of such a prince alone, it may be said with strict propriety and truth,

> Volentes
> Per populos dat jura, viamque affectat Olympo.

Civil fury will have no place in this draught: or, if the monster is seen, he must be seen as Virgil describes him,

> Centum vinctus ahennis
> Post tergum nodis, fremit horridus ore cruento.

He must be seen subdued, bound, chained, and deprived entirely of power to do hurt. In his place, concord will appear, brooding peace and prosperity on the happy land; joy sitting in every face, content in every heart; a people unoppressed, undisturbed, unalarmed; busy to improve their private property and the public stock; fleets covering the ocean, bringing home wealth by the returns of industry, carrying assistance or terror abroad by the direction of wisdom, and asserting triumphantly the right and the honor of Great Britain, as far as waters roll and as winds can waft them. (428–9)

Gardens and Parks

The first quotation is from the end of the *Georgics*, the Virgilian text to which *Windsor-Forest* chiefly alludes. It is Virgil's image of Caesar. The second is from the first book of the *Aeneid*, Jupiter's reassurance to Venus. But Rome is not even close to founding; eleven books of suffering remain. Not all readers of the *Aeneid* would by any means read the text as apocalyptically as Bolingbroke.

Long ago Isaac Kramnick subtitled his book on St John and his circle "The Politics of Nostalgia in the Age of Walpole." As his comments on Elizabeth I in the *Idea* indicate, he sees the theatrical dimension of Bolingbroke's effort to create an image for England and for her king. The problem, however, is that the theatre is melodramatic. Like melodrama, it creaks between the equal impossibilities of hero and villain. St John's recreation of a place in one of Donne's satires suggests some of the problem. In his third satire, *Of Religion*, Donne writes:

> doubt wisely, in strange way
> To stand inquiring right, is not to stray;
> To sleepe, or runne wrong, is: on a huge hill,
> Cragged, and steep, Truth stands, and hee that will
> Reach her, about must, and about must goe;
> And what the hills suddennes resists, winne so;
> Yet strive so, that before age, deaths twilight,
> Thy Soule rest, for none can worke in that night. (77–84)

In what sounds like a recollection of this place, Bolingbroke says:

> We have been long coming to this point of depravation: and the progress from confirmed habits of evil is much more slow than the progress to them. Virtue is not placed on a rugged mountain of difficult and dangerous access, as they who would excuse the indolence of their temper, or the perverseness of their will, desire to have it believed; but she is seated, however, on an eminence. We may go up to her with ease, but we must go up gradually, according to the natural progression of reason, who is to lead the way, and to guide our steps. On the other hand, if we fall from thence, we are sure to be hurried down the hill with a blind impetuosity, according to the natural violence of those appetites and passions that caused our fall at first, and urged it on the faster, the further they are removed from the control that before restrained them. (374)

The most obvious modification of this re-situated image, apart from the important smoothing out of its deliberately difficult syntax, is the adjustment of the labour of mounting the hill, mirrored in the twists of Donne's phrasing. Bolingbroke makes the hill a possible climb, stopped only by violence. The consequence of abandoning the corporate image of kingship or, more precisely, the notion of the mediating king and the attendant theology of this position, is humanist elaboration and gesture. The king is then either as other men and so lost in what Kramnick approvingly calls the "administrative image" (168), or, necessarily, like *no* man, a "sort of standing miracle" and hence, in a special way, a new burlesque Jupiter casting out devils. The shifts of Bolingbroke's treatise are stylistic mirrors of this division. He sees, alternately, two radically opposed models that are inevitable consequences of his suspicion, not just of Stuarts and Jacobites but of any kind of mediating theology. And here the humanist gestures that in themselves reflect something of the same suspicion, lack of faith, or whatever come with only spasmodic echoes of the past great tradition of mirror for princes. Desperation seems to demand an even more radical version of pastoral than earlier images even begin to suggest.

At a later date Washington Irving's Diedrich Knickerbocker, a pastoral figure in his own way, alludes to Bolingbroke in his reflections on politics, specifically with reference to the *Letters on History*. William Hedges comments as follows: "Bolingbroke's monumental casualness practically reduces all knowledge to history and then at least by assumption reduces history to little more than private experience."[39] "In the end," he goes on to say, with an interesting allusion to Sterne: "*Letters on History* describes, to a certain extent, and still more suggests, perhaps as well as any document of the age, even including *Tristram Shandy*, the ultimately incomprehensible universe of experience which is the background to a world of common sense" (324).

The Idea of a Patriot King may seem far removed from Dryden's projections of ideal monarchs in his poems about the return and coronation of Charles II, but in these early poems, and later, in *Absalom and Achitophel*, there is also some desperation as old models, hedged with more than near divinity, are proposed for a new king with no intention of fulfilling them.[40] Milton had long since sought his pastorals and paradises elsewhere.[41] Increasingly pastoral is located in the New World, in Jefferson's Virginia or, like Gay's *Polly*, in the West Indies. If true, says Milton, speaking of the Golden Age, then *only* in the Golden Age – or later, in the novel, where a Paradise Hall can be fictionally asserted and, on occasion, actually built and used to assert a pastoral vision, as for the political gardens of Stowe.

St John's views, written in 1738 if not published until 1749, must have been part of Scriblerian conversations. As such they are important in delineating the Scriblerian ideal. His treatise extends the idea of pastoral past the conventional notion of a deliberately evoked country scene to a larger simplicity, viewed not only in the individual lives of a little world, like Pope's shepherds, but in the greater world of the monarchy as well. The standing miracle who will be able, in Fielding's terms, to be wise, moderate, and unselfishly good, however, *is* a miracle. While he does not speak like a gypsy, he is just as far from the real laws of England as their leader and just as unlikely to enter and transform the city into a shining palace, an urbane pastoral place.

If the *Patriot King* establishes an essentially pastoral version of kingship, it is possible to see *An Essay on Man* as a pastoral too. Indeed, it seems to make more sense to read the poem in this way than as Pope transcribing (or not transcribing) Bolingbroke's deism. Swift's comments about Bolingbroke, Pope, and philosophy reflect his own bitterness about the failure of the image he wanted for England, partially, of course, because he was unable to be at Dawley to join the conversation. Pope and St John were themselves in retirement, cultivating their gardens or *fermes ornées*, literally and metaphorically, galling the horsemen, but from the *locus amoenus* of pastoral. The conversation intended at the urgent beginning of *An Essay on Man* and resumed at the end may dissolve rapidly as the poem proceeds, but pastoral encounter is present throughout, not simply in the initial insistence on dialogue but (especially in the Third Epistle) in the proposed revision of our view of the world as we cease to scan the divine.

Pope begins by inviting St John to what looks to be a meditative experience in the literal sense. He is to "leave all meaner things / To low ambition, and the pride of Kings" (1.1–2), to return to the ample fields, to philosophical exploration, from the baser concerns about court and king. He is to return, in other words, to the *locus amoenus* of house and garden so that as poet and patriot – shepherd kings – he and Pope may "restore / The Faith and Morals Nature gave before" (3.285–6). The design for restoration, through experience of the maze, so as to discern its plan, relates the project and the poem to Milton, as in *Windsor-Forest*. Pope means to allude both to that first garden and to the internal landscape in which he searches to justify the ways of God to men. His phrase ("vindicate the ways of God to man") is different from Milton's. "Vindicate" and "men" are both more secular and less personal than the critical words in the lines they recall. The new churches are Palladian mansions in landscaped grounds, with the rough places built into the plan and the crooked made serpentine line. I have argued elsewhere that there is a strong biblical presence in *An Essay on Man*, drawn from scriptural places projecting suffering servants.[42] This presence, however, is felt less strongly than Pope's insistence upon nature and upon the shining palaces that can emerge from natural and complementary scenes. The poem provides a turn on the more courtly pastoral of Pope's early poems, for it urges the primacy of instinct, learned from the animal kingdom. This is also a "bright tradition of the golden age" but, as Wordsworth would argue in the *Prelude*:

> Not such as, 'mid Arcadian fastnesses
> Sequestered, handed down among themselves
> Felicity, in Grecian song renowned;
> Nor such as, when an adverse fate had driven,
> From house and home, the courtly band whose fortunes
> Entered, with Shakspeare's genius, the wild wood
> Of Arden, amid sunshine or in shade
> Culled the best fruits of Time's uncounted hours,
> Ere Phoebe sighed for the false Ganymede;
> Or there where Perdita and Florizel
> Together danced, Queen of the feast, and King;
> Nor such as Spenser fabled. (8.133–44)

Pope's world is an early version of Wordsworth's "unconscious love and reverence" (8.278, 283), a state of mind that will, as the *Essay* finally says, take its centre as social love and human nature. If the human form does not become "an index of delight," the larger polity becomes a source of admiration and still, even in 1733, at least for Pope, of possibility. At no point does *An Essay on Man* espouse real monarchy; at no point does the poem deify reason. Rather the liveliest moments visualize the scene of man in a literally sensational way, in the evocation of the *scala naturae* in Epistle 1.207ff, in the anaphoral verbal series (warms, glows, lives, and so forth) that manifest "God the soul" (268) and in the account of the golden age in the Third Epistle, where to "copy Instinct then was Reason's part" (170).

The vignettes of evil in *An Essay on Man*, like the critical view of those who attempt to scan the almighty, come from that artful wit that distinguishes Fielding's female gypsy when she disturbs the pastoral harmony her king tries to achieve. Law, finds John Bull, that dweller in a happy rural village, is a bottomless pit because the language of law is also the language of crafty wit, where words can be so changed that it is possible to argue, for example, for the virtues of cuckoldom against family and social relation. The clear physical and psychological air of Bull's village and the "Chearfulness and Mirth" (95) vanish into wrangle and the destruction of the estate as well as in the destruction of friendly relations. In his preface to the translation of Huygens on chance, Arbuthnot says that "*There are very few Things which we know, which are not capable of being reduced to a Mathematical Reasoning; and when they cannot, it is a sign the Knowledge of them is very small and confused; and where a Mathematical Reasoning can be had, it is as great Folly to make use of any other, as to grope for a Thing in the Dark, when you have a Candle standing by you.*"[43]

This praise of mathematics may seem an odd passage to introduce into a discussion of pastoral and the pastoral ideal, but Arbuthnot's fascination with mathematics, with the possibility of a rational and demonstrable world, is related to and consistent with his concerns for clean air and his wish to make physicians turn city planners. All these are meant to move us to that clarity of design and purpose central to pastoral and to the expressions of it in poems, in gardens, and in parks. In the end, all are organizations of the sensations and instincts found in Nature. In that shining image that is composed from many shining buildings, all move as well in harmony with the sociability and discourse these buildings were to accommodate and to radiate. In *An Essay on Man* this extended sociability is constricted to Pope and Bolingbroke, with only small vignettes of other dramatic scenes, but the dialogue, or the attempt at it, stresses the need for conversation in a sequestered place. In the dialogue of the *Essay* we have realized before us another aspect of one of Alpers' observations, in his essay on Empson, that "it is of the essence of traditional pastoral to find styles of speech that express the possibilities of freedom and community within acknowledged, sometimes deeply felt, limitations."[44] One of the rhetorical problems of *An Essay on Man* is that it is neither fully aware of its own pastoralism nor clear about what poet and patriot may accomplish, especially in a world in which no Patriot King appears.

Alpers makes his observation about pastoral and styles of speech in his discussion of Empson's account of the versions possible for pastoral.[45] In *The Beggar's Opera* Macheath, in a style little different from the gypsies, is a pastoral hero *because* he is an outlaw, one who acts outside John Bull's bottomless pit. Gay's concern for the pastoral life is a constant, beginning with the declaration of *Rural Sports* about the "happy fields, unknown to noise and strife" (436). This line is an early echo of Milton, from Satan's farewell to the happy fields in *Paradise Lost*, 1.251. In the *What D'Ye Call It* Kitty will echo this line again (2.8.1). The rightness of Pope's decision not to write a pastoral tragedy in the fashion of the *Aminta* is probably validated by the infelicities of Gay's *Dione*, but this play itself shows Gay's concern with pastoral places. Dione flees "a life of care" (3.4.52) at Court to "the blissful plains" (3.4.59). That her "mien and dress / The polish'd manners of the Court confess" (3.3.45–6) does not invalidate her retreat. Swift complains that Gay could not "distinguish Rye from Barly, or an Oak from a crab-tree" (Swift to Gay, 4 May 1732, 4.16), but wishes that Gay had "as good a house & gardens as Mr Pope" (10 Nov. 1730, 1.418). When Gay revised *Rural Sports*, he made it, as John Aden has shown, a georgic, and so changed the original subtitle from "poem."[46] It is, I think, perverse and wrongly nostalgic to argue that *The Shepherd's Week*, begun as a contribution to the pastoral battle between Pope and the wits of Button's, became a document in the tradition of realistic pastoral represented by Philips.[47] The splendid preface that defines the language Gay proposes to use serves to amplify the principles of Pope's *Discourse* ironically:

> soothly to say, such as is neither spoken by the country Maiden nor the courtly Dame; nay, not only such as in the present Times is not uttered, but was never uttered in Times past; and, if I judge aright, will never be uttered in Times future. It having too much of the Country to be fit for the Court: too much of the Court to be fit for the Country, too much of the Language of old Times to be fit for the Present, too much of the Present to have been fit for the Old, and too much of both to be fit for any time to come. Granted also it is, that in this my Language, I seem unto my self, as a *London* Mason, who calculateth his Work for a Term of Years, when he buildeth with old Materials upon a Groundrent that is not his own, which soon turneth to Rubbish and Ruins. (1.92)

Pastorals, as this passage makes very plain, are by no means crude representations of the country, in crude language.

W.D. Ellis established the relation between the popularity of D'Urfey and Gay's parodies of this popular butt in *The Shepherd's Week*.[48] The literary character of these allusions and especially the comic notes remove the series from any easy idealized nostalgia for Devon.

Gay is certainly able to present the conventional pattern of the city versus the country, as in "The Lady's Lamentation":

Love in cities never dwells
He delights in rural cells
Which sweet wood-bine covers. (1.7–9)

When Merit praises Florinda in Gay's *The Wife of Bath* (1713) as a "plain, simple *Kentish* Yeoman's Daughter" because she has "Virtue without Formality," he adds that she has "all the good Breeding of the Court with the Country Simplicity – Beauty without Vanity, and Wit without Affectation" (1.1.57–60). Although the "gentillesse" speech from Chaucer's tale of the Wife of Bath does not make its way into Gay's transformation of his original, his comment that there is "no true Nobility without" (1.1.64–5) suggests that the original of the tale may be present in his mind. That original is also in its own way pastoral, even though the desire for a primitive world of wish fulfilment is snarled by the Wife's confusions. Her story is about that knightly mode that, as Poggioli observes, the "pastoral dream may ... replace, without being able to reach."⁴⁹ When Mrs Clackit, in *The Distress'd Wife*, protests that she "wou'd not marry a man that had a country house. – I should be in perpetual apprehensions, when a husband had such a hideous mortifying thing in his power" (5.9.37–40), like most of her sisters in the period she thinks of the country house as a prison, not as that oasis whose strengths make it possible to establish a city. *Trivia* is chiefly a poem of darkness and labyrinth, but there are pastoral lights. Commenting shrewdly on Gay's oasis of the sensibility, the *locus amoenus* of Burlington House, Dianne Ames observes that

Gay goes beyond traditional satire's facile antithesis of the city and the country to rhapsodize on the cultural advantages of urbanity itself. This attitude is actually perfectly attuned to Vergil's view of culture in the *Georgics*. To him the rightful domain of culture was the city, which became "*pulcherrima*" only by labor and art. To Gay, as to his patron and Vergil, the proper realization of *urbs* was not *rus* but the cultivation of *urbanitas*.⁵⁰

The sparrow in the *Fables* may eulogize her "thatch'd retreat" (Fable 38, 2.287), but she does so as a trope from fabular fiction. Gay does not in the least mean, any more than Pamela, to make his way back to the thatch. In the language of his *Epistle to Paul Methuen*, it is "*Burlington's* proportion'd columns" (1.216) that represent the ideal, in their proportion and in the ability of this shining palace to light up London. For Gay, of course, Burlington House served as particular example, as Pope says in a note to the *Iliad*, 6.16, of "that ancient Hospitality which we now only read of" (7.323n). The "wonderful Simplicity of the old heroic Ages," celebrated in a note in Book 7 (387n), was concretely expressed in sociability in the literal sense of that term. Ideally, the retired man, as the literature on the topos shows, is not to be alone in a rural landscape, except very briefly. He (and even she)[51] retired to reflect, to regain equilibrium and to entertain.[52] The process and the ideal are nicely illustrated by Matthew Bramble, that grouchy latter-day Allworthy. Brambleton Hall, with all its natural advantages, should be a paradise. But Bramble has been a virtual recluse. His old friend Charles Dennison has rebuilt a wilderness into a lively country house with the aid of all social classes, and has achieved, as Bramble says, the felicity Bramble has himself sought for twenty years. He has failed to find it not simply because of his solitude but because of the corrosive ironic wit his kind of solitude has engendered and emphasized. Unlike Fielding's female gypsy, Bramble does not use this wit to deceive, except in so far as he is self-deceived. His natural son, Humphry Clinker, the product of a positive instinct long since suppressed, writes no letters at all and, as a variety of comic episodes in the novel indicate, has no irony at all. He responds to words literally. The end of the novel is also the end of letters, actually and figuratively construed.

Positive instinct, vivid in the natural world praised in *An Essay on Man*, is central to *The Beggar's Opera*, as it is in Pope's *Eloisa*, whose heroine desires only a paradise where "love is liberty and nature law" (92), a mutuality of affection needing no legal bond for ratification. Pope's "Elegy to the Memory of an Unfortunate Lady," a study in the harm worked by the tyranny of law, is the other side of Eloisa's insistence that an ideal world is one where love rules, without laws of any kind. The *Opera*, as Empson argues, works out pastoral in ways that are both different from and related to the issues I have been arguing. "There is," he says, "a natural connection between heroic and pastoral before they are parodied" (196), a point established seriously, if unconsciously, by St John in *The Idea of a Patriot King*. In a Golden Age kings are shepherds and shepherds kings. Pope observes that the "general design and moral of the *Odyssey*, is to inform us of the mischievous effects which the Absence of a King and Father of a family produces" (2.33n). In an earlier note (1.540n), he says that "The simplicity of these Heroic times is remarkable ... Greatness then consisted not in shew, but in the mind: this conduct proceeded not from the meanness of poverty, but from the simplicity of manners." The difficulty, when Dunce the Second reigns like Dunce the First, is finding a hero and a habitation for him, in an age in which kingship no longer meant the charisma Dryden tried to project for Charles in *Absalom and Achitophel.*

Derek Hughes's account of the varying views of the heroes of Dryden's plays does not (nor does he mean it so) solve the problem of whether Dryden meant to view Almanzor and his brothers seriously, ironically, or with some tone in between. The critical dilemma of later readers highlights Dryden's own insecurity about monarchy.[53] Within the Homeric world heroic virtue was still possible. It is seen vividly in passages that memorialize friendship (like the speech of Patroclus), in Sarpedon's cry for honourable holding fast, a speech Pope translated early and commented upon movingly. In his note in Book 24 of the *Iliad*, Pope describes how Homer fixes the "Idea of [Achilles'] Greatness upon our Minds" (653n). Felicity Rosslyn says that, as he appears at the end of Pope's translation, Achilles' wrath removes his *philophrosyne*, so that he loses *aidos*, that "instinct that teaches us to love the way things are."[54] When he listens with compassion to Priam, Achilles recovers the moral heroism he had lost. Perhaps no gloss is necessary, but the centre of the matter is that he behaves in a sympathetic pastoral style, like a Patriot King, like a friend. In Gay's *Achilles*, we are aware, as Peter Lewis argues, of "childish posturing" and "theatrical honour."[55] "But you know," says Periphas to Ajax, "we were so very valiant that we did not know what we were fighting for" (3.12.35–6). Gay is rather sharper about war and personal experience in his "*Epistle* to her Grace Henrietta, Dutchess of MARLBOROUGH" (1.283–5), in the first two fables of the first book, and in his representation of Achelous and Hercules in his translation of Ovid's Book 9 (1.185–98). Homeric and medieval heroes and kings were clear about their functions because they worked in a context more extended than a social landscape. The revival of a hero now would have to come from a Newgate pastoral and, as Empson says, would work out that hero's passions as a "laird of the open ground where he robs people ... king of the Waste Land" (201).

Amidst the cheating worlds of lawyer and thieftaker, Macheath is a noble and free spirit. One might even argue that his thievery, the removal of money, is itself a pastoral gesture. In his *Tables and Measures* Arbuthnot, sounding very medieval, says that the Inventor of Money was by some *Jewish* Writers believed to be *Cain, Adam's* eldest son, to whom *Josephus* ascribes it: this author tells you that *Cain* was the first monied man, that he taught his band luxury and rapine; and broke the publick tranquility by introducing the use of Weights and Measures ... If arguments *a posteriore* were to be used in this case, I should be very apt to give *Cain* the honour of the Invention; were he now alive, I'm sure it would rejoice his soul to see what mischief it had made among mankind ... money ... has been a great conveniency in the commerce and affairs of mankind: but whether that will balance the mischief it has done, I shall not determine.[56]

In *The Four Last Years of the Queen* Swift remarks that, "by all I have yet read of the History of our own Country, it appears to me, That National Debts secured upon Parliamentary Funds of Interest, were things unknown in *England* before the last Revolution under the Prince of *Orange* ... I am very well satisfyed, That the pernicious Counsels of borrowing Money upon publick Funds of Interest ... were taken indigested from the like Practices among the *Dutch*, without allowing in the least for any Difference in Government, Religion, Law, Custom, extent of Country, or Manners and Dispositions of the People" (68–9).

Pope's epistles, to his several political persons and to others, make his own suspicions known, not just of "blest paper-credit" ("To Bathurst," 70) but of anything other than land and barter as proper commerce, *pace* his own investment in the South Sea Bubble and his subscriptions for Homer and for Shakespeare. Macheath is a pastoral hero to the extent that he is independent of the system to which Scriblerus took consistent and vivid exception. Certainly Gay's hero's independence from permanent ties to women associates him, however comically, with a world in which love is liberty and nature law. As he stands like the Turk with his doxies around, Macheath *is*, however oddly, the free man, a new version not just of pastoral but of Marvell's thought in "The Garden" that "two Paradises 'twere in one / To live in Paradise alone" (49). To live with many, and with no commitment, is the obvious other side of the proposition. Empson is right in tracing the "knot that sacred love hath tied" in matrimony to the hangman's knot and to Polly's hanging about Macheath's neck, with her later visions of him in her own romantic fantasies about the tree: "Where is my dear Husband? Was a Rope ever intended for this Neck! O let me throw my Arms about it, and throttle thee with Love!" (2.12.21-3) The betrayal scene with Jenny Diver and the others, with the echo of the Judas kiss, and the throttling, are the restriction of this pastoral hero. He may not be an owner of a shining palace, in town or, in reduced scale, on the banks of the Thames, but he *is* a gentleman in his own upside-down way, with pastoral freedom. John Rees and Joan Owen use Jean Hagstrum's discussion of the icon of Hercules' choice as a way of looking at Macheath's choice between Polly and Lucy.[57] He chooses Polly but really wishes to be the legal property of neither the whore nor the woman whose desire for respectability comes to much the same thing. As the son of the Heath he wants the freedom of the road, to inhabit paradise alone, to be a man alone, or at least an imperial animal in an exclusive group.

The focal point of Owen's study, however, is not the *Opera* but *Polly*, the sequel never performed until 1777, an appropriate time in dramatic history, given the transformation of sentiment and tone. Gay alters not only his characters but (more significantly) his scene, as he transports all, in one way or another, to the West Indies, another version of pastoral, or at least of pastoral in potential. I want later to return to Gay and his early drama, with special emphasis on his rewriting not just of the *Opera* but of the *Fables* and the *Wife of Bath*. Here I want simply to concentrate on what happens to the characters in their new scene. Macheath's energetic and free sexuality becomes predatory, and he is in league with Jenny Diver. Polly emerges as heroine, no longer wanting to hang about her love (or simply to hang him) but as heiress of the old tradition of the woman prepared to go through any trial for reunion with her lover, including the trials often associated with the assumption of male dress, like Fidelia in *The Plain-Dealer*, Margery in *The Country Wife*, Florimell in *Secret Love*, Hellena in *The Rover*. As Owen argues, Polly is also faced with the choice of Hercules, but this is not the choice of the *Opera*. Faithful to Macheath even when his vices as Morana are known, she is finally won by another. We are nearly back in Fielding's gypsyland when we meet the Indian Cawwakwee. As Owen comments:

the real Cult of Independence depends on the survival of innocence ... genuine primitivism disengaged from irony. Supported only by her intuitive, humane sense of respect, Polly becomes the real outsider and judge, the orphan driven from European hypocrisy to the company of natural man: an aristocracy of naivete ... *Polly* emerges as a rich idyll of pastoral care and independence ... As a goddess educated in the meaning and responsibility of her own virtue, Polly is finally elevated above all private abuse of ethical abstractions. To borrow a Cheyenne phrase from Thomas Berger's novel *Little Big Man*, when she joins the Indians she becomes a Human Being. (404–5)

Transportation to another land to find deeds answerable for a paradise not within but without (and happier far) provides a natural transition to Swift, hater of the pastoral cant of Strephon and Chloe but most committed of all the Scriblerians to the pastoral ideal, the style of life as it might be fictively rendered. The inability of the hero of *Travels into Several Remote Nations of the World* to stay at home is so easily seen as a comment on the insufficiencies of Lemuel Gulliver that we forget that he does not in fact wish to leave Houyhnhnmland at the end of the fourth book but is forced out because the horses (quite properly) fear that he may become a natural leader of a Yahoo rebellion. It is also now fashionable to assume that if we are supposed to look critically at Gulliver, not least because he looks on young Yahoos as shoe leather, we are also supposed to regard the horses, if not as silly, then perhaps as deists (the label is supposed to do the job), but certainly not as ideals. The language of Eden informs Gulliver's experience in this fourth book, not least in the mythical account of the arrival of the Yahoos, paw in paw. It is impossible to find anything positive about these creatures, certainly from Swift's point of view. Quite apart from their bad behaviour, sometimes inadvertently commended as only human, they are much too dirty for a writer committed to a near obsession with the clean, the neat, and the plain.

Without deceit, except for a single place near the end of the voyage, when they meet to discuss Gulliver without his knowledge, the horses deal with each other as if they were Golden Age Egyptians. Although they may be without passion, they are certainly not without feeling. The episode most often adduced as indicative of their chill is the behaviour of the horsy wife to the death of her spouse. She goes to a gathering after the funeral. Only Donald Greene has noted that she dies soon after, evidently missing her mate but disinclined to neurotic display and thus to a disturbance for the rest of the polity.[58] While Gulliver's version of European society, made acutely worse by his isolation from it in a much less complicated world, may be what the horses reject, as the King of Brobdingnag rejects English society in Book 2, it does not follow necessarily that none of this negative account is true and that the critics of his history are misguided. Like More's Hythloday in *Utopia*, Gulliver learns only negation and literalism from Houyhnhnmland. He hates his family and trots like a horse. Pope's mischievous poem on Mrs Mary Gulliver hints that he may be consorting with the sorrel mare in his home stable (6.276–9). Like Hythloday, he has had an experience but missed its meaning.

That the ideal world should turn out to be run by horses does not mean that Swift does not take its pastoral values seriously but that he cannot imagine this ideal realized among humans. "I cannot tell," says Arbuthnot, "by what chance, but the most honorable Profession of a Foot Soldier has always been reckon'd as one of the lowest kinds of Day labour, and it has cost Mankind less to kill their own *Species*, than any other sort of *Animal*" (*Tables*, 180). Gay's *Fables*, intended as a speculum for the young Prince William, often introduce us to animals whose natures are no better than humans, but these have a certain licence in their natures as animals. Mainly they do not "imitate the restless mind / And proud ambition of mankind" (Fable 4, 2.49–50). Gay's introduction to the *Fables* makes it clear that the shepherd learns from nature, and that theme, as I have earlier argued, is central to the pastoralism of *An Essay on Man*. The voice of Nature, scriptural in undertone, urges men to take instruction from creatures:

"Learn from the beasts the physic of the field;
"Thy arts of building from the bee receive:
"Learn of the mole to plow, the worm to weave;
"Learn of the little Nautilus to sail,
"Spread the thin oar, and catch the driving gale. (3.173–7)

Pope's translation of the *Odyssey* includes a long note on the death of Argus that illustrates his interest in and trust of natural observation. "In my judgment," he says, commenting upon Ulysses' tears, "*Ulysses* appears more amiable while he weeps over his faithful Dog, than when he drives an army of enemies before him: That shews him to be a great Heroe, This a good Man. It was undoubtedly an instance of an excellent disposition in one of the Fathers ... who pray'd for the *Grace of Tears*" (17.364n). In the *Iliad*, remarking on Fate's preservation of goat and hind, he says:

Dacier has a pretty Remark on this Passage, that *Homer* extended Destiny (that is, the Care of Providence) even over the Beasts of the Field; an Opinion that agrees perfectly with true Theology. In the Book of *Jonas*, the Regard of the Creator extending to the meanest Rank of his Creatures, is strongly express'd in those Words of the Almighty, where he makes his Compassion to the Brute Beasts one of the Reasons against destroying *Nineveh*. *Shall I not spare the great City, in which there are more than sixscore thousand Persons, and also much Cattel?* And what is still more parallel to this Passage, in St. *Matth*. Ch. 10.

Are not two Sparrows sold for a Farthing? And yet one of them shall not fall to the Ground, without your Father. (15.311n).⁵⁹

Pope's care for animals, reflected in his household in the large figure of Bounce, is an anticipation of a new epic focus, partially engendered by Lucretius. The poor Indian of *An Essay on Man* who hopes to see his dog and bottle in the next life might do much worse. Natural creatures, in addition to offering educational models for various skills, are precisely that – natural – and as such both predictable and manageable. If they do not always render the image of a peaceable kingdom, they give instinctive responses and feeling.

One of the most usual arguments against the Houynhynms, apart from their apparent deism, is their poetry, distinguished, Gulliver tells us, for its plainness and obvious lack of wit. This lack is made metaphorically manifest by the long account in the second chapter of the fourth book of Gulliver's attempts to find suitable food, and especially of his initial "great Loss for Salt" (10.232). I have written elsewhere about this passage, principally in terms of Gulliver's failure in natural observation and metaphorical history. Some of the same comments can be made about the horses, whose closed society makes them primitives too. With the notoriously short sight of their kind (and no telescopes), they have "no Conception of any Country beside [their] own" (281). With enough for simple survival and no distracting commerce, they need not think of preservation and they take no long voyages. The use of salt as a condiment would introduce awkward prudential decisions into their virtuous cloisters.⁶⁰ The horses, in other words, are primitives, in some ways resembling Fielding's gypsies. There is no need for prudential decision in cloisters where virtue mostly reigns. And the salt that was a synonym for wit and a hallmark of Scriblerian writing *is* missing until Gulliver extracts salt from seawater – without ever lecturing on the implications of the mineral. In another fit of inventiveness he is the person who devises the solution of castration for control and extermination of the Yahoos. He uses gypsy "wit oblique" to break the steady light of Nature, to stop the species to which he is clearly related.

With all that we imagine about the meetings of the Club, and all we know about the manner in which they conducted their correspondence, their final rhetorical ideal is also a version of pastoral, for the ideal is clarity and plainness in speech. That is the centre of John Bull's vexed situation, as it is of Swift's political essays, his sermons, his views of women and dress. For the simple problem of who is to have which horse in *Stradling versus Stiles*, the narrator crazily proposes that "first of all it seemeth expedient to consider, what is the *Nature of Horses*, and also what is the *Nature of Colours*; and so the Argument will consequentially divide itself into a two-fold Way, that is to say, the *Formal Part*, and the *Substantial Part*."[61] Now this is as mad as Martinus Scriblerus eating his gingerbread letters to learn the Greek alphabet, but it is not any more to the point than the residents of the third voyage of the *Travels* who, through excess of wit, build houses from the top down. Responding to Swift's complaints about his loss of memory, Pope writes on 12 October 1738: "You lose little by *not hearing* such things as this idle and base generation has to tell you: you lose not much by *forgetting* most of what of what *now* passes in it. Perhaps, to have a memory that retains the past scenes of our country and forgets the present, is the means to be happier and better contented." (4.135) The phrase "past scenes" takes us back to the world imagined by Bolingbroke in the *Patriot King*, to the world of *Windsor-Forest* and *Rural Sports*. If the language is elegantly proper in these, its writers long for a language that is direct. That is what I take Swift to mean when he speaks of proper words in proper places.

No Scriblerian says so, but the final validation of the friendship they held as the highest of human goods is not witty exchange but communicative silence, among persons genuinely correspondent. The letter about gathering "three or four Cotemporaries" for an assault on the world sounds like a clarion call for manifestos, for action. But the real direction is a move backwards to a reconstruction of the Golden Age. There speech will be as plain as Houyhnhnm poetry, whose force will strike immediately. As I have earlier noted, the tone of the rest of this letter is bitter. Swift begins by saying that he has "no very strong Faith in you pretenders to retirement; you are not of an age for it, nor have you gone through either good or bad Fortune enough to go into a Corner and form Conclusions de contemptu mundi et fuga Seculi" (2.464–5). He understands what true retirement might mean. His own efforts to garden received little attention until Carole Fabricant's *Swift's Landscape*. His letters are full of references to gardening but they have a tone rather different from Pope's on the state of the art. On 12 December 1721, Swift writes to Knightley Chetwode: "I hope you are grown regular in your plantations, and have got some skill to know where and what trees to place, and how to make them grow. For want of better I have been planting elms in the Deanery garden, and what is worse, in the Cathedral churchyard where I disturbed the dead, and angered the living, by removing tombstones, that people will be at a loss how to rest with the bones of their ancestors" (2.412).

Edward Malins and the Knight of Glin remind us of Deane Swift's observation that the only presents Swift ever gave were in fact some trees.[62] "If you had told me," he writes to Charles Ford as early as 12 November 1708, "you began to take a Relish in planting and improving the Scene, I should begin to have favourable Thoughts of your Conversion" (1.110). He took a considerable interest in Delany's more expansive spaces at Delville, comments upon his expenses in "An Epistle upon an Epistle" (2.475–9), and establishes his values when, in "An Apology to the Lady C—R—T," he observes that "He'd treat with nothing that was Rare, / But winding Walks and purer Air" (2.99–100). More comically, in "My Lady's Lamentation" he declares

> How proudly he talks
> Of zigzacks and walks;
> And all the day raves
> Of cradles and caves;
> And boasts of his feats
> His grottos and seats;
> Shews all his gew-gaws,
> And gapes for applause?
> A fine occupation
> For one of his station!
> A hole where a rabbit
> Would scorn to inhabit,
> Dug out in an hour,
> He calls it a bow'r.   (3.173–86)

On 8 July 1713 he writes to Vanessa that "My River walk is extremely pretty, and my Canal in great Beauty, and I see Trout playing in it" and adds that he is "now fitter to look after Willows, and to cutt Hedges than meddle with Affairs of State" (1.73). "Do you find," he writes to Chetwode some ten years later, "that your trees thrive and your drained bog gets a new coat? I know nothing so well worth the enquiry of an honest man, as times run. I am as busy in my little spot of a town garden, as ever I was in the *grand monde*" (12 Feb. 1722/23, 2.449). He makes the same observation to Pope in a letter of 8 July 1733 (4.170). The centrality of the garden in his Dublin experience is perhaps best shown in a letter to Chetwode on 14 February 1726/27: "I know nothing

I should more desire than some spot upon which I could spend the rest of my life in improving. But I shall live and die friendless, and a sorry Dublin inhabitant, and yet I have spirit still left to keep a clatter about my little garden, where I pretend to have the finest paradise stocks of their age in Ireland. But I grow so old, that I despond, and think nothing worth my care except ease and indolence, and walking to keep my health" (3.199).

The garden had a name. Mrs Pendarves writes to Swift on 24 October 1733. She has been to see Lord Bathurst, and "we did not," she says, "forget to talk of *Naboth*'s vineyard and *Delville*" (4.200). In a later letter of 9 September 1734 Mrs Pendarves speaks of North-End as "the *Delville* of this part of the world. I hope *Naboth*'s Vineyard flourishes: it always has my good wishes, though I am not near enough to partake of its fruits" (4.252). Pope was invited to come to have "two Gardens for amusement" (10 May 1728, 3.286). In 1731 Swift writes that the winds "have almost ruined my fruit, for I suffer peach and Nectarin and pear-weeds to grow in my famous Garden of Naboth's Vineyard, that you have heard me boast of" (20 Apr., 3.458). Swift's choice of name for his garden is as right and as resonant as his other namings. It reflects his sense of the problems in achieving the pastoral ideal and the assaults to which it is liable. The tenth chapter of Poggioli's *The Oaten Flute* is called "Naboth's Vineyard: The Pastoral View of the Social Order." "The bucolic reaction to might and violence," he says,

is primarily sentimental; the consciousness of its own innocence, merging with the awareness that the precariousness of its happiness is due to acts of men rather than to "acts of God," produces in the pastoral soul a sense of outraged justice. The very concept of natural justice had been predicated not only on the inner voice of man's conscience but also on the state of nature, when mankind was supposed to be either an unruly horde or a docile herd. Hence, the important role the idea of justice has always played within the pastoral dream. (195)

Poggioli's first subject in this chapter is Virgil, who realized, he says, that political peace was the basis for the

reestablishment of an order based on justice. He did so in the Fourth Eclogue, in which he conveyed that expectation through the fabulous images of the restoration of the Golden Age and of the return of Astraea to the earth. Yet the peace and justice announced in the Fourth Eclogue were still conceived, so to speak, in aristocratic terms – as the gift of a wise shepherd of men to his herd. Only after the foundation of the empire, while writing the *Aeneid*, was Vergil able to celebrate peace and justice as the rule of a universal law.   (198–99)

The hollow tones of Pope's imitation of Virgil's Fourth Eclogue may reflect his own uneasiness at the possibility of realizing expectation. His own eclogues, as I have argued above, do not battle out political issues as Virgil's do. They articulate a world nearly detached from the practical concerns of the real, except in the dedicatees. Poggioli goes from Virgil to a pastoral biblical city: "that of Naboth of Jezreel, whose vineyard lay close to the palace of Ahab" (199). Ahab asks Naboth for his vineyard, offering a better or money (his assumption being, I suppose, that every man has his price). Naboth properly replies that he will not give over the inheritance of his fathers. We know the rest. Jezebel, wife to Ahab, has Naboth denounced; he is stoned to death, and Ahab goes to take the vineyard. As Poggioli observes, the story up to this point is not unlike the story of the First Eclogue, except that Naboth has lost both life and land (199–200). God sends Elijah to curse Ahab; Ahab is humbled, but his punishment is that the evil will be brought into his son's days – an Old Testament resolution.

Naboth's vineyard was a favourite scriptural place for reflection on tyranny and the social order.[63] It is striking that Swift should adopt it for his own garden and thus invoke some darker tones for pastoral oasis, the menace so constantly present, not just by wind and water and falling walls but by human agents, like witty gypsies and those who, for falsely alleged pastoral motives, release birds from young ladies' cages. He is much more alive to menace than Pope or Bolingbroke, and his perception of this menace doubtless helps to account for his impatience with his friends and what he took to be their posturing retirement. He would have agreed sadly with Pope (Pope to Swift, Aug. 1723) that a wish for constant companionship with friends is "as vain as to wish to live to see the millenium, & the Kingdom of the Just upon Earth" (Swift, *Corr.*, 2.460). He might, however, have responded with ill temper to Bolingbroke, who wrote to Swift on 24 July 1725: "will you leave yr Hibernian flock to some other shepherd, and transplant yr self wth me into the middle of the Atlantick Ocean? We will form a society, more reasonable, & more useful than that of Dr Berkley's Colledge, and I promise you solemnly, as Supreme Magistrat, not to suffer the currency of Wood's halfpence, nay the Coyner of them shall be hang'd if he presumes to set foot on our Island" (Swift, *Corr.* 3.82). The Dean's bagatelles are never in quite this tone, possibly because of his more complicated sense of the forces moving against pastoral and those manifestations of it in poetical forms. As Claude Rawson has remarked: "This most unremittingly parodic of eighteenth-century writers hardly ever attempted mock-*epic* (though he mocked most other forms of poetic inflation), as though anxious to avoid damaging the originals."[64]

Actual damage in the garden was not foreign to Swift. In March of 1729/30 he writes to Bolingbroke: "I built a wall five years ago, and when the masons played the knaves, nothing delighted me so much as to stand by while my servants threw down what was amiss: I have likewise seen a Monkey overthrow all the dishes and plates in a kitchen, merely for the pleasure of seeing them tumble and hearing the clatter they make in their fall" (3.383). The wall was a constant problem, a literalization of the difficulties of Naboth, and Swift's tones rise to the characteristic *saeva indignatio*, complete with the monkeys (visiting Yahoos) and here involving his own mixed response to the failure of the structure. As Pope wrote to Swift on 15 October 1725:

I have often imagined to myself, that if ever All of us met again, after so many Varieties and Changes, after so much of the Old world, and of the Old man in each of us, had been alter'd ... we shou'd meet like the Righteous in the Millenium, quite in peace, divested of all our former passions, smiling at all our own designs, and content to enjoy the Kingdome of the Just in Tranquillity. But I find you would rather be employ'd as an Avenging Angel of Wrath, to break your Vial of Indignation over the heads of the wretched pityful creatures of this World; nay would make them *Eat your Book*, which you have made as bitter a pill for them as possible.   (Swift *Corr.*, 3.107–8)

The avenging angel reminds us of Elijah (as well as of the avenging gnome in the fourth canto of *The Rape of the Lock*) sent to chastise Ahab for his usurpation of the vineyard, to work retributive justice, even as the monkey passage shows a more passionately direct act of vengeance, worked towards the masons.

Both these allusions take us to another strain in the Scriblerians which has its own relation to pastoral. That is the world of the child, especially a child's passionately expressed indignation that nothing seems to be fair. This strain reminds us again of Poggioli's comments about the distance between the bucolic and the Christian experience, or of his later observation, in the chapter on Naboth's vineyard, that a New Testament resolution of the crisis would not be retributive justice but a mercy and charity that recognize the deep flaws of human nature and, without approving of them, get past, accept, and occasionally make things less bad. This child quality has both a negative and a positive side. We see the negative in Scriblerus in the revenges worked upon Curll and on other dunces and, given the ideals of other versions of pastoral, in the frivolity of the Scriblerian invitations to meeting in friendly pastoral experience. We also see it in their zany quality, not so wild as Sterne but verging on occasion on that wildness. The better part of the impulse lies in the pastoral clarity a child-world might provide, in a century when the child was being discovered and protected.[65]

On 14 December 1725 Pope and Bolingbroke wrote to Swift about Gay's *Fables*: "[We] suppose Philips will take this very ill, for two reasons; one, that he thinks all childish things belong to him; and the other because he'll take it ill to be taught, that one may write things to a Child, without being childish" (Swift, *Corr.*, 3.120–1). What Pope and Bolingbroke have in mind is that simplicity Pope so much admired in Homer, in everything from his poetic style to Juno's dress (*Iliad*, 14.203n), in contrast to the "innumerable Equipage" of the modern world and to the labyrinths of that political lying of which Arbuthnot wrote an art. Labyrinth becomes a metaphor for the deceit practised by those grown far away from a world of innocence. Charles Martindale speaks of the "childlike imaginative world" of the poem.[66] I have written elsewhere of some elements in Pope's Roman Catholic background that may shape parts of his work.[67] Catholic retirement, with its strong pull to the pastoralism of the mystical tradition, stills human wit in favour of contemplation. Martindale is concerned rather to underline Pope and his toyshop. To this one would want to add the tramgrams for his crammed garden, the velvet suit, and the tye-wig. The little language of the *Journal to Stella* shows a similar pull to the pre-adult world. Among the facts we have about the Scriblerians are the simple ones that Swift, Gay, and Pope never married. The muted tones of the poems to Stella and the fantastical letters of Pope to Lady Mary may tell us that the child impulse is also related to the projections of ideal orders and that it militates against the trying order of marriage. Uncle Toby never does get to the Widow Wadman from his bowling green. The John Bull papers are, quite simply, more domestic. The search for a perfect past makes acceptance of a flawed present a particularly difficult task, and those who search swing between near sentiment and angry satire.

"Pastoral poets leave the theater and the agora," says Poggioli, "to cultivate, like Candide, their own garden where they grow other flowers than those of communal myth and public belief" (4). It seems, said the hero of More's *Utopia* as he sits himself in a garden with More and Peter Giles, that "there is nothing which their founder seems to have cared for so much as for these gardens."[68] Utopian gardens have two doors, one to the inner garden and one to the public world. Shining palaces, gardens, and parks – constant images of efforts to realize ideals. My title, "Gardens and Parks," is drawn from Vladimir Nabokov, a modern Scriblerian, who used it for the autobiographical essay he printed first in the *New Yorker* and later made the final chapter of his completed autobiography, *Speak Memory*.[69] That chapter, like the first in Nabokov's recomposed account of his life, is really about children and about the gardens and parks of Europe to which he and his wife, deprived of the shining palace and aristocratic pastoral spaces of his native country, took their son in the days before they emigrated to America, where he wrote his labyrinthine novels. These were made partially possible by the oases from which Nabokov came. He asserts these, not always so seriously, in many places in his fiction, from the backyards of the Haze house, where he first sees the child Lolita, to the child-scenes in *Invitation to a Beheading*, to the natural paradises of *Ada*. The topoi set down for him early are as central to him as to those eighteenth-century writers he knew in remarkable detail. They sustained him through other places, complicated these, and created a special style whose operations, achievements, and limitations are like those of Pope and Swift and Gay and Arbuthnot, designing their own parks and gardens.

Royal masquerade, Somerset House. Engraving by William Hogarth. Courtesy Thomas Fisher Rare Book Library, University of Toronto

3 Monsters and Metropolis

When Mr Allworthy retreats to his study at the end of chapter 4 in Book 1 of *Tom Jones*, leaving the foundling to the tender mercies of Miss Bridget and Mrs Deborah, he does not exit like Horace's *beatus vir*, central to the retirement topos in the gardens and parks of the seventeenth and eighteenth centuries. He is not bound for creative reflection and action in the styles of Pope's Trumbull, Lansdown, Cobham, Bathurst, and Burlington. Rather he goes as one of those solitary figures who increasingly populate the novelistic scene, eloquent or semi-eloquent I's:[1] saddlers living uncertainly through a plague that becomes a metaphor for non-communication at many levels, whores with a passion for memorandums without understanding why they keep them, shipwrecked sailors frightened by footprints, hard-pressed servant girls, and, especially, consumptive frenetics warding off death by searching for the stories of their lives.[2] At the end of *Tom Jones* Allworthy can rest comfortably as his Paradise Hall, augmented by the Western lands, comes to the godson and namesake who has found wisdom (or at least Sophia) and reached his majority after nine gestational months on an increasingly labyrinthine road that leads to the maze of an often ruinous city undistinguished by shining palaces.

But no reader quite believes in all this romance, and no reader is in fact allowed to do so, for another solitary voice, in the person of the narrator, is always there to tell him that this is only a story and that he, like a new epic machine, has made it up.[3] Unlike the teller of *The*

Pilgrim's Progress, he is not perpetually surrounded by the comfort of providential biblical narrative and he does not go on, like Bunyan in Part 2, to provide for the fetching and redeeming of a family in what is essentially a cheerfully unmenacing tale, in which it is possible to seek and find true valour and to be a pilgrim. Fielding's view of the real world and of those good reptiles for whom he writes is a dark one.[4] He exits with irony, as he had already done in *Joseph Andrews*, knowing, like the teller of that tale, that not even country estates are free from Lady Boobys and Peter Pounces. Parson Adams, meant as the best of wayfaring, warfaring Christians, a new Adam and Abraham, emerges torn, tattered, and bloody from his attempted pilgrimage from his country village to the city, lucky to be alive and really only able to cope with flock or family when he stands in his surplice, only now clearly recognizable as the good shepherd, in the narrow confines of his pulpit. Howard D. Weinbrot's study of the digressions in *Joseph Andrews* reminds us that these interpolated tales introduce reminders of hard reality into that romantic world where everybody turns out to be related to the right person in the right way, with that "utmost merriment" of which most critics write nostalgically when they speak of Fielding's first novel.[5] The digressions end either unhappily, as for Leonora, the unfortunate jilt, or not at all, as for the story told by Parson Adams' son Dick of the miseries of marriage and friendship in the story of Paul and Lennard. Even in the demi-paradise of Mr Wilson's country house (and it is clear that Wilson, like Tom Jones, cannot survive in the city) there are marauding squires who wantonly kill a dog no bigger than one's fist.

In some parts of the green and pleasant land, specifically in Yorkshire, domestic matters are even worse. The fourth chapter of the first book of *Tom Jones*, as I have earlier argued, gives us paradise in every positive feature valued by eighteenth-century builders. We slide down together with our controlling narrator from this prime sublime into Allworthy's breakfast room. We query his retreat from that room only upon reflection, without asking questions about the hinges of the door through which he goes. However much we feel his limitations as he mistakenly lectures Jenny Jones, we never doubt the harmonious prospect of the park we can see from his sash windows. Most critically we are sure that these, unlike Mr Shandy's, do in fact work. Tom's birth is doubtful, but nobody's obstetrical bag is impossibly knotted. Mr Allworthy, unlike Walter Shandy, is devoted to the memory of his deceased wife, but he preaches no funeral orations, and we are quite sure that his marital habits were never governed by the winding of a clock. The view from Shandy Hall is not a fine prospect of another Eden, but an ox-moor "full in view before the house," "a fine, large, whinny, undrained, unimproved common" that "exclusive of the purchase-money, which was eight hundred pounds ... had cost the family eight hundred pounds more in a law-suit about fifteen years before" (4.31.395-7). Arbuthnot's sense of the law as a bottomless pit is here rendered literally and metaphorically. As we know from his study of the importance of good air, Arbuthnot the physician would have agreed with Burton about one of the causes of melancholy: "The worst of the three is a thick, cloudy, misty, foggy air, or such as come from fens, moorish grounds, lakes, muckhills, draughts, sinks, where any carcasses or carrion lies, or from whence any stinking fulsome smell comes."[6]

In its own way Shandy Hall is a verbal equivalent of Dürer's *Melencolia* I.[7] The detailed iconography of this familiar engraving of a portly woman, idly slumped in the midst of ill-sorted objects, is highly complex, but the most obvious problem in the scene, which contrasts in every detail so sharply to the engraving of St Jerome that is meant to face it, is its sheer clutter, like the chaos of the Shandy household. This condition comes from the inattentions of its owner, a classic melancholic obsessive, the very opposite to the ordered and communicative gentlemen of gardens and parks. Walter Shandy speaks incessantly, but never to the immediate point. As he digresses, his house is steadily dismantled by Trim and Toby. His wife is reduced to acting out her sexual needs in green satin nightgowns, twice scoured, and in a variety of other colourful dresses. The hall is being rebuilt in Uncle Toby's bowling green, but Toby's world is also obsessive. It is really neither garden nor park but a memorial to a variety of ruinations in the bodies politic and particular. It is also a child-world, and while it is supposed to end in Toby's march to the Widow Wadman's door, to silence forever that corking pin in her nightdress that comes forever unstuck, the march is interrupted, as is the match.[8] The timing of Mr Shandy's sciatica casts doubt on his own ability to father a child. The Shandy bull is impotent. Tristram writes his book elegiacally, when all his family is dead and the line thus about to become extinct.

We are not surprised to trip over Burton frequently in the pages of *Tristram Shandy*, and not just in the epigraphs that decorate the first page of every brace of books. Building on the work of Ferriar, Heather Jackson has shown the importance of the Burtonian sources for some of these.[9] The works themselves have much in common in their encyclopaedism. Artfully stuffed trunks both, each was written, as Sterne says, against the spleen, with learned fragments shored against perceived ruins.

We are also not surprised to find in the Shandean world a character called Yorick from another work much concerned with melancholy. Its chief character, as oppressed by intellectual doubt and agony as Walter Shandy or Burton, wishes that his too too solid (sullied) flesh would melt, thaw, and resolve itself into a dew. Anguished for a paradisal Denmark where nothing was rotten, and fresh from the utopia of a university, Hamlet cannot cope with the ruin of his father's kingdom except at second hand. The medium he chooses, the only mode in which he feels comfortable, apart from impenetrable wit, is the mode of theatre. This image is also much in Sterne's mind as he lowers curtains and sets scenes and entices his audience to join the action. Sterne is aware, like all writers on theatricality, that the theatrical can be, as it is here, often a crucial sign of uncertainty about identity.[10] In *The Rhetorical World of Augustan Humanism* Paul Fussell speaks of the century's varied fascination with Hamlet, not least in the elegiac notes the graveyard school of poets struck from the melancholy tones of Shakespeare's most famous hero. He writes that "every serious Augustan writer conceives of his role as that of *laudator temporis acti* ... To write satire is implicitly to undertake elegiac action, for all satire assumes some identifiable paradigm of virtue which folly has willingly let die."[11] In Gay's *The What D'Ye Call It* Sir Roger orders his play: "I will have a Ghost; nay I will have a Competence of Ghosts. What, shall our Neighbours think we are not able to make a Ghost? A Play without a Ghost is like, is like – i'gad it is like nothing" (introductory scene, 48–51).

Writing of "Tristram's Sorrow: The Crisis of European Life," James Swearingen links Tristram's experience and elegiac sense with that crisis, a new response to a newer philosophy calling even more in doubt.[12] The microscopical observations characteristic of the new science of the late eighteenth century brought some coherence. Through writers like Locke, clearing the underbrush, there was, as A.G.H Bachrach writes: "a new picture of man as a reasonable creature, capable of intelligently observing the world and of rearranging his experience in a meaningful pattern of certainties and accepted doubts. Thereby one more step had been taken on the road leading from the theocentric to the anthropocentric world."[13]

"Pray, Sir, in all the reading which you have ever read," asks a voice in *Shandy*, "did you ever read such a book as *Locke*'s Essay upon the Human Understanding? ... It is a history-book, Sir, ... of what passes in a man's own mind" (2.2.98). This is not the only reference to Locke in Sterne's book. 'Tis all, as its narrative voice would assert, associated. Unlike Bachrach, Sterne is as ambiguous about the "meaningful pattern" as Locke himself would have been. As Christopher Fox has argued, the Scriblerians were well aware of the doubts Locke cast on earlier perceptions of these matters, and able to make some comedy of them.[14] Mack's edition of *An Essay on Man* leans heavily in its annotation on early humanist sources. It has not been remarked, I think, how Lockean the pyschology is, here in the *Essay* and also in the *Epistles to Several Persons*. Sterne is prepared to treat Locke both seriously, precisely as a source for an associative method, and comically, as the source for mechanical operations of the spirit. On another occasion Tristram says with the apparent confidence we come to distrust, "as sure as I am I – and you are you." The response is: "And who are you? said he. – Don't puzzle me; said I" (7.33.633). This uncertainty is a rather larger problem than Tom's search for his parentage and real name. The presiding feature of a garden or a park or any kind of pastoral is clarity, or clarity finally achieved through retreat. The Shandean world defeats garden and park, simply because it is a deliberately dramatized ruin of this pastoral clarity.

So far as we know, no Scriblerian got out of bed earlier than he meant to to read Burton's book, a work not fashionable again in England until the mid-century and not reissued until 1800. But their enthusiasm for gardens, parks, pastoral scenes, and *loci amoeni* was considerably tempered by their sense that folly had let much of this die and meant to go on so doing. Louis Bredvold's classic study of the "Gloom of the Tory Satirists" documents their concern, as does C.S. Lewis's study of Addison. Addison's determined cheerfulness and firm resolution to exclude the inelegance of loud mirth in the new and wondrous world of observation, where one could make a word mean something exact and banish witty acrostics, whilst testing wit by translation, contrasts with the gloom and, at the same time, with the guffaws of Pope and Swift. Although Pope gives inverted commas in his edition of *Hamlet* only to 1.4 (Polonius, "Give thy thoughts ... Take each man's censure") and to 3.9, the King as he speaks of his "offence" to "give in evidence," his contrived black velvet suit, and frequent theatrical poses, memorialized by W.K. Wimsatt's account of the number of times and in what poses he was painted, suggest that earlier figure, even though Pope was given more to grottos than to Danish battlements.[15] The grotto was created to solve a practical problem on Pope's miniature estate, but his furnishing of the shadowy cave and his way of using his retreat have tones of melancholy, in the position of the grotto, in the traditions associated with such structures, and in the sheer volume and character of the collection of ornaments with which he decorated it.

Burton is behind the lines in *The Rape of the Lock* at 1.130 and the representation of the Cave of Spleen in the fourth canto, that place where the dreaded East is all the wind that blows, where extravagances of imagination are worked out as pieces of theatrical machinery. Burton is part of the context of *An Essay on Man* in the Second Epistle, that section given to the unreliability of the operations of the mind:

As Man, perhaps, the moment of his breath,
Receives the lurking principle of death;
The young disease, that must subdue at length,
Grows with his growth, and strengthens with his strength:
So, cast and mingled with his very frame,
The Mind's disease, its ruling Passion came;
Each vital humour which should feed the whole,
Soon flows to this, in body and in soul.
Whatever warms the heart, or fills the head,
As the mind opens, and its functions spread,
Imagination plies her dang'rous art,
And pours it all upon the peccant part.   (133–44)

Burton appears a little more remotely in the Third Epistle, in the invocation of the old topos of elm and vine, astronomically adjusted to a more mechanical contemporary rendition.[16] In the second edition of *The Dunciad* Pope may be recollecting Burton again. "*List'ning delighted to the jest unclean*" is glossed with a tale from White Kennet's account of Burton at Oxford. "When he fell into a particularly wretched state of melancholy, he could get relief only by going to Folly Bridge to listen to the bargemen swear at one another, at which he would set his hands to his sides and laugh most profusely." The parallel to Swift's delight in watching monkeys demolishing kitchens is irresistible. "My Lord," he writes to Bolingbroke on 31 October 1729, "I hate and love to write to you, it gives me pleasure, and kills me with Melancholy" (3.355). This violent polarization is characteristic of Swift.[17] His choices for scriptural echo underline his sense of siege. To Mrs Whiteway he writes on 27 November 1738: "I hope at least things will be better on *Thursday*, else I shall be full of the spleen, because it is a day you seem to regard, although I detest it, and I read the third chapter of *Job* that morning" (5.128). In the note for this letter we find: "This chapter he always read upon his birth-day. – Deane Swift. 'Let the clay perish wherein I was born, and the night in which it was said. There is a man child conceived.'"[18] In a letter to Oxford on 14 August 1725 he tells us of the "little obscure Irish Cabbin about fourty miles from Dublin, whither I fled to avoyd Company in frequent Returns of Deafness" (3.84). Parnell suffered often from bouts of the spleen. His habit of coping echoes Burton on the bargemen. Goldsmith tells us that when Parnell

found his fits of spleen and uneasiness, which sometimes lasted for weeks together, returning, he returned with all expedition to the remote parts of Ireland, and there made out a gloomy kind of satisfaction, in giving hideous descriptions of the solitude to which he retired. It is said of a famous painter, that, being confined in prison for debt, his whole delight consisted in drawing the faces of his creditors in caricatura. It was just so with Parnell. From many of his unpublished pieces which I have seen, and from others that have appeared, it would seem that scarcely a bog in his neighbourhood was left without reproach, *and scarce a mountain reared its head unsung.*[19]

Gay's flippant epitaph "Life is a jest; and all things show it, / I thought so once, but now I know it," and our habit of reading him very selectively in texts like the *Opera*, conceal the elegiac strain in his poems and plays and in works like the *Acis and Galatea* done with Handel in 1718. Act 2 of *Dione* takes place at Menalcas's tomb. It is not unlike a graveyard poem. We find, in 3.5.123–30, a maid "at the dead of night" outfitted with glimmering tapers and other stock features of a scene earlier worked out in considerable detail in Pope's *Elegy*, and especially in the movement and psychology of *Eloisa*.[20] There are even gloomier strains in *Dione* 4.7.7–10, with its darkness, hanging mountains, and grave, and in "Panthea" yet another "melancholy Cave," dark rocks, ivy, and craggy walls (1.82–3.89–92). "Araminta" has a "Croaking Raven," and the speaker thinks of retiring to "some old Ruine lost in Thought" (1.86.96–7). "Melancholy's self" presides over the disputed "Elegiac Epistle" (2.446.51), no surprising poem from the author of "A Thought on *Eternity*" and "A Contemplation on *Night*." Polonius and Hamlet are recalled in *The What d'Ye Call It* in the introductory scene: "And is the Play as I ordered it, both a Tragedy and a Comedy? I would have it a Pastoral too: and if you could make it a Farce, so much the better – and what if you crown'd all with a Spice of your Opera? You know my Neighbours never saw a Play before; and d'ye see, I would shew them all sorts of Plays under one" (53–8). In *The Distress'd Wife*, a play whose first act Howard Erskine-Hill describes as showing "an overt moral desperation quite new in the drama of Gay,"[21] there is another echo of a familiar place, comic in effect but evocative of the darker place from which it came. Forward, recycled from Macbeth, says, "To wed, to sleep; – no more!" and Sprightly replies, "Am I to be terrified with *Shakespeare*?" (3.4.8–9). Even *The Shepherd's Week* has spurned maids, frustrated suicides, and a deathbed scene.

In a letter to John Caryll, Gay seems to dissociate himself from high seriousness: "for my part who doe not deall in Heroes or ravish'd Ladys, I may perhaps celebrate a milkmaid, describe the amours of your Parson's Daughter, or write an Elegy upon the death of a Hare" (24). The context of the Hare's death casts a different light on the rural simplicity that Gay seems here to invoke. In the fiftieth fable of the first series, climactic because it is also the last, we hear of "A Hare, who, in a civil way, / Comply'd with ev'ry thing, like *Gay*" (2.7–8). This is the tale of the "Hare and Many Friends." All desert the Hare at the end, when "the hounds are just in view" (64).[22] I shall return to the effects of this sensibility on Gay's style later, but would register now Erskine-Hill's view, from the vantage point of *The Distress'd Wife* – that truth cannot really be found in the dramatic events as they unfold, that the sheer variety of genres signals this incertitude (162). "It is not," he says, "absurd to detect a modernistic indeterminacy in some of [Gay's] best drama" (163). Erskine-Hill associates this incertitude with similar feelings in Swift's *Tale* and in *The Dunciad*, which he describes as "formally problematic and multi-perspective."

Some of Gay's less well-known poems have unexpected or abrupt conclusions. In "A True Story of an Apparition" he begins with sceptics, who assert that "sprites are pure delusions rais'd by fear" (1.4), but continues with a tale of a traveller taking his "solitary way" through "*Arden*'s forest," whose "branching paths the doubtful road divide." The story is familiar enough. The inn is an "ancient lonely house." In a hall "where Ivy hung the half-demolish'd wall" we meet a ghost who has been murdered by the "barb'rous hostess" of the inn. The ghost gives directions to the field where his treasure lies, and adds:

Call loud on justice, bid her not retard
To punish murder; lay my ghost at rest,
So shall with peace secure thy nights be blest;

> And when beneath these boards my bones are found,
> Decent interr them in some sacred ground.   (120–4)

The stranger follows the phantom down "half-worn stony stairs" through gloomy passages to the fields. But the spectre "ascends in flame." We read of our hero:

> What cou'd he do? the night was hideous dark,
> Fear shook his joints, and nature dropt the mark:
> With that he starting wak'd, and rais'd his head,
> But found the golden mark was left in bed.   (135–8)

We expect some kind of action – denunciation of the murderers, decent burial as requested, but the poem ends abruptly, translating the action and the moral valence elsewhere:

> What is the statesman's vast ambitious scheme,
> But a short vision, and a golden dream?
> Power, wealth, and title elevate his hope;
> He wakes. But for a garter finds a rope.   (139–42)

Gay has subverted a conventional adventure, with some graveyard touches of its own. The treasure is gone. There is no funeral. The statesman is hanged.

In the tale of "The Mad-Dog" there is a similar effect. A prude who cannot stay chaste from week to week keeps visiting her confessor, who, as "wak'd by wanton thought" (1.33) as judges questioning pregnant women at the bench, demands to know why she cannot stop:

> She tells him now with meekest voice,
> That she had never err'd by choice,
> Nor was there known a virgin chaster,
> Till ruin'd by a sad disaster.
> That she a fav'rite lap-dog had,
> Which, (as she stroak'd, and kiss'd) grew mad;
> And on her lip a wound indenting,
> First set her youthful blood fermenting.   (83–90)

This early account of the Lady with the Dog is itself salacious – more directly so than Pope's account of Belinda's affair with Shock, leaping up to wake his mistress with his tongue. The remedy for the lady's condition is total immersion, but her modesty defeats the cure. Her

> modest hand, by nature guided,
> Debarr'd at once from human eyes
> The seat where female honour lyes,
> And though thrice dipt from top to toe,
> I still secur'd the post below,
> And guarded it with grasp so fast
> Not one drop thro' my fingers past;
> Thus owe I to my bashful care,
> That all the rage is settled there.   (110–17)

We leave the lady when the speaker invites us to "weigh well the project of mankind":

> Then tell me, Reader, canst thou find
> The man from madness wholly free?
> They all are mad – save you and me.

After a review of others who preserve whatever part is crucial above the cleansing tide, we return to our heroine, but for a different, unexpected view:

> All women dread a watry death:
> They shut their lips to hold their breath,
> And though you duck them ne'er so long,
> Not one salt drop e'er wet their tongue;
> 'Tis hence they scandal have at will,
> And that this member ne'er lyes still.   (139–44)

The apparent focus on chastity is converted to looseness of tongue. The members are shifted but made analogues of one another. The poem stops here – having once more, in a slightly different way, frustrated the expected ending of a tale, the shape of a clear story.

Violence appears differently in one of the plays. A character in *The Rehearsal at Goatham* remarks, "My Puppet-Shew, to be sure, hath one great Sign of Merit, in its Time it hath suffer'd violent Persecution. My little Actors have still the Wounds and Scars upon 'em that they receiv'd by the Sword of Don *Quixote*" (4.38–42).

Swift's melancholy is shown even in the midst of his garden in Dublin, where the troublesome walls, trying, as it were, to be ruins, militate against the pastoral of real and poetical gardens and parks. Marjorie Beam, in an essay on the *Tale* and *Hamlet*, suggests that there are conscious echoes of *Hamlet* in the *Tale*, so that the lonely figure of Elsinore stands both with and in contrast to the solitary dweller in his dark London garret. "The tale-teller," she says, "is a frustrated, bitter little Hamlet: like Hamlet, very self-conscious about his own suffering and the spiritual purity which it implies; like him, an alienated observer of a society which he regards as both obtuse and corrupt."[23] Images of death, decay, and ruin inform both works, and the expression of the chief figures often takes similar rhetorical form, as well as the shape of the echo itself. "Both exhibit a queasy sensibility which transmutes moral and intellectual disgust into physical revulsion and expresses it in obscenity and scatology. There is a neurotic extravagance in their responses which gives a baroque edge to their language: images of rottenness, poison, worms, disease, and decay are dwelt over with the loving ingenuity which characterizes obsession" (5). Although Hamlet, properly distressed by unweeded gardens, is not the teller, the borrowed imagery suggests a strongly felt and highly instructive parallel. Unable to deal with the ruination he perceives as Denmark, Hamlet wishes that his solid or sullied flesh would melt. As Robert Erickson has pointed out, Arbuthnot's *Gnothi Seauton* (1734) sharply divides the world of the flesh and the world of the spirit in a way that only a final leap of faith could resolve.[24]

For all its sense of the voice of God, present to extend succour to his suffering servants, human or animal, we are vividly aware from the opening of *An Essay on Man* that we do exist in a maze. It is worth remarking that the first version of the famous lines about the mighty maze asserted that it did *not* have a plan. Mack says that "Either reading ... suggests that there is both intricacy and plan ... The earlier text placed the emphasis on man's not having a chart of the maze (*plan* as a drawing or sketch: OED sense 1) and was misinterpreted ... The new reading placed an emphasis on there being an order in the maze" (1.6n). Like some of the rewriting of philosophical notes for the poem into the rhetoric of orthodox Christian humanism, this explication seems a little stretched, although Pope would have welcomed the defence. On an isthmus of a middle state, man is a being darkly wise and rudely great, but torn between reason and passion. While Pope's notion of reason does not make this faculty into a power that is "rational" in the modern sense, there *is* a division: reason is the card and passion the gale (2.108). The couplets of the *Epistles to Several Persons* are elegantly balanced, and this formal balance is often Pope's only real containment of melancholy perception. But these testimonials to the gardens and parks of Cobham, Bathurst, and Burlington are also preoccupied with the divisions of men, driven by ruling passions out of control and, simply, divided, not knowing what to prefer.

As Earl Wasserman has shown, in both these apparently "moral essays" and other poems Pope writes against a framework of biblical story and classical precedent.[25] This story and this precedent are, however, by no means so firmly felt as they are in, say, the world of Bunyan, the world of Donne, or even a world where a displaced hero is in constant soliloquy to question why times are out of joint and to meet a ghost who comes to give him part of the answer. Most of the ghosts in the Scriblerian world, *pace* the visions of Eloisa or Gay's "Apparition," are comically viewed, like those who turn up in his farces or, in Rosicrucian dress, materialize to help a young woman dress for a ball at Hampton Court. Gay's apparition is ultimately unsuccessful; Pope's opening sceptical denial of sprites is only affirmed by the ironic conclusion of *The Rape of the Lock*. As W.J. Howard has shown, in his "The Mystery of the Cibberian *Dunciad*," Pope makes conscious use of the mystery cults to lend theological context to the activity of the dunces as they destroy words, even as the cult of the Great Mother destroyed *logos*. This argument about *The Dunciad*, first adumbrated by Aubrey Williams' chapter on the anti-Christ of wit, seems strongly to support a more unified view of human personality than we find in the *Essay* and in others of the later satires. Yet while the Christian world is invoked, it functions *only* as image, literary feeling, nearly as melodrama. The poem contains the menace of the dunces and universal darkness, but it does so only by secular satirical effort. If it is true, it is true for this world and this world only.

Jean Hagstrum's *Sex and Sensibility* addresses some forgotten parts of Dryden in the later translations and in those plays that illustrate his sensuality.[26] His reading of these texts is supported by Judith Sloman's study of Dryden's choices of material for translation, from the *Fables* to *Sylvae* to *Examen Poeticum*.[27] Hagstrum is less comfortable with the two strains he sees in Swift on love and women – the intensity of the language of disgust in the "unprintable" poems, especially in the reverse blason in Corinna's slow disintegration at night, and the fascination with the horror of the flesh in the Yahoos and in the other ruined or grotesque figures Gulliver encounters in his travels.[28] According to him, we are supposed to laugh when Gulliver returns home for the last time, able to re-enact the virtue of the horses only in trotting and neighing. We are also supposed to sympathize with Mrs Mary as she pines and suspects the sorrel mare and the stable boy. But surely in the *Travels* we only infer her distress at being left so often by her wandering husband. If Swift himself wishes us to see this domestic consequence of his chief character's adventures, he does so only in the faintest of voices.

The whimsically suggestive poem on Mrs Mary was written by Pope. Swift's sexual strictures are always much more severe; I have already quoted him on the value of violent friendship over violent love. There is attractive whimsy in poems commemorating ladies of thirty-five, an age, he suggests by implication, when women are usually past courtly compliment. Swift's feeling for Stella is clear, but there is, as well as his admiration for her as "an able alert companion," also a careful distance maintained.[29] The vexed question of the marriage may never be solved, but it is hard to believe the relation anything more than Platonic, for Swift was, as the letters, the *Journal*, and the poems show, able to deal with women only at some distance, across the seas to Stella and Rebecca Dingley or as persons to be not a little feared. We know of the grief of Parnell at his wife's death, and there are tales of Arbuthnot letting his children play with his papers, but the rest were unmarried. There is a considerable misogynist strain in the group as a whole, even, in a paradoxical way, in Pope's ostensible devotion to "A Lady" and indeed in his way of presenting it, even in his help for the Blounts and others, and his melodramatic early commitment to Lady Mary.[30] It may be dangerous to say so, but this quality in the Scriblerians represents a fear of commitment to those variegated (that is, overbred) tulips who may assault the body and distress the soul. This was, after all, a male group, for those who can live in paradise alone. "Nature is nature," says Jonathan in *Tristram Shandy*, "And that is the reason, cried Susannah, I so pity my mistress" (5.10.457).

In his *Illustrations of Sterne* John Ferriar says that he cannot "help thinking, that the first chapter or two of the Memoirs of Scriblerus whetted Sterne's invention, in this, as well as in other instances of Mr Shandy's peculiarities."[31] Like Erickson in his "Situations of Identity in the *Memoirs*," Ferriar seems to be responding to the wild schemes for education in *Shandy* and to the consonance between schemes like the

Tristrapaedia and the learning of Greek by eating the alphabet in gingerbread. Since Ferriar's principal subject in the *Illustrations* is in fact Burton, one wonders how he read the opening of the *Memoirs*:

In the Reign of Queen Anne ... thou may'st possibly, gentle Reader, have seen a certain Venerable Person, who frequented the Out-side of the Palace of St James's; and who, by the Gravity of his Deportment and Habit, was generally taken for a decay'd Gentleman of Spain. His stature was tall, his visage long, his complexion olive, his brows were black and even, his eyes hollow yet piercing, his nose inclin'd to aquiline, his beard neglected and mix'd with grey: All this contributed to spread a solemn Melancholy over his countenance. Pythagoras was not more silent, Pyrrho more motionless, nor Zeno more austere ... His whole figure was so utterly unlike any thing of this world, that it was not natural for any man to ask him a question without blessing himself first. Those who never saw a *Jesuit* took him for one, and others believed him some *High Priest of the Jews*. (91)

As he remarks shortly thereafter, his body is "exhausted by the labours of the mind" (92), one who has found in "Dame Nature not indeed an unkind, but a very coy Mistress: Watchful nights, anxious days, slender means, and endless labours must be the lot of all who pursue her, through her labyrinths and meanders" (92). His "first vital air," he says, "I drew in this Island (a soil fruitful of Philosophers) but my complexion is become adust, and my body arid, by visiting lands (as the Poet has it) *alio sub sole calentes*" (92). Martinus's experience will reflect the clutter of Dürer's *Melencolia* I.

In these passages other aspects of the classic melancholic are revived – the mystery of the melancholy person, his brooding over intellectual matters in labyrinthine style, his adust complexion. Melancholy is bad enough, even though it is associated, as it is for Hamlet, with exceptional sensitivity and even with genius. Hamlet himself has this humour in an extraordinary degree, for he has been "too much i' the sun." Those who suffer thus from too much illumination are said to be "adust" in their complexions. In its Latin origin the word means "sunburnt."[32] The most famous of such melancholics is one of Hamlet's predecessors, not the other Spanish Don whom the first figure in the *Memoirs* recalls but Thomas More's Hythloday. Raphael is described in terms very close to the language of the *Memoirs*. His face is described as *vultu adusto* (1.48).[33] This is a countenance natural enough for a sailor, but with its metaphoric resonance it is also one appropriate for a seafarer who has not, as he remarks, sailed as Palinurus but rather as Plato (1.49).[34] He is a seeker after wisdom, in his own way a looker out for a northwest passage to the intellectual world, if not quite to Walter Shandy's, at least for a perfection he has never managed to find. Melancholy, that potentially creative but also potentially ruinous humour, links Hamlet, Hythloday, Martinus, and Lemuel Gulliver. All are seized in a very real sense with a curious kind of pastoral vision, and that vision is frustrated. None is ever really at home, and none is able to sustain a family or any kind of human relationship.

The conduct of Martinus's family strongly resembles the operation of the gloomy house in Yorkshire. There are prodigies attendant upon his birth, but the narrator's account of them casts doubt for the future. Instead of the expected bees, signalling honeyed discourse, "a great swarm of *Wasps* play'd around his cradle" (98). While these do not hurt him, they "were very troublesome to all in the room besides," as no doubt was the "Dunghill ... covered all over with Mushrooms," which rose "in the space of one night" (98). We hear the tones and rhythms of *A Tale of a Tub* in

what was of all most wonderful, was a thing that seemed a monstrous *Fowl*, which just then dropt through the sky-light ... It had a large body, two little disproportioned wings, a prodigious tail, but no head. As its colour was white, he [Cornelius] took it at first sight for a Swan, and was concluding his son would be a Poet; but on a nearer view, he perceived it to be speckled with black, in the form of letters; and that it was indeed a Paper kite which had broken its leash by the impetuosity of the wind. His back was armed with the Art Military, his belly was filled with Physick, his wings were the wings of Quarles and Withers, the several Nodes of his voluminous tail were diversify'd with several branches of science; where the Doctor beheld with great joy a knot of Logick, a knot of Metaphysick, a knot of Casuistry, a knot of Polemical Divinity, and a knot of Common Law, with a *Lanthorn of Jacob Behmen*. (98–9)

The early nurturing of Martinus is equally menaced, from the daily argument about his suction and food, long before Greek and gingerbread, by his instructor, a tristrapaedic with two radically different pupils:

Martin's understanding was so totally immers'd in *sensible objects*, that he demanded examples from Material things of the abstracted Ideas of Logick: As for Crambe, he contented himself with the Words, and when he could but form some conceit upon them, was fully satisfied. Thus Crambe would tell his Instructor, that All men were not *singular*, that Individuality could hardly be praedicated of any man, for it was commonly said that a man *is* not the same he *was*, that madmen are *beside themselves*, and drunken men *come to themselves*; which shews, that few men have that most valuable logical endowment, Individuality. (119)

This passage stresses a radical division in human personality, with a natural consequence in a failure in communication between the two schoolfellows. As Charles Kerby-Miller points out, following William Warburton, it is also a satire on a passage in Locke's *Essay* where Locke argues that if "the same man" has "distinct incommunicable consciousness at different times, it is past doubt the same man would at different times make different persons."[35] "Locke's theory," Kerby-Miller adds, "is that individuality is based on identity of consciousness or memory." Although it is clear that this passage is meant satirically, and that it is all of a piece with the general Scriblerian suspicion of philosophic speculation, Locke's notion of memory is not fundamentally opposed to the Scriblerians' own constructions of satiric butts. These are persons who become non-persons either because they have no ability to build from ancient experience or because they are rooted in a single obsession, like Martinus and his schoolfellow, so that they are unable to use knowledge to create normal human experience.

The effect of Cornelius's toleration and fostering of the divisions of his son and his companion is predictable. They issue in the most comic part of the *Memoirs*, Martinus's attempted love affair with Lindamira-Indamora, Siamese twins joined at the genitals. Martinus is enchanted by the plenitude of his lady's doubleness:

Heavens! how I wonder at the Stupidity of mankind, who can affix the opprobrious Name of Monstrosity to what is only Variety of Beauty, and a Profusion of generous Nature? If there are charms in two eyes, two breasts, two arms; are they not all redoubled in the Object of my Passion? What tho' she be the common Gaze of the multitude, and is follow'd about by the stupid and ignorant; does she not herein resemble the greatest Princes, and the greatest Beauties? only with this difference, that her Admirers are more numerous, and more lasting. (147–8)

Fugitives, as their names suggest, from the more extravagant parts of heroic drama, Lindamira and Indamora elicit not only the extravagance of Martinus's affections, and scenes of romantic melancholy that beggar the highest parts of heroic drama, a little tarnished by the six-pence admission fee for a viewing of her/their parts; they are also a source of infinite and infamous theological, philosophical, and legal speculation, with doctors of every persuasion attempting to resolve the dilemmas presented by two as one, with two putative spouses:

the Advocate for the Plaintiff asserteth, that if there were two persons, and one Organ of Generation, this System would constitute but one Wife. This will put the Plaintiff still in a worse condition, and render him plainly guilty of Bigamy, Rape or Incest. For if there be but one such Organ of Generation, then both the persons of Lindamira and Indamora have an equal property in it; and what is Indamora's property cannot be dispos'd of without her consent. We therefore bring the whole to this short issue; Whether the Plaintiff *Martinus Scriblerus* had the *Consent* of Indamora, or *not*? If he hath *had* her consent, he is guilty of *Bigamy*; if *not*, he is guilty of a *Rape*, or *Incest*, or *both*. (161–2)

The chief issue, as for the discussion of "person" (or what here becomes a "common tenement") is the unnatural ground of Martin's affection for this double mistress, conceived in what amounts to a travelling circus:

How great is the power of Love in human breasts! In vain has the Wise man recourse to his Reason, when the insinuating Arrow touches his heart, and the pleasing Poison is diffused through his veins. But then how violent, how transporting must that passion prove, where not only the Fire of Youth, but the unquenchable Curiosity of a Philosopher, pitch'd upon the same object! For how much soever our Martin was enamour'd on her as a beautiful Woman, he was infinitely more ravish'd with her as a charming Monster. (146–7)

As I have noted above, the names send us to heroic drama,[36] but however comic the rendition of the language of love, the chief point is curiosity and its correlative in inhumanity, so that the creature does become merely a tenement. A monstrosity, a version of ruin, is loved because she/they are precisely that, even as Fossile in *Three Hours after Marriage* will welcome his wife as the "best of [his] Curiosities" (1.26). "I am ... affrighted," said David Hume, "and confounded with that forlorn solitude, in which I am plac'd in my philosophy, and fancy myself some strange, uncouth monster ... left utterly abandon'd and disconsolate." He goes on to say:

Fain wou'd I run into the crowd for shelter and warmth; but cannot prevail with myself to mix with such deformity. I call upon others to join me, in order to make a company apart; but no one will hearken to me. Every one keeps at a distance, and dreads the storm, which beats upon me from every side. I have exposed myself to the enmity of all metaphysicians, logicians, mathematicians, and even theologians; and can I wonder at the insults I must suffer? I have declar'd my dis-approbation of their systems; and can I be surpriz'd, if they shou'd express a hatred of mine and of my person? When I look abroad, I foresee on every side, dispute, contradiction, anger, calumny and detraction. When I turn my eye inward, I find nothing but doubt and ignorance. All the world conspires to oppose and contradict me; tho' such is my weakness, that I feel all my opinions loosen and fall of themselves, when unsupported by the approbation of others. Every step I take is with hesitation and every new reflection makes me dread an error and absurdity in my reasoning.[37]

In a solitude of this kind we are doomed to be curiosities; without comparative, we are all monsters. The monstrous and the grotesque, themselves icons and aspects of ruin and often presented as icons of cities, later rendered as monstrously overgrown, even, as in Smollett, dropsical, are central matters for the Scriblerians once out of their gardens and parks. Swift's *Tale* is a central text in this perception of the world. Its physically and psychologically ruined city-dweller reads the books of both God and Nature as if Cornelius or Walter Shandy had been his early instructor. In the *Travels*, quite apart from the grotesquerie of the Yahoos, Lemuel Gulliver, deliberately sent by his creator to Emmanuel and its science and then to Leyden for even more (his physic seems to issue only in many dead sailors), is fascinated by what he can observe in Brobdingnag, nearly as microscopically as he is himself observed by the Lilliputians in the first voyage. While he is perceived as human in all his travels until the last, when he is horrified by being reclassified with the Yahoos, notably when his clothes wear out, he is never part of any group but some kind of monster, a Man-Mountain or, more tellingly in the second voyage, a subhuman creature whom a mother monkey tries to adopt.

The source of this perception of life and living and learning, as these become monstrous, is related to what Bachrach sees as the age's emphasis on observation, a habit of mind not suited finally to the grandeur of generality or to pastoral as I have sketched it. I have noted that Sterne would not entirely have shared Bachrach's enthusiasm or the optimism said to obtain in many writers, especially Pope. If scientists delighted in what they could find under microscopes, the Scriblerians were either horrified at the flaws in what should be ideal – as in Swift's account of what really lay beneath one whore's dress or of how another one looked when she was flayed – or persistently and satirically critical. Anyone who concentrates on minutiae in any way is a subject for attack, like the philosophers in *An Essay on Man*. Because these are cousins german to obsessive students of texts and carnations, they are as blind as those who ask why man has not a microscopic eye. Only rarely do we reflect on the literal background of Pope's title for *The Dunciad* and its association with earlier schoolmen, like Duns Scotus, preoccupied with the particularities, or quiddities, of individual objects and subjects, thus splitting the universal – and the grandeur of generality – in the world's great wonders. In the dunces Pope represents the inheritors of this early tradition and works against them as Ulrich von Hutten did in his *Epistolae Obscurorum Virorum*. This Renaissance satire was composed in a cultural situation parallel to the crisis the Scriblerians felt. A zealous convert to Christianity from Judaism campaigned to have Jewish books burnt. Johannes Reuchlin, the famous student of these books, assembled signatures from distinguished men. Von Hutten's title is self-explanatory: he makes the book-burners into duncical fools. Pope refers to the *Letters* in the Advertisement to the first edition of Book 4 of *The Dunciad* when he says:

If any person be possessed of a more perfect copy of this work, or of any other fragments of it, and will communicate them to the publisher, we shall make the next edition more complete: In which, we also promise to insert any *Criticisms* that shall be published (if at all to the purpose) with the *Names* of the *Authors*; or any letters sent us (tho' not to the purpose) shall yet be printed under the title of *Epistolae Obscurorum Virorum*; which, together with some others of the same kind formerly laid by for that end, may make no unpleasant addition to the future impressions of this poem. (5.411)

The Twickenham editor gives neither notes nor identification in the concluding table for von Hutten's proto-Scriblerian Renaissance text, nor for its author, but says only that the paragraph was "intended to satirize Curll's methods of publication." Curll often filled out "a pamphlet with letters sent to him 'tho not to the purpose,'" and published as Pope's "anything that was 'communicated' to him" (5.411, n. 22).

The passage can be read in this way, but it is more important to see the association with the original author – another member of a distressed group, but one who had success in his satirical enterprise.³⁸ Pope gave a copy of the 1710 *Epistolae* to Swift. As early as an *An Essay on Criticism* Pope envisages the monks finishing what the Goths began. He singles out in special their hounding of Erasmus, one of his humanist heroes, himself part of a group who sought, with varying degrees of intensity, battles similar to those of Scriblerus – and sometimes identified as author of the *Epistolae*. Pope left his eleven-volume set of the Basel edition of Erasmus to Bolingbroke.

I have alluded earlier to Howard's study of the Cibberian *Dunciad* and its argument about Pope's deliberate use of the cults to lend added significance to the activities of those he attacks. It is worth noting that the initiate were, in their own ways, exclusive and thus divisive professors, monstrously rendered with one eye up and one eye inward, like the philosophers on the Flying Island in Book 3 of Swift's *Travels*. Each destroyed or ruined words in different ways, although the philosophers are not here attempting to move city to court in the fashion of the dunces. Gentlemen in gardens and parks do not engage in this kind of speculation, nor in writing for money, nor in quibbling or piddling over texts.

Pope's strategies in *The Dunciad* were all present in Swift's *Tale* volume. I describe it thus to stress the need for seeing all three parts, although not "unified" in the usual sense of that term, as aspects of a single work: the *Tale* proper, *The Battle of the Books*, and *The Mechanical Operation of the Spirit*. The last is the logical and monstrous consequence of the misreadings and increasing confusion of the ruinous Tale-teller. If the teller's rending of the garments of Scripture takes him finally to the madness of section 9, the Goddess Criticism, sitting high on a mountain in Nova Zembla, achieves, through analogous microscopical observations, the same kind of destruction in the world of letters, so that only the generation of the spirits loose at the end of the *Operation* is possible. The amount of writing about the third voyage of the *Travels* suggests nearly as much unease as the writing about Swift's final position in the fourth book, but the third is paradigmatic of the work as a whole, precisely in its fragmentary quality and in its attack on the scientists.³⁹ Gulliver himself is fascinated by the Grand Academy of Lagado, for, as he says, he has been something of a projector in his youth.

The sleep of reason, said Goya, produces monsters, ruins of nature. For Scriblerus reason did not mean scanning either God or nature too closely but surveying the whole instead of seeking slight faults to find.

The monstrous and the curious, those related phenomena, are central to the madly ruinous world of the *Memoirs*, but they are even more manifest in *Three Hours after Marriage*, a group production in a very literal way. I have already cited Fossile on his wife as a curiosity. When Fossile discovers Townley's shortcomings later (and it *is* Townley, not a shepherdess but a creature of the city), he continues the language of the cheated antiquarian: she is a bristol stone instead of a diamond. Like Walter Shandy on the time of conception, he deals with his imagined marriage and hoped-for pregnancy in medical terms: "in this Vial are included Sons and Daughters. Oh, for a Draught of the *Aqua Magnanimitatis* for a Vehicle! fifty drops of *Liquid Laudanum* for her Dose would but just put us upon a *Par. Laudanum* would settle the present Ataxy of her Animal Spirits, and prevent her being too watchful" (1.48–53).

Phoebe Clinket is the play's most classic instance of obsession. The nature of that obsession – that her poems and plays are her children – are familiar to readers of other Scriblerian material. The "Titillation of the Generative Faculty of the Brain," we hear in Pope's *Peri Bathous*, leads a person to conceive (*Prose Works*, 2:189). The generational imagery of *The Mechanical Operation of the Spirit* echoes in the background. We hear Hamlet as well, for Phoebe is so convinced of her theatrical powers that she echoes his speech to the players: "Read me the last Lines I writ ... and take care to pronounce them as I taught you" (1.90–1). Fossile sounds like Polonius when he says "Yonder she comes in her usual Occupation. Let us mark her a while" (1.71–2).[40]

The immediate human consequence of the tunnel vision of both Fossile and Phoebe is that Townley, Plotwell, and Underplot have little difficulty in getting what they want, although even they suffer from the claustrophobic world created in part by the comically rigid insistence on the unities, so that the stage is often crammed with its awkward cast. Characters act out their futility by tripping over each other physically even as they consistently misunderstand speech. There are twenty-six asides in the play, as if to dramatize the absence of communication even further, in a mode that recalls Hamlet and anticipates Sterne as it renders rhetorically yet another unhappy family. The solitudes and claustrophobic prisons thus created are actualized in the disguises of the crocodile and the mummy, especially the last. If the age craved the microscope and Newton demanded the muse, it also reached for other exotica. If conservative Scriblerus consistently viewed the new science satirically (at least as it claimed to replace the old world), the group also regarded with suspicion those who did not stay at home to cultivate English gardens, of the earth and of the mind, so that these, as in *Windsor-Forest*, might be rendered politically. The mummy is an especially good choice in this static and uncommunicative world, for it is both exotic and dead, or is at least supposed to be. Possum echoes Hamlet comically when he says, seeing the mummy stir: "Speak, I conjure thee. Art thou the Ghost of some murder'd *Egyptian* monarch?" (3.199–200)

Death, or denial of human personality, is central to the play, either through direct allusions to death or to Ovid. That the writers are quite aware of their choice of disguise emerges in Plotwell's description of his costume. It is "this Habit of Death" (3.50–1). To seduce Townley, he must adopt a habit that is also a prison. Townley does not believe that he is human, and, in a perhaps Apuleian mode, he must refuse to assume human shape when Fossile demands it.[41] Disguise, the central matter of theatre, runs literally riot in the play, whose authors are as much taken by theatre and questions of identity as are Hamlet and the later creator of Tristram's "whimsical theatre" (3.39).

If the satire on those who insist on the unities, and often, like Phoebe and Sir Tremendous, rant in an ancient style, becomes a metaphor for the dehumanization and stagnation induced by this rigidification of art, the ending is equally resonant. The play is called a comedy. We end, if not with a dance, at least with each character apparently in possession of what each one wishes. Fossile, to whom "Nothing has happen'd … in the common Course of Human Life" (3.205–6) since he married, is delighted to have his desired heir without having to have a wife. Phoebe leaves her tragic muse to write a comedy. But we have no confidence that she will not have as many of these returned upon her hands as were her tragedies. The child, left to Fossile, will doubtless get an education like that of Martinus or Tristram. Nothing, in short, *has* happened; the effect is nearly absurdist.[42] In its preoccupation with theatre the play also looks back to Jonson's *Poetaster*, like the *Letters* another response to literary crisis, especially in its epigraph. This is Martial's "Rumpatur, quisquis rumpitur invidia" – "Let he who wishes to burst with envy, burst."

The allusions to *Hamlet* underline the fascination in *Three Hours after Marriage* with theatricality as a way of denying identity and with ruination in a new place. The more pervasive strain of allusion, however, is to Ovid. These allusions are as appropriate as the echoes of *Hamlet*. Elizabeth Sewell has called Ovid's *carmen perpetuum* a "vast postlogic."[43] It is composed, as Dryden remarked, of "fictions made against the order of nature." The notion that all coherence was gone, as in Donne's *Anniversaries*, lent itself in a very obvious way to a mode of representation of ruin through Ovidian allusion.[44] Pope translated two of Donne's satires, but one of his favourites among Donne's works was the *Metempsychosis*, another song without end, as if taken by this literary rendition of the impossibility of a completed form. He contributed, with Gay, after the establishment of the Club, to Garth's Ovid of 1717 and claimed to have translated above a quarter of the *Metamorphoses* in his youth.[45] The years around Garth's Ovid also show other interest in the Roman poet, for 1717 is also the date of *Three Hours after Marriage*. In 1716 Gay published *Trivia*, with allusions to Niobe, Philomela, Phaethon, Theseus, and Orpheus. In the same year, as Kerby-Miller has shown, there were two Ovidian additions to the growing *Memoirs* (277–80, 293–307). The Case of the Young Nobleman, chapter 11, concerns the trials of love. The "long description of both the symptoms of love and the methods of its cure in Burton's *Anatomy of Melancholy* [3.2.3–5] offered an easy source for some of the ideas and references in the chapter" (278). Kerby-Miller also cites the *Remedia amoris* in some of his notes (279, 280).

Pope's first version of *The Rape of the Lock* was written in 1712 in an attempt to compose a family quarrel, as a favour to John Caryll. There was no Game at Ombre, no sylph machinery, and no Cave of Spleen. The second version of 1714 is in effect a new poem, one that is Ovidian in tendency and in tone. It is worth underlining that *after* meeting the group, notably Swift, Pope made radical alterations, so that a minor piece of heroic became a serious heroi-comical poem, a dense epyllion with, as Earl Wasserman has shown, nearly no limits in allusion. Although the poem is shaped in a way that Scriblerian works usually are not, it *is* a Scriblerian document. Given their origins in both the Rosicrucian philosophy and in Fontenelle's *Treatise on the Plurality of Worlds*, the sylphs provide further texts for the Scriblerian concern with the mechanical operation of spirits. They act out once more that split between mind and body that both animated and agitated the Club. I have argued elsewhere that (Dennis and Johnson to the contrary) Pope has in fact given the poem appropriate epic machinery, from the religion of its time.[46] Ricardo Quintana is one of the few modern readers to see the darker side developed in the 1714 version. He speaks of Pope's use of "the Ovidian theme of ceaseless change" in which "one thing perpetually blend[s] into something else."[47] The most overtly Ovidian part of the poem occurs in Canto 4, where "Bodies [are] chang'd to various forms by *Spleen*" (2.48). In this conventional and revelatory epic descent to the underworld, we see the realities of other Ovidian conduct above. Figures are now fixed, some simply unmoving and others changed, or presented so that their earthly obsessions are now made plain. For all practical purposes, some of those at Hampton Court are really only so many teapots.

Pope's illustrators responded to this expanded version of the poem.[48] Du Guernier points up a very dark side, for the airy sylphs, who might on first glance be mistaken for pastoral folk, are, as Halsband notes, transformed into pudgy putti. Belinda herself sits with exposed leg, with a satyr to her right, a literalization of what Geoffrey Tillotson described as that "ingenious obscenity" that "is sometimes curling and uncurling itself" beneath the surface of the poem.[49] Halsband observes that "nowhere in the poem is there any mention of a satyr, a pagan figure (one of Pope's contemporaries wrote) used by the ancients for a 'passion too gross to be named,' representing the 'vice and brutality of the sensual appetite'" (20). The contemporary was Lady Mary. In a note Halsband remarks "that Pope's use of 'satyr' in this sense is remarkably rare. He uses it only twice in all his works: in his 'Pastorals' (1709) and unavoidably in a translation from Ovid (1712)" (20, n13). Neither of these satyrs fits Lady Mary's tone, but the fact that a contemporary artist thought one right for *The Rape of the Lock* suggests a serious response. This was felt within Scriblerus too, for Parnell's "To Mr. Pope" includes lines that were used in a later eighteenth-century artist's response to the poem. Halsband quotes these:

The Graces stand in sight; a Satyr train
Peeps o'er their head, and laughs behind the scene.   (27–8)

The work that most catches the potential nightmare and Ovidian world of the poem, and hence its darkly Scriblerian quality, is Füseli's *The Dream of Belinda*.[50] Though Halsband thinks that Füseli "goes far beyond Pope's poem" (53), on the contrary, he *interprets*. He stresses unreality, potential transformation, and, with the unnatural, the obsessively erotic. Parnell's first couplet in "To Mr Pope" speaks to this: "But know, ye fair, a point conceal'd with art / The Sylphs and Gnomes are but a woman's heart." Halsband also makes no comment about Belinda's spots in the Du Guernier illustrations. While Pope's heroine obviously does not have pox of either kind, the illustrator uses the conventional symptoms graphically to hint at moral insufficiency beneath the skin. That Pope should choose the Polyphemus story as one of his translations of Ovid and that Gay did Acis and Galatea stresses what attracted the group to Ovid. As Addison says,

> *Ovid*, in his *Metamorphosis*, has shewn us how the Imagination may be affected by what is Strange. He describes a Miracle in every Story, and always gives us the Sight of some new Creature at the end of it. His Art consists chiefly in well-timing his Description, before the first Shape is quite worn off, and the new one perfectly finish'd; so that he every where entertains us with something we never saw before, and shews Monster after Monster, to the end of the *Metamorphosis*. (3.417.565–6).

This observation contrasts sharply to Addison's sense of Virgil, whose *Aeneid* "is like a well-ordered Garden, where it is impossible to find out any Part unadorned, or to cast our Eyes upon a single Spot, that does not produce some beautiful Plant or Flower" (3.564). Virgil is deliberately presented in the language of garden and park. In the same essay we are told that the *Georgics* give "the most delightful Landskips that can be made out of Fields and Woods, Herds of Cattle, and Swarms of Bees" (565). Ovid, whom Addison first describes as the poet of "enchanted Ground," with "nothing but scenes of Magick," is unfixed and finally, whilst still entertaining, at least for Addison, a creator of monsters, suitable for a house (or a cave) of fiction.

I have stressed the fact that although Pope translated, as he said to Spence, "above a quarter of the *Metamorphoses*," the revisions in the *Rape* were made after his meeting with Swift – that is, at the time of Scriblerus.[51] Ovid's chief concern is the loss of fixity, the permanent loss of human shape, in tales that are, nearly without exception, violent icons of ruin. Sheila Watson traces Swift's habitual use of Ovid and comments on its effects in "Swift and Ovid: The Development of Meta-satire." She argues that this strain in Swift is not simply a reflection of a fashion for Ovid as this is reflected in, say, Addison's thirty-seven tags for issues of the *Spectator*. Noting that when "he was writing *The Battle of the Books* and *A Tale of a Tub* Swift, in his poetry, abandoned the use of the Pindaric Ode," she goes on to remark that "the first major poem after the three short ones attributed to the years between 1698 and 1700 is the 'Humble Petition of Frances Harris,' a poem in the style of the *Heroical Epistles*" (142). In "VanBrug House," she observes, "the emphasis ... is on transformation. The wit of the verses is raised, as Sprat suggested it should be, from the works of nature, the literal metamorphosis of the silkworm, from the masculine and durable arts of men's hands, the spinning of cloth and the building of houses, and also from the labours of the chemists" (142). We ought also to note that "other poems of the same period reflect the same interest in Ovid. They suggest that for Swift the Ovidian technique had become a probe for exploring the temper of the age in which he lived" (143).

It is not only in the poetry that Ovid informs Swift's text. The epigraph for the fourteenth *Examiner* comes from *Metamorphoses* 2.56–61 and "is concerned with the doubling and transformation of words into noise, error, and panic fear" (3.8). The change alters clarity into unintelligibility, chaos, and irrational behaviour. The epigraph for the fifteenth *Examiner* is from 8.203–5 (3.13). The twentieth epigraph comes from 13.352–7. One of Swift's favourite Ovidian places was the story of Daedalus and Icarus (8.183). We are reminded of Icarus, the classic example of false aspiration, in the *Travels* when Gulliver's box descends to the sea at the end of his second voyage, although he himself, with a dim view of the implications of the reference, does not much like the comparison. While Watson finds "no specific reference to Ovid" in the *Battle* (144), the whole tale is really Ovidian in the transformation of books into battlers; the fable of the spider and bee is itself Ovidian in manner.

The main text of the *Tale* is about a coat subject to constant change, to gradual ruin. The sheer frenzy of the process is speeding Ovidian flux. At the end of *The Rape of the Lock* the star twinkling over the new world is not the soul of Caesar, speaking of a new Rome, but only Belinda's transmuted lock, shining delusively over Hampton Court, attracting false visions like the fate of Louis or the fall of Rome. This star is *said* to lend new glory to the shining sphere, but as everyone, especially its creator, knew, the lock is a comet. These burn out and were still, in the popular imagination, signs of impending disaster, as in Dürer's *Melencolia* 1. Among a plethora of images of ill fortune in the engraving, a comet, with a trail, is shooting from left to right. Scriblerian use of Ovid focuses almost exclusively on translations downwards. The dunces become animals, by echo and allusion. Pope knew, as well as Fielding in the Trulliber episode of *Joseph Andrews*, about what happened when Circe caught Odysseus's sailors.[52] Her power dulls his blunted purpose to return either to Ithaca or to sense and sensibility.

In other, different ways the animal world becomes more attractive, like the horses of the *Travels*. Most of the animals in the first series of the *Fables*, although often deterred by men, act out a positive essay on man in their own world. Because we do not in fact learn, as we are advised to do, "of the little Nautilus to sail" but concentrate instead on metaphorical sinkings of ships, we are not only a little less than angels but also not nearly so attractive as Great Danes. Pope's devotion to Bounce fits into the context of his filial piety to his parents. He is not wholly melodramatic when he writes from Twickenham to say that he finds only Bounce and that only Bounce can communicate with him. This is a radical pastoral statement. It is both odd and inescapable that a writer so persistently identified with spinning wit and play with words should have so vivid a sense of the satisfaction of a creature who can engage in none of these activities, except when we reflect that, properly treated and trained, many animals, certainly dogs, will respond with the predictability absent in flawed human nature and in the spinning world of Ovid, where destructive activity is so often fixed (and hence stopped) by translations into other forms. It is frightening to work out the logic of Sewell's "post logic" of Ovid: that many are saved in the *Metamorphoses* by being permanently changed from the human state into the animal. A contemporary who rendered the story of Berenice, supposedly, in her transformation, an emblem of fidelity, hears the heroine wishing instead for her old natural place on earth. So transformation works in two ways: dehumanization through obsession, and the fascination with being an animal, not entirely like the hero in Apuleius, who could at any point, had he made an act of will, go back to being human. There is paradoxical nostalgia for the primitive and predictable, and for that final consonance between man and nature that is also present in the *Metamorphoses*, a wish again for the ancient, or least for a peaceful kingdom.

Addison stresses the theatrical quality of the Ovidian when he talks of the magical dimension of Ovid's verse, as contrasted to the very different verse effects of Homer and Virgil, the first admired for his simplicity and the last for his formality and order. Pope's Cave of Spleen, together with his own grotto the scene of considerable theatrical pose, operates in part by incorporating the excesses of the stage and its machines to suggest the worst effects of disabling spleen (melancholy) in its move to inhibit properly human activity. The persistently theatrical, in its most radical form, may emerge as caricature or the grotesque.[53] Hogarth's brilliantly slow alteration of the standard human countenance in his *Characters and Caricaturas*, so that the first and human face is finally distorted, is a slow-motion account of what the

Scriblerians perceive and render rather more rapidly, almost as if, by satirical fiat, they regarded themselves, in their province as satirists, as "so nearly divine," so nearly Patriot Kings.[54] Fielding's preface to *Joseph Andrews*, as he continues to make the transition from the H. Scriblerus Secundus of his days on the stage and in *Shamela* to the fiction that would become *Tom Jones* and *Amelia*, reflects the issues raised by his ingenious friend Mr Hogarth, so often a part of both *Joseph Andrews* and *Tom Jones*, especially with regard to burlesque and caricature. Hogarth may seem on the surface to belong in these works more to the ambience of the amiable humorist than to a tougher world of progresses and declines, but exploration of Fielding's references suggests a sharp subtext. The true burlesque for him is distortion, a Slipslop or, at the other end of the scale, what he calls, in the preface to *Joseph Andrews*, that "most glaring example" (10) of the mode, Parson Adams.

I shall return to these issues later in some observations on Scriblerus and *Don Quixote*. I emphasize here that the Scriblerians, especially Swift and then Pope, are increasingly inclined to a more severe view. Theirs is not the ingenious Mr Hogarth who did the illustrations for *Shandy* but the Hogarth to whom Swift responded, the creator of *Gin Lane* and the *Rake's Progress*, where progress is a dramatic decline into disease, decay, and death – ruin in cities. This process is "contained" in *Joseph Andrews* in the account of Mr Wilson, and in the Man of the Hill episode in *Tom Jones*. These stories are not so dark because we do not see them happen or in progress of happening, as we do in the Scriblerian reduction of person to the absurd and the grotesque. The latter quality has been aptly described as an artistically consistent response when a society feels in a state of uncertainty or threat.[55]

The evocation of the grotesque is also the evocation of masque, especially of antimasque. It is striking that some kind of comic and resolving dance was originally contemplated for the end of *Three Hours After Marriage*. This, however, would have been a parody of the resolving dance, for resolution of the usual kind is impossible in a world of satirically theatrical change and disguises, a world where disguises only *seem* to be penetrated but in which masks cannot come off and stay off. In the *Essay* Locke says that "The Senses at first let in particular *Ideas*, and furnish the yet empty Cabinet."[56] But we are all in the dark, for, so far as he can tell, only sensations are "the Windows by which light is let into this *dark Room*. For, methinks, the *Understanding* is not so much unlike a Closet wholly shut from light, with only some little openings left, to let in external visible Resemblances, or *Ideas* of things without" (2.12.162–3). In the years after the *Essay*, lights went on in the theatre. As Pope stresses in *The Dunciad*, there was a passion for masquerade, an event to which all manner of sins were attached. "The whole Design of this libidinous Assembly seems to terminate in Assignations and Intrigues," says Mr Spectator (1.8.37). In addition to substituting, by rule, false identity for true, the masquerades, as Matthew Bramble later complained in louder tones, reduced the clarities of social class. Disasters suffered by the heroines of eighteenth-century novels often begin in attendance at a masquerade, that peculiar aspect of subversive misrule whose history Terry Castle has written in part.[57] Tom Jones is at his lowest ebb in London. He meets Lady Bellaston at a masque, grotesquely got up as the Queen of the Fairies. The central issues of disguise and ruination of identity are summed up in a passage from the scene:

Some of these answered by a Question, in a squeaking Voice, *Do you know me?* Much the greater Numbers said, *I don't know you, Sir*, and nothing more. Some called him an impertinent Fellow; some made him no Answer at all; some said, *Indeed I don't know your Voice, and I shall have nothing to say to you*; and many gave him as kind Answers as he could wish, but not in the Voice he desired to hear. (13.7.713)

Humans become merely masks or dominos in a new Ovidian change and, simultaneously, as Fox's study makes clear, act out Locke's thoughts on person in a serious version of the comic discussion of person in *The Memoirs of Martinus Scriblerus*. Moll Flanders, whose true name we shall never know, goes through a series of shape-changes. While she refuses paint and abortion with the same kind of intensity, she will finally assume the guise of a man, even if with some reluctance. Roxana is the quintessence of name-calling in what Maximillian Novak calls this age of disguise.[58] She acquires her name, a more exotic one than her real "Susan," at a masquerade attended by the king, dancing in an equally exotic Turkish costume in a dance supposed to be Turkish but actually French, although not recognized as such by her audience. Now while this "Roxana" is later revealed by a replay of the Turkish costume, the mask serves only to alert her daughter, to whom she has bequeathed her "own Name" (248), to seek out the mother who has denied her. The adventure ends with Amy's offstage murder of Susan. Pamela becomes

Shamela partially through her translation from the loft of the pastoral thatched cottage to the display balcony of a brothel, itself represented as a stage.

As David Blewett has shown, the masquerades were associated with George II and the depravity of his court. Blewett also relates the title-page of *Roxana* to the court of Charles II, to point up the double time-scheme of the novel, which associates the heroine with two reigns of corruption, made so by a theatrical penchant for vice.[59] Moll's horror of paint, and hence unconsciously of theatre, is, however, beggared by Swift's distress at Corinna, the ruin of the dismantled and uncostumed actress, but his sense of the world as a stage is equally strong elsewhere. Swift's Tale-teller is highly theatrical in his language and behaviour. His action is situated on three stages at the beginning of the work. Pope's ladies in the second of the *Epistles to Several Persons* are done in the language of painting, but that language is itself a language of theatre, pose, and denial of identity. We do not see the celebrated lady herself to whom the poem is addressed. Unlike most women, who have, as she is said to have remarked, "no Characters at all" (2.2), she also has a variety of talents, including, says the male speaker, the good sense not to be known. I have already spoken of the theatrics of the Cave of Spleen; the most central place for Pope and theatre, however, is *The Dunciad*, from the first hero to the second, for both were associated with the theatrical world. Pope attacks Cibber not simply because he was an enemy and the laureate but especially because he was also a theatre manager, a creator of spectacle, the lowest of Aristotle's ranking of the qualities of the arts. The fourth book concludes in a theatrical scene, as art after art goes out, when the Great Anarch lets the curtain fall, even as the Great Apologist has feared lest his follies die (4.407–9).

London, as we have heard Joseph Andrews say, is a bad place. He is glad to make his way back across the dark landscape to his village, for even though the Boobys and Pounces are there to menace the clarity of pastoral, there are at least no theatres. In London, Joseph cut his hair "after the newest Fashion … was a little too forward in Riots at the Play-Houses and Assemblies," and, less frequently at Church, "behaved with less seeming Devotion than formerly (1.4.27). Tom Jones's worst trials come in the last six of the eighteen books in that city, which becomes an analogue for theatre.[60] He is lured to Lady Bellaston's house after a theatrical encounter in which Fielding speaks of the powers of the great Rich in a style reminiscent of the Circe episode of the tenth book of the *Odyssey*. Just before Lady Bellaston comes up to him, he speaks to one masker who has a kind voice. Not surprisingly, she is dressed as a shepherdess, a wistful survivor of pastoral. The chapter begins with Fielding's larger description of masquerade, with what seems a plain echo of Petronius: "Our Cavaliers now arrived at that Temple, where *Heydegger*, the great *Arbiter Deliciarum*, the great High-Priest of Pleasure presides; and, like other Heathen Priests, imposes on his Votaries by the pretended Presence of the Deity, when in reality no such Deity is there" (13.7.712). Fielding's imagery recalls the activities of Book 4 of *The Dunciad* or parts of the *Mechanical Operation of the Spirit*. His tone is ironic, but the narrator introduces the masking events in theological tones. There is a deity in Somerset, as there is another presiding in the narrator of the novel in this new epical world. Allworthy may withdraw after his slide from the sublime in Book 1, but he is no priest of pleasure, and his temple will ask for revivification from a person who finally knows who he is and gives up city costume for country dress and the plain speech of which that dress is an image.

The Scriblerians were not so simple-minded as to establish a crude opposition between city and country. Gay is very plain spoken, not least in his Chaucerian glosses and certainly in the events of his text. Not all shepherdesses carry ribboned crooks. It is just as possible to be "bedight" with a green gown on a country field, although the process is perhaps both less clumsy and more in the way of what Susannah means in *Tristram Shandy* when she speaks of nature. While the clap of those lovers Pope wittily memorialized for Lady Mary was in fact lightning, no one in the group thought that the pox stopped at the limits of London or Dublin or any other urban place. Although no one of them went so far as to say that the man who had lost interest in London had lost interest in life, one of the paradoxes of the Scriblerian position is that all members of the group were, for varying reasons, strongly attracted to the city and its ruin, for all their talk of Horace and rural seats left behind. Swift and Parnell felt isolated at home in Ireland, and Pope's villa was close to the city. Their attraction was not entirely like the tale-teller's fascination with corruption but at least in part an attraction to the potential of the city as a possible secular paradise. Their response was monumental distress at the confused labyrinth that was its actuality, dirty by day and menaced not only by Gay's Mohocks but more generally, as Swift says in *The Four Last Years of the Queen*, by "those disorderly People that often infest the streets at Midnight" (7.27). Gay means deliberately to invoke ancient images of the labyrinth as he sends his walker through the streets in *Trivia*, where the city (as elsewhere) is an emblem of every sort of corruption.[61] The mighty maze of its experience, now clearly quite without a plan, is parallel to the labyrinth of Crete, with life as violent and as monstrous as "that which Theseus found." Battestin says that London "is Gay's emblem for actuality, for Life itself" (671). If we view *Trivia* in this way, and not as a cheerfully urbanized georgic, despite one notably Orphic beheading, then the fire at the end becomes apocalyptic, a scene worthy of the descent of the dark and the end of *The Dunciad*. Battestin relates it to the cities of Sodom and Troy, to the prodigies of Caesar, and finally to the fire in Naples (673). Gay's tones are less edgy than Pepys's reading of the fire and the plague in the *Diary*, and there is nothing about divine vengeance, as in Defoe's *Journal* and in the *Diary*, but there is a purgation at the end that is meant to sweep all away, possibly to make it new.

The London of 1716 needed renovation, for the planning projected after the fire of 1665 had proved only a project. While country values can be brought into the city, as Burlington brings them in *Trivia*, to create a shining palace and possibly the virtue of which this palace is an image, there is too much surrounding dark to give enough light to make the values of this house articulate. James D. Yoch, in his study of the topos of the shining palace, observes that cities "rarely appeared in masque scenery" in the last decades of masque production, but that the "cityscape … was merely part of the antimasque" and that when it was "not forgotten, the city was distant or condemned."[62]

Book 8 of *The Prelude* invokes the pastoral, but Book 7 records Wordsworth's residence in London, that "monstrous ant-hill on the plain / Of a too busy world" (149–50). His vision of the city makes it as unreal as Eliot's in *The Waste Land*, a piece of jumbled theatre where

> Shop after shop, with symbols, blazoned names,
> And all the tradesman's honours overhead:
> Here, fronts of houses, like a title-page,
> With letters huge inscribed from top to toe;
> Stationed above the door, like guardian saints;
> There, allegoric shapes, female or male,
> Or physiognomies of real men,
> Land-warriors, kings, or admirals of the sea,
> Boyle, Shakspeare, Newton, or the attractive head
> Of some quack doctor, famous in his day.   (158–67)

The viewer's steps are "Conducted through those labyrinths, unawares, / To privileged regions" (185–6). There are, of course, *loci amoeni* in the Inns of Court, where lawyers "Look out on waters, walks, and gardens green" (188). This, however, is only a temporary oasis from a city of mob scene, the grotesque of the travelling cripple and the "true epitome / Of what the mighty City is herself" (722–3), the "blank confusion" (722) of Bartholomew Fair,

> A work completed to our hands, that lays,
> If any spectacle on earth can do,
> The whole creative powers of man asleep! (679–81)

Martinus Scriblerus falls in love with Lindamira-Indamora at a curiosity show, here for Wordsworth extended (and the city is emphasized always) to the "Horse of knowledge and the learned Pig" (707):

> All Freaks of nature, all Promethean thoughts
> Of man, his dullness, madness, and their feats
> All jumbled up together, to compose
> A Parliament of Monsters. (715–16)

The effect of the curiosities, the monsters, the confusions that form this epitome is that all are "melted and reduced / To one identity, by differences / That have no law, no meaning, and no end" (726–8). Wordsworth's recollection of "the [pastoral] early converse with the works of God" (742) allows him to "move / With order and relation" (760–1) to "feel, in London's vast domain" (765). Gay's walker is an earlier, cruder version of this moving figure. Neither can transform the city, which ruins earlier gardens and most often does not establish buildings of virtue.

But while the imagery of *The Prelude* recalls some of the imagery of the Scriblerians, in the confused anthill of the city, seen most vividly in fairs and shows and distortions, their response was not to move with order and relation, at least not in Wordsworth's style, although his method leads from theirs and composes it. In the nostalgia Kramnick describes and Mack amplifies in *The Garden and the City* in literary terms, they were still in many ways persuaded that the shining palace in danger of ruination might be bright enough to restore more than the idea of a Patriot King. Some of the implications of *An Essay on Man* suggest Thomson's view of nature as a potentially permanent oasis, so that Poet and Patriot might in fact rise to restore the faith and morals nature gave before. Swift had long since given up, as his bitter remarks on the letters of his friends illustrate. The war from the *loci amoeni* of Twickenham and Stowe, a little theatrically conceived themselves and with as little ultimate effect, went on.

But it *was* nostalgia, for Walpole's response to the world created by the philosophical perceptions of the seventeenth century and articulated in its political philosophy was appropriate, if not ideal, and modern instead of ancient and medieval. Once the balm of an anointed king was no longer sacred, a scientist might analyse its components, and other forms of desacralization were free to operate. The vision of government held by, say, Clarendon and his circle was intimately bound up with the notion of a king who was not a man like other men but touched by another sphere, as he could then touch others, as others had, generation upon generation, even to a David from pious times, e'er priestcraft had begun. The last line of *Absalom and Achitophel*, with its evocation of the new time that begins when an anointed monarch rises to take possession once more of his kingly body, "And willing Nations [know] their lawful lord" (1031), is also deliberately chosen as the last line of Pope's *Odyssey*.[63] It is put into quotation marks to send the reader back to its source (10.378). With these lines Odysseus regains his paradise in Ithaca and his line goes on, in those golden – pastoral – days of the grandeur of majestic simplicity. Pope also thinks of Dryden, as R.A. Miller points out, in his description of William in *Windsor-Forest*, viewing his subject as unfavourably as Dryden had as he looks to what ought to be at once the monarch's and the muses' seats.[64] His looking to Dryden is perhaps the critical issue, an authority from the past, however immediate, but still resonant, especially with the ruination of earlier ideals.

The varied efforts to make it new, from the Royal Society to Locke's deliberate deletion of authority from his *Essay*, with its concentration on "the history of a man's own mind," created an epistemology and a psychology that could not allow for a theocratic kingship. That view, whatever Scriblerians thought of individual kings and queens, is central to what they wished to restore, as Bolingbroke's treatise makes clear, although he secularizes. What was possible was Locke's *Treatises of Government* or, much later, what Gary Wills has called Jefferson's invention of America. That these new conceptions of the state also had strong pastoral pulls did not, I think, strike the Club, but if it had, they would probably have thought the issue irrelevant. I have deliberately included figures like Defoe and Fielding (the last easily enough) to suggest how many of the same anxieties affected and afflicted those who appear to have belonged to opposite camps. Burke's later effort to create political sublimity in his denunciation of the French Revolution failed. The pervasive dress metaphor in the *Reflections* lights up the problem, in a way that also stresses ruination, as Swift had already represented it long ago in the *Tale*: "All the decent drapery of life is to be rudely torn off. All the super-added ideas, furnished from the wardrobe of a moral imagination, which the heart owns, and the understanding ratifies, as mercenary to cover the defects of our naked shivering nature, and to raise it to a dignity in our own estimation, are to be exploded as a ridiculous, absurd and antiquated fashion."[65] The naked style that was the aim of the Royal Society was also the design of those who executed the king, precisely as a burlesque metaphor and no standing miracle.

So while there might be country houses, some of them owned by one's friends, there was no hope for a central palace from which a queen might order peaches without labyrinthine negotiation. In that way even *Windsor-Forest*, a pastoral about a garden and a park and cities, written early in Pope's career, has a hollow ring, unconvincing Ovidian transformation and out-of-date speeches from river gods that would have worked in *The Faerie Queene*. England, as a live force so often rendered in Swift's political pamphlets, in Pope's early and late materials, in Gay's efforts to propose fables for the education of a prince, was menaced in a quite obvious way when a monarch was not simply secular but illiterate in the tongue of his folk. Even in pastoral scenes, as Anne McWhir has shown, there is menace.[66] If Dunce the Second reigned like Dunce the First, then the realm of Albion was in confusion at every level, not least that imaged in *The Dunciad*, as the vast anthill of the city moved to take over what still remained of the court. All this echoes that earlier city scene in the *Tale*, a world in which, even in later editions, there is no court at all, but vanishing pairs of stairs and the tinselled theatrical figures of those who are presumably both courtiers and men of the church. The Prince William who was supposed to become civilized by reading the *Fables* went on to become the Butcher of Culloden, a character who might have figured in the most dismal of the stories rather than being a learner from them. The lines echoed from *Dr Faustus* at the end of the prologue to *The Shepherd's Week* (addressed to Viscount Bolingbroke), "I swear by holy *Paul* / I'd burn Book, Preface, Notes and all" (1.95–6), are comically meant, but the sheer sense of defeat is very strong in places, notably in Swift, reduced to Ireland and finally to frustration. Pope and Bolingbroke were not entirely posing in their respective retreats. Even in *The Dunciad*, although Pope rather than the Great Anarch controls the curtains at the end, there is also a sense in which the world of the Scriblerians is coming to a close, a sense that every man has his price, with tags for the laureateship and for those in whose gift it lies, as for gifts of places in the church.

William Kinsley, commenting on *The Dunciad* as mock-book, speaks of Pope's perception of the effect of the printer's art and new technology on eighteenth-century culture.[67] He cites Marshall McLuhan's work on media in partial documentation of his study, an account of how Pope uses "all aspects of contemporary ... bookmaking procedures for his own satiric purposes" (29). He concludes: "We end where we began, with the awareness that Pope is using for his own ends, and with full understanding, techniques and media that have betrayed or numbed his contemporaries. Pope may have shared one of Blake's visions – 'I was in a Printing house in Hell, & saw the method in which knowledge is transmitted from generation to generation' – but the source of his glory is that he was able to build a poetic heaven in hell's despite, to reclaim Pandemonium from Dulness and make it sing the glory of the Word" (47). Earlier, Kinsley directs readers to Hugh Kenner's study of *The Dunciad* and to his essay in *The Stoic Comedians* on the *Tale* as mock-book. Kinsley and Kenner and McLuhan, as I have in part suggested before, see *The Dunciad* as the central eighteenth-century response to print, especially manipulated print, a triumphant reply from what Pope earlier called, in *An Essay on Criticism*, "the juster Ancient Cause." In the end this cause (print is the script of witty gypsies) failed, at least in so far as their wish to drive the world before them failed, at least in so far as this wish was to restore the ruins of that ancient cause.

I have echoed and altered Milton in *On Education*. Education is what the fourth book of *The Dunciad* is about, as promised in Pope's grand design, along with an epic and an epic catalogue of other works. The crises the Scriblerians faced were different from Milton's, although they read him as a near contemporary and everywhere echoed him, as part of the juster ancient cause. The difference in perspective, however, is radical in at least one central way. At the end of *Paradise Lost*, having made ruin of a garden by failing to discover what to make of their wide landscape, Adam and Eve exit from Eden, forever barred by a flaming sword. While they are said to take their solitary way, they are, of course, not solitary at all, for they go hand in hand, having been told and shown the future and conjured to perform what Milton calls "deeds answerable" to achieve a paradise within that will be happier far because of the performance and the perception. Pope's difference from the Milton he recalls so strongly, notably at the beginning and end of *An Essay on Man*, is more than the shift of "justify": to "vindicate" and "men" to "Man." Here at least we stop over different responses of Milton and Pope to gardens, edenic and otherwise, and to cities and ruins. Milton is figuring forth God's ways, to men, individuals – like those who are forever looking out of the similes in *Paradise Lost* so that the garden and even the halls of Pandemonium have always more persons than the characters directly before us on stage. They are contained in the similes, in the dramatic action as they work it out in reality. Pope's design in *An Essay on Man* is not to write an essay in the usual sense of that term in his own century and the one that preceded it. He addresses it to Bolingbroke, speaks to him at the beginning and returns to him at the end. In between, however, the familiarity that ought to go with this kind of colloquy disappears, and the voice of the poet is very often a surrogate for the voice of God. The voice that speaks to us from the proems to Books 1, 3, 7, and 9 of *Paradise Lost* is the voice of one himself involved, like the persons of the similes, in the fall, attempting to present not just the ruin and repair of Adam and Eve, and, by extension, all their sons and daughters, but his own ruin as well. This is here no longer perceived as a ruin like those represented in the political pamphlets, simply that of the inheritor of the original sin that makes the wretched world temporary, a place of pilgrimage. The paradise within may make its possessor a member of the City of God, as the confused on earth are already members of the city of Babylon, but Milton, no more than Augustine, saw either city as more than a metaphor or symbol for an inner state. Each knew that the fulfilment of that state lay beyond the boundaries of fortune. These are not finally counsels of despair about the world but a definition of boundary. While they may seem to send us principally inward, and in many ways initiate in part strains of solitude, they do not deny the possible improvement of the estate outside but say only that one can perhaps make that external garden less unweeded, less bad, whilst cultivating the inner terrain.

That balanced statement would finally suit no Scriblerian. That it would not might lead one to speculate on Scriblerian perceptions of gardens and parks, cities and monsters, in somewhat Augustinian terms. Perhaps the most striking visual rendition of the Scriblerian view of things as they were is presented in Pope's drawing at the beginning of *An Essay on Man.* There are two versions of this drawing. The first is filled with ruins – statues, columns, houses. The half-figure of a statue bears the engraving "viro immort.," and the structure next to it "sic transit gloria mundi." The ruined building in the background is labelled "Roma aeterna." In front there is an ancient man blowing bubbles. Music and a recorder without a recordist are just below the *sic transit.* In the second rendition, as Mack notes in his edition, there is "an added central figure: an emaciated rake, obviously out at elbow (and knee) holding an engraving which depicts the Prodigal Son in an attitude of prayer beside the trough where he has just fed the swine. One or two details in the engraving are curiously reminiscent of Dürer's treatment of this subject, but the engraving is not a copy of Dürer, nor have I been able to establish any original for it – if indeed it had one" (3.90). Despite the two versions, Pope did not in the end print this drawing of architectural, urban, and human ruin. It speaks, like many other parts of the *Essay,* not least its evocation of the topos of the suffering servant, to the less optimistic strains in the poem. Like Gay, whose revisions in poems or plays seem always to make them less complex, less interesting, Pope edited to stress the positive.

All saw cities and gardens as creations of the world. The light from the shining palace did not come from light radiating over Delectable Mountains but from the strong friendship of what Parnell called "the Knot of Souls."[68] Although he was a cleric, his efforts at scriptural translation produce rather lifeless verse, and his holy sonnets lack conviction. Swift's sermons have a flat practicality. Although Pope's Roman Catholicism sometimes gives context for his poems, his response to his own tradition was often sentimental, even pietist in feeling, and not simply because he wanted to please John Caryll.

Part of the anguish that distinguishes and energizes Swift comes from his felt perception that one worked, as in Naboth's vineyard, to make gardens and cities come about on earth, every scriptural injunction to the contrary notwithstanding. The church as an institution was crucial from the beginning. The letters persistently argue for the Irish church, in highly practical ways. These are often marked by angry tones, but his concerns are not spiritual in a tradition like Milton's and certainly not in Donne's. The plainness of the preserved sermons and their practical subjects are analogues to the plainness of the poems to Stella. It is something at least if worshippers do not sleep and the lower sort do not query the Trinity. The church must be established; otherwise, form and order or garden and park cannot obtain in England. His urgency that these must obtain is as acute as Dryden's in *Absalom and Achitophel*, although they have, as I have earlier noted, no theocratic argument about a king. Swift's verses on his own death are deliberately backward- as well as forward-looking, and they concentrate on deeds answerable, without letting us know much, if anything, of a paradise within. Pope's observation that if they do meet in an afterlife, Swift will be an avenging angel is both accurate in his understanding of the Dean's temperament and, to my mind, completely metaphorical (Swift, *Corr.*, 3.107–8).

Poggioli writes of the pastoral vision as essentially secular, one that moves within its own ambience to compose suffering. I believe the Scriblerians to be exactly that – secular, at times desperate about so being, but with a desperation emerging from a conviction that if we are to repair ruins, we had better do so here and turn, not mystic, but town planners. "*I bless the Lord Jesus,*" says Christopher Smart, "*for the memory of GAY, POPE AND SWIFT.*"[69] His benediction comes, I think, from his perception that they were, as he was, experimenters with language.[70]

I shall later return to this theme in a discussion of the relevance of the Scriblerian ethos and mythos for the lexis of their group style. Unlike Johnson, Swift would not have preferred praying in the street with Kit Smart to other activities, but Johnson's preference is grounded both in his own religious sensibility, susceptible to every kind of documentation, and on the distance between 1745, when the last of the group died, and the later part of the century, when those responsive to new pressures were writing more inward verse. Life was a not a jest, and all things did not show it. Pope's final poetical lines tie him both to Chaucer's *Knight's Tale*, that poem Dryden described in the preface to the *Fables* as the epic of our nation, and to that animal world of which I have earlier spoken. A dog no bigger than one's fist can be menaced by a marauding squire, and mad dogs can bite Great Danes. "I doubt not," he writes to Orrery on 10 April 1724, "how much Bounce was lamented: They might say as the Athenians did to Arcite, in Chaucer,

Ah Arcite! gentle Knight! why would'st thou die,
When thou had'st Gold enough, and Emilye?

Ah Bounce! ah gentle Beast! why wou'dst thou dye.
When thou hadst Meat enough, and Orrery?" (*Corr.*, 4.517)

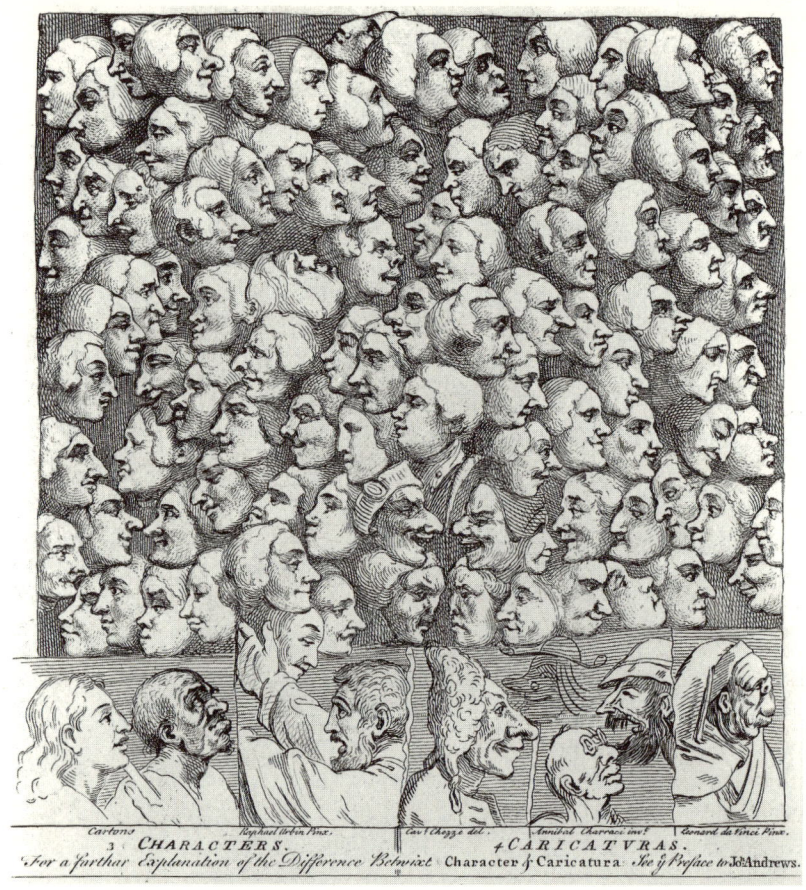

Characters and caricaturas. Engraved by William Hogarth. Courtesy Thomas Fisher Rare Book Library, University of Toronto

4 Scriblerian Fictions

Somerset and London are, if not opposite, at least diagonal poles in English geography. The halls of Paradise and Shandyland are, at least on the surface, spiritually as far apart as garden and city, park and ruin are, on the surface, diametrically opposed. The critical phrase is "on the surface," for although his door hinges work, Mr Allworthy's estate is in danger, not just from the projected improvements of the ill-fated Captain Blifil (2.8.108–9) or the more morally destructive schemes of his cold and calculating son. We are so used to hearing of the perfect plot of *Tom Jones*, and so unused to reading Fielding's plays and the lesser novels, to say nothing of his journalistic pieces, that we do not usually think, even post Hunter and Rawson, of the dark side of this comic novelist. Nor do we reflect on how this dark side, created by what Rawson calls the Augustan ideal under stress, affected and effected the many windows of his particular houses of fiction. The stress refracts light and creates cracks as well as faulty sash windows and the recognizable pecularities of early and mid-eighteenth-century styles. It is worth reflecting a little on Fielding's and then on Sterne's styles for a perspective on the special stylistic manner produced by the matters of Scriblerus in their long correspondence.

Paul Hunter has well described Fielding's plays in his *Occasional Form*, adding "the chains of circumstance" appropriately as his subtitle. Fielding's earlier plays belong to a tradition of comedy whose targets are outworn stock devices and situations. The main targets are some

Restoration plays. But as the writer of that paradoxical essay "Upon Nothing," which recalls in part Rochester, early perceiver of doubt's boundless sea amidst the court of the plays that are most often Fielding's sources,[1] Fielding seems to have come gradually to distrust the art and form of drama itself. As his plays become more allusive, more plays for readers than for viewers, he enjoys the more limited society of that audience who could go from laughing at *Tom Thumb* and *The Grub Street Opera* to reading the footnotes to their texts. These notes, like those Pope enthusiastically wrote earlier in *The Dunciad*, threaten to creep up to take over the pages, scholarship menacing art or, what is in the end more important here, becoming a part of that art in itself.

The "real" action becomes the dramatic conflict between the author and the reader. An insistent demand for active involvement of readers in the action, a demand made in an even more consciously urgent way than art usually does, is the central force behind Scriblerian style, the feature from which all other aspects of it come. The nonsense of the mere stage action, preferred by the pit, natural victims of Rich, the manager Fielding later described in *Tom Jones* as "high priest," working literal Circean magic, is slowly abandoned for a play of wit circling round the action. This play – and the notion of play is also central to Fielding, as it was to Sterne and to the Club and to their predecessors, Apuleius, Rabelais, Cervantes, Lucian[2] – exercises no magic, no transformation. Rather readers are consistently *made* by Scriblerian techniques to be disengaged, and thus necessarily and most centrally engaged with the text. If they are not, they are caught in a romantic trap of the claptrap that Fielding's plays, at another level, aim to parody.

After necessarily leaving the stage, having begun the process artistically himself before the action of the Lord Chamberlain, Fielding's first major effort was *Shamela*, a brilliant reading, however prejudiced, of the chief moments of Pamela's experience, not omitting, in his survey of the epistolary, an allusion to the wedding-night letter that is said to be lost. Quite apart from Fielding's cynical view of Pamela and her creator, and, I think, much more important in his overall perspective on the function of art, was his sense of the effect of Richardson's fiction on the audience, as his frame suggests. As Parson Tickletext's opening salacious rhapsodies over the heroine show, the novel and dear pretty Pamela had literally captured Richardson's audience in what Fielding regarded as a catastrophic suspension of disbelief. Surrounding the central text by two parsons glosses this belief in yet another way. Those who write of the novel and the parody concentrate chiefly on Fielding's witty march through the novel and his annoyance, shared with many others, at the crassness of a virtue that is certainly not cloistered but out front to be rewarded. This is an important part of Fielding's satiric purpose.

The real comedy, the Scriblerian comedy of the piece, however, is best approached through Eric Rothstein's brilliant analysis of the allusions in "The Framework of *Shamela*." For those who are not, as Fielding would later say, with the contempt often characteristic of his controlling narrators, "mere *English* Reader[s]" (*Joseph Andrews*, preface, 3), *Shamela* becomes not simply an attack on Richardson but a tightly allusive text whose title-page alone reaches out to touch and to unite the arts, the state, and the church. Richardson becomes an occasion for the investigation of many kinds of sins, and Cibber, in Fielding's view, along with Middleton and Hervey, are much more dangerous villains because of their high places in the cities of ruins. *Shamela* works allusively, not simply in the title-page but on every page, so that the reader, active rather than passive, must be in full possession of all the meanings invoked, or, at the very least, trying to sort them out.

As Rothstein demonstrates, Fielding knew all of Richardson's text and created much of his comedy from that other central Scriblerian stylistic feature – deliberate displacement. Pastoral figures lose their radiance when they are re-situated in city showers or in the green fields of Devon; rhetorical topoi cease to have power when they are confined in a bathetic chest of drawers. The disparity further engenders comic detachment.

Rothstein's gloss shows clearly that Fielding did not limit himself to Richardson, who was only, in his view, symptomatic of larger problems in the arts, the state, and the church. Fielding's linkage of these organizers of his ethos has another side, for he implies not simply that these *can* be linked but that they *are* and that perceiving the linkage is in fact the central issue he is representing and addressing. Cibber, Middleton, and Hervey, whom Pope perceived as dangerous in *The Dunciad* and in later satires, are identified as creatures for expulsion from their realms of influence because they were exponents of the arts of sinking in poetry, religion, and statecraft. The ability to see this linkage and to describe it in an appropriate cast of characters is a familiar Scriblerian theme, from *A Tale of a Tub* to *The Shepherd's Week* to the *Memoirs* itself. The mode of inducing this perception is even more critical. *Shamela*, quite simply, tells no story. Nor, in the end, do any of the Scriblerians "tell" in this way. Novels were the improbable province of the grotesqueries of the Double Mistress in the *Memoirs*. The episode is in fact explicitly labelled a "Novel" at the beginning of that section of the *Memoirs*. Story is not Fielding's purpose, for "story" is itself a mode of deception, of putting critical faculties to sleep, as they are in the most famous scenes of *The Dunciad*, where Cibber nods off in the lap of Mother Dulness. His sleep prefigures the dark scenes of typically Scriblerian metamorphosis in the Greater Dunciad of Book 4. There, after the wizard old has extended his cup to put all into a trance where anything may be done, art after art goes out and all is night, and human shapes are lost, not least the human art of meaningful speech.

Perhaps the most important device in the Scriblerian mode, one evidently related to disengagement and displacement, is allusion, a rhetorical tool designed to send the reader *out of* the immediate text for critical revaluation, even as Tickletext is brought to his senses by Parson Oliver by being made to reread the signs. As John Sitter has recently observed, allusion is central to the seventeenth- and eighteenth-century concept of wit: "Quotations, echoes, invocations of clichés, historical symmetries, and stylistic impersonations ... emphasize that literary works are parts of a continual dialogue and are made out of available material."[3] *Shamela* and other works like it hope not just to discover the "true name" of a wench or any other subject or object but the true names and ancestors of words and things and actions and to find, paradoxically, that this discovery makes fresh the stale and the simple-minded excitingly complex.

Those who write praises of nothing and of silence, or, in earlier days, of Virgil's gnat or Seneca's pumpkinification of Caesar or von Hutten's obscure men or of Erasmian folly itself, are committed to paradox, that "strange saying" that startles ordinary perception, further disorients, disengages, and displaces the reader in order to make perception new. The problem for the reader is the topicality often inherent in the technique and our general resistance, *as* "mere English readers," to searching it out. The search can seem to demand here, as elsewhere in Scriblerian writing, a nearly formidable knowledge of modern and ancient history and experience. It asks, minimally, a desire to acquire this knowledge, and an understanding that it can never be fully possessed, only perpetually sought. The effect is the creation of a special kind of audience, beginning with a solitary reader who reconstructs community not from single fictions but from the history and perception of fiction and rhetorical forms.

In 1943 Marshall McLuhan, beginning with an account of Newton on language in his scriptural commentary on Daniel, charted the background for Thomas Nashe in the logic and grammar and rhetoric of the Middle Ages and Renaissance. He filled his text, well before the renewal of interest in the eighteenth century, with elaborate notes on Swift and Pope.[4] Aubrey Williams recognized his considerable debt to McLuhan in his 1955 study of *The Dunciad*, in his account of Pope's parody of the notion of *translatio studii* in the procession of the dunces from city to court, but notably in his chapter on the anti-Christ of wit. More than any other commentator Williams has a vivid sense of the wedding of the theological and the literary in Pope's last revision of *The Dunciad*, an assertion, once more, of the linkage of the arts and other forms of human thought and endeavour. Martin Price's study of Swift's rhetorical art and the constant Scriblerian play with the figures and tropes of rhetoric sets the bottom line for the qualifications of an author as one who must have mastered speaking.[5] The noise in the dance of Thunder and Lightning in *Tom Thumb* is very funny, like the habit of other characters in Fielding's later plays of repeating lines in a desperate effort to get at meaning. Like Eliot's infamous characters, they've gotta have words when they talk to you. And like his lower sort, words are what they cannot find. It is no coincidence that, in a ruined park of a modern world with a single tree, and a world where words are badly needed, Beckett's Lucky, in *Waiting for Godot*, leashed by Pozzo, should enter stuttering in tags from eighteenth-century philosophers. He sounds like a choking fugitive from the philosophical parts of the *Memoirs*, the madder parts of *The Dunciad*, and, perhaps most of all, from *A Tale of a Tub*.

When Fielding moved from *Shamela* to *Joseph Andrews*, he did not abandon his *Pamela* context to "write a novel" as we mainly understand that term. He used it as a frame for the experiences of his two heroes, the allegedly eponymous Joseph and his mentor, equal occupier of the title-page, one as instructive as the title-page for *Shamela*. The most interesting part of the title-page, however, is not its evocation of a double hero, although that doubleness itself may suggest a certain ambiguity about direction, as does the description of the history as "Written in Imitation of The Manner of CERVANTES, Author of Don Quixote." Many writers have made us aware of the fascination of the century with Cervantes, originator, it is usually argued, of the "amiable humorist." Parson Adams is perhaps the most striking instance of this odd figure, although Uncle Toby might finally take pride of place. No one from the Scriblerian era, with the possible exception of Arbuthnot's Jack in *John Bull* (a vivid contrast in his geniality to Swift's destructively dangerous fool), not even John Bull himself, is a candidate for this amiability. This humorist, having acquired approval over time, is a character of a later and gentler age. While it would be wrong to deny the comic sense of *Joseph Andrews*, it is, I think, equally wrong to emphasize only the cherry-coloured caps and flourishing dairies that romantically dominate the end of the novel. Although nobody has been raped or killed or allowed to come into property not his or her own, a great deal of dark violence has been represented. The apparently neat cheer of the ending, moreover, should alert the more than English reader to the fact that fiction is being made and shown off to the gentle reader as such. Swallowing the apparent perfection of the ending aesthetically confirms the darkness that has consistently swirled around the major figures in the tale. Further reflection on *Don Quixote*, however amiably read by some, should at least suggest another side to the Cervantic story and, through reflection on the mode of Cervantes, raise other issues for Fielding's experiments with narrative. These were followed later by Sterne and preceded by the allusions made to the Don by the members of the Club, whose interest in Cervantes has not, I think, been sufficiently emphasized.

In a letter to Warburton (Pope, *Corr.*, 4.455), Pope cries "Aut Erasmus, aut Diabolus!" when he responds to Warburton's dissertation published as an insert to his friend Charles Jervas's preface to *Don Quixote*. He observes of Jervas himself that the translator of Cervantes is in Ireland, like Sancho, as governor of his island. In a letter to Judith Cowper (2.141) he speaks of Sancho's diet of wafers and marmalade and, in a letter to John Caryll, compares himself to the Squire (1.114) – as he does in another letter, this time to Wycherley (1.10). Gay is teased by a parallel (3.251) between the Don's queens and duchesses and Gay's Queensberrys. Jervas, Pope, and Bolingbroke write to Swift that Jervas is finished with and by his translation (2.350), and Martha Blount is asked (4.212) to assure Cleland that she is reading *Don Quixote*. Lord Bathurst speaks of Swift's lineal descent from Cervantes in a letter to the Dean (Swift, *Corr.*, 4.290). *The Memoirs of Martinus Scriblerus*, prototype for *Shandy*, most clearly in its first drafts, begins with a Spanish gentleman, a kind of cross between the Don and Thomas More's sunburnt traveller, Raphael Hythloday. There are no windmills here, but the madness of Martinus's education suggests that we are in a Cervantic world and should expect its characteristic ethos and features of its style.

Don Quixote is not the piece of amiability it has been seen to be by some of its readers. The Don is lost in illusions and treated miserably by those he meets on his impossible journey. Bolingbroke, who took a less forgiving view than some readers, speaks sharply of him: "Imposed on by authority, and assisted by artifice, the delusion hardly prevails over common sense; blind ignorance almost sees, and rash superstition hesitates: nothing less than enthusiasm and phrensy can give credit to such histories, or apply such examples. Don Quixote believed; but even Sancho Panza doubted."[6] Because the Don is out of touch with what seems to be reality, he is the constant prey of the landscape and the scamps who people it. Books where human persons are hung upside-down for uncomfortably long periods of time, or lured into even more illusions by those who enjoy discomfiture, are not quite so amiable as all that. As an analogue, most of *Joseph Andrews* takes place in the literal dark, as the characters seem to fall into one inn after another as they make their way in a linear fashion across the landscape.[7] The scene of the parson being tried by the squires has so obvious a scriptural antecedent in the trial and mocking of Christ that it is perhaps easy to overlook it, although the episode with Trulliber has been explicated. It is a combination of the transformation of Odysseus's men under Circe into hogs and, with exact propriety, a parody of a communion scene, with the parson-farmer gone wrong at every turn. Adams's experiences are like those of the Don. While we laugh at his insulation from the world around him and the consequences of this insulation for his wife and six children, and perhaps wonder at a parson whose most precious book is an Aeschylus, we cannot laugh, at least not ultimately, when Adams is pursued as if he were an animal, tried by the wicked, refused by the greedy, and unrecognized as a cleric because he is tattered, torn, and bloody. We can only be grateful at the end, when he mercifully gets not to London but back to his village and his pulpit.

But not just the cruelty links Adams to the Don. Allusion here takes on a new twist. As Homer Goldberg points out in his article on the interpolated stories in *Joseph Andrews*, passages traced to Cervantes turn out themselves to be allusions to other sources.[8] The name of this particular game *is* a very special kind of allusion – a constant spinning of the reader-viewer from the immediacies of the text to other texts against which they are measured, compared, and enlarged into what John Barth might call an ocean of story, as contrasted to captivating "story" itself.

The structure of the "History of the Adventures" is quixotic too, in the now usual meaning of that term. Don Quixote, after all, set off on his journey to attempt to create a Golden Age anew – a garden and a park to replace the ruination of chivalry. Very probably because Cervantes did not believe in this romance, his book deliberately goes nowhere or, to put it more clearly, moves straight across a landscape as if it were, to echo a famous Scriblerian title, travels into some remote parts of the Spanish world. The Don's island paradise, later recalled in that gypsy episode in *Tom Jones*, cannot last any longer than any other *locus amoenus*. In a prevailing scene of ruin it is all a joke or, more accurately, a shaggy-dog story that illustrates that there can *be* no real story able to resist the powers of Lady Booby. She is not confined to the town but invades the world of Adams, even if she cannot cancel his power to ensure the marriage of Fanny and Joseph.

While we romantically come full circle to the happy ending of *Joseph Andrews*, we move Cervantically in the rest of the text, with one adventure after another, travelling into several parts of the Augustan landscape. This process of composing one scene after another is characteristic of nearly all the productions of the Scriblerus Club – even as it is one of the most obvious features of *Don Quixote*. As one reader of Cervantes says: "the narrator of Cervantes' prose epic frequently exercises a subversive role in the 'neo-classical' masterpiece, undermining the aesthetic principles on which it is based, reminding the reader that the 'lofty' text is quite individually and subjectively determined, and suggesting that the traditional classical assumptions concerning poetic truth, decorum, and the imitation of nature as sanctions of a literary text and its fictional characters are questionable."[9]

There are beginnings in this special kind of narrative, but no middles and no ends, except ones imposed from wishful imagination or from a narrator who dictates what he recognizes and underlines as essentially *invented* closure. "When Don Quixote left his village," Carlos Fuentes has noted, "the modern world began."[10] The Don is in effect spending his time attempting to make sense of a new world, one in which the old signs and the things they are to signify have become separate. If there are no knights, no chivalric forces, and certainly no Patriot Kings presiding over pastoral oases, there can be no centres for organically conceived fiction. In *Imagining the Penitentiary* John Bender sees the novel and the new prison as related, with the former perhaps creating the latter. The new prison, unlike the open old one, focuses, panoptically, on single figures in an enclosed space, under watchful eyes. Don Quixote, says Michel Foucault, in the chapter on Cervantes in his *The Order of Things*, is, without knowing it, in search of lost similitudes.[11] Without these it is impossible to have anything but perpetually extended lands or landscapes, across which fictional figures or writers go on this search.

In the midst of working out the parallels between criticism and church history and sorting out references, it is easy to forget that *A Tale of a Tub* is exactly that: a tale. It is a grossly oversimplified *story* of the history of religion, in the mode of once upon a time. This tale, *qua* tale, is as much a part of the satire as the rest. The story, told by a fool who is mad or syphilitic or both, is perpetually interrupted, as are most Scriblerian works and their prototypes. The interruptions can be made into an organic structure only by readers as nostalgic as the Don for a world where there *were* compelling similitudes.[12]

The eruption of Cervantes into the eighteenth-century scene is a cultural sign of dislocation, a perception, often fogged, that one could not in fact be sure of anything, least of all human character, as Pope argues in his discontinuous *Epistles*, and not just in the second, where The Lady says that most women have no characters at all. I have earlier alluded to Weinbrot's study of the interpolations in *Joseph Andrews*. These "real" stories render an unsatisfying world where lovers are jilted and stories like Paul's and Lennard's are left without ending. They play against the constructed world of fiction, where a powerful narrator can make all come right, in his place as the new epic machinery, imposing order on a chaotic world but expecting readers to see that this imposition is only a construction.

Fielding's preface is a useful place for mapping out the new stylistic problems addressed in *Joseph Andrews* and for looking at the special problems with form that the Scriblerians had faced earlier. While it is possible to write the preface off as a joke, the narrator already in charge, sending up a variety of learnings, it seems to make more sense to take it as it is. If we read the preface, it presents a host of problems. It is supposed to be a preamble to explain this new kind of writing, this "comic Epic-Poem in Prose" (4). It attempts the definitions of a critical treatise, but, in addition to alerting us to Hogarth and Ben Jonson,[13] each also important to Fielding's predecessors in the Club, all its statements are ambiguous. Ambiguity pervades the discussion of the comic and the burlesque, character and caricatura. However firmly put the logical structure of the lecture, or its effort at logic, and its insistence that in *Joseph Andrews* we will find, even as for "the Ingenious *Hogarth*" (6), characters rather than caricatures and comedy rather than burlesque, the ambiguity remains. The novel or history may not be like "the Productions of Romance Writers on the one hand, and Burlesque Writers on the other" (10), but it is unlike these because of its mixture, what Fielding earlier called "medleian," as he did the *Historical Register*, as we might well call the *Memoirs* or *A Tale of a Tub* or *The Travels* or *John Bull* or the constantly growing *Dunciad*. Certainly it would be hard to argue that Slipslop and Pounce are not caricatures, even though the book itself may well span at least part of Hogarth's sketch in his *Characters and Caricaturas*; there we are sent in the note at the bottom of the sketches, for further enlightenment, to *Joseph Andrews*. The introduction of a somewhat breathless narrator, who surfaces in three of the prefaces to the four books and leans over our shoulders in the books themselves, is a further way of ensuring that we do not take the fiction, at least not the fiction as resolved, seriously, although we obviously take very seriously the shape of the book itself, especially as it is under narratorial control.

If the narrator of *Joseph Andrews*, still connected to those early plays, seems breathless, the narrator in *Tom Jones* gives no such impression as he scores off some of his readers as "good Reptile[s]" (10.1.525). Far from genial, he is assaultive, although not quite in Swift's way, and this assault is meant to bring reaction — and reform, if only for exclusion from the circle of contempt in which some of the readers are found. Even without the introductory chapters to the eighteen books, the narrator is always with us, dropping hints, making judgments, and so forth. Here the art of allusion is brought to perfection. The story is certainly readable without tracing the Horatian memorial of the Captain's fall, just as the Captain meditates on improving the Allworthy estate, or the assorted parallels to Mr Hogarth. But if these are lost, their loss is deeply felt. The Hogarthian dimension, much more interesting here than in the preface to *Joseph Andrews*, insists, once more, on the unity of the arts and the insufficiency of words.

These last were issues central to the establishment of the Scriblerus Club and to its characteristic modes of allusion, paradox, and denial of story. The *Tale* is centred in these issues and is even more negative than its early critics saw. If the ideal was to be, by implication, a reflection of the union of the books of God and Nature, the process of the narrative, comically but with considerable despair, denies that this is possible except in a mechanical operation of the spirit or an invented fiction in the *Battle*, where Swift is hardly proposing that only the Ancients have a right to exist. This fable is exactly that. The *Tale* is, as I have observed above, not just that part with that title, but only the first element in a literal olio of story to which the other texts are super-added. It seems to me right to call them obvious spin-offs from the *Tale* (and possibly right to think of the one as coming from the critical, the other from the religious), but it also seems to make more sense to focus on the sheerly disintegrative, figured in a literal way by the fact that the volume itself has actual holes in the manuscript (62, 170, 200). It also has a remarkable use of asterisks to indicate what is missing. Print itself is suspect as a medium for the preservation of wisdom, even as are all the shows and shadows of things. Swift might have made *his* gypsies wear badges like the Dublin beggars, but he would, at least intuitively, have known what Fielding was trying to do when he somewhat clumsily invented that dialect for his pastoral folk, to place them outside the usual speech forms of corrupt society, where speech is a lie. Everywhere in the Scriblerian universe words, so wildly tossed about, are ultimately traps. The final paradoxical gospel, from these supremely witty writers, is a counsel of silence or of reflection in a closed garden. Terry Castle's splendid essay, "Why the Houyhnhnms Don't Write: Swift, Satire and the Fear of the Text," argues this point, if partially by implication. The Yahoos have primitive modes of communication, born from aggression. The horses have poetry, but it is not *written*.

Tom Jones ends on the same upbeat note that characterizes *Joseph Andrews*. We view it, I think, with the same suspicion, as the creation of that remote and learned voice who is more interested in his digressive introductions than he is in the creation of the perfect plot – perhaps because he knows that it is made up, that it can only *be* made up. The infinite regress of the chapter headings for the final sections is a sign of the comic sense of the process itself. The whole has been another kind of masquerade, perhaps not so dangerous as the one to which Tom goes, but yet another effort to find a highly elusive reality. The cry of "I don't know you" *should* come from *Shandy*, but it comes instead from the chapter with the angry overtones as Tom is led to the lowest part of his experience with Lady Bellaston. We may be quite sure that he is not finally born to be hanged, but the sense of theatre is still present. Fielding helps in his own way to pull orthodox humanism out of the fire only by insisting on coming into his text. The Club habitually entered its own, especially in the *Memoirs*, constantly playing, as Fielding does, with text and with genre. The deliberately Quixotic beginning of the *Memoirs*, with the mysterious stranger, rapidly shifts into the strange educational career of the hero himself. With the zany exception of the novel of Lindamira-Indamora, the *Memoirs*, rather like *Shandy*, often seems to write a sentence and to trust to God Almighty for the next. In Fielding's own fictional world, apart from the plays, the text that exhibits the most radical dislocation in styles, as Claude Rawson has shown, is *Jonathan Wild*.

But however close Fielding's fractured world to that depicted in the Club, the most instructive analogue for a reflection on Scriblerian style is *Tristram Shandy*. The first version of *Shandy* was more like the *Memoirs* than the "novel" we now have, with its fully articulated cast of characters living in a strange but realized world. In his *Illustrations of Sterne* John Ferriar specifically relates the *Memoirs* to Sterne without arguing for the plagiarism he sees Sterne perpetrating for the Burtonian allusions. After working his way through the *Political Romance*, a topical satire much in the fashion of, say, Pope's *Imitations of Horace* or Swift's political treatises or Arbuthnot's *History of John Bull*, and after playing with fiction in early letters and in the *Political Romance*, Sterne manages to make a fiction of the materials that beset his forerunners.

Reflection on some of the features of his style will illuminate problems faced by the Scriblerians. These remain, to my mind, unsolved and in part account for the selective reading we make of their works, a reading that has distorted or oversimplified what they wrote and, paradoxically, kept a portion of it alive for the English reader. Although we are in the end persuaded that Sterne's insistence on his own randomness is as false as it is true, the insistence has its own importance. He illuminates the problems felt by those wanting the fictions of gardens and parks but aesthetically depressed by ruination. Indeed, the notion of the incomplete, the fragment, as the ultimate beauty, one common in the century, is right for the Scriblerians and those who write in their style, a modern version of Bacon on the virtue of the method of probation as contrasted to the magistral way. The effect is to draw attention to the holes in the fabric of existence itself and not to blink at what the asterisks signal.[14] The notion of the unfinished work lends a special context to Hogarth's insistence on the beauty of the serpentine line, a beauty founded in mystery, in not knowing what lies round the bend. Writing recently on *Sterne's Fiction and the Double Principle*, Jonathan Lamb notes that although all readers of Sterne must be grateful for the work of the Florida annotators, an unhappy result of their labours has been to re-position Sterne in a grid of borrowings, quotations and allusions that considerably restricts the freedom to read beyond the annotated pale. Melvyn New sets out these restrictions in a couple of essays where he describes the annotator's job as mediation between the uninformed reader and the potentially infinite library predicated as Sterne's source. In his rather odd image, the annotator is posted at the "backside" of the Sternean text, reporting to an eager audience on the provenance of what passes through, and consoled for the meanness of his position by the conviction that the more he notes of this fattening stream, the more he will have to note.[15]

Lamb is not opposed to annotation. He merely wishes to suggest that identification is not the central issue in those who practice in a tradition of learned wit. He is delicate about the oddness of New's image. It recollects Swift's parody of those students who discover the problems of patients by paddling in their excrement, and of Pope's diving contests in *The Dunciad*, along with Gay's greengowns of *The Shepherd's Week*, which turn the pastoral and its ladies upsidedown. In a similar fashion – annotation as refrigeration of the mind (I echo Johnson) – the notes to the Twickenham edition (like those of the pretended annotators for the *Tale* or for the *Travels*) are sometimes hard to disentangle from the comic notes of Scriblerus or PW (Pope Warburton). Allusions are supposed to send readers out of the text but paradoxically *not* to stop them at the comfort of identification. Discomfort, the aim of much of this kind of writing, can be fatally soothed by an annotational hour in a library.[16] From the first word to the last (if indeed it was the last) Sterne does not joust only with literal death in the consumptive figure of his hero, solitarily telling the tale of the Shandy tribe long after all his relatives are gone. He also jousts with the death of words, as aware as Pope and Locke that the bright creation would fade, that such as Chaucer was should Dryden be. Print might keep work alive, but the sheer amount of it, Hamlet's words, words, words, could make human speech a highly doubtful, even dangerous mode of permanent communication.

From the beginning, gardens could be places of ruinous danger as well as of holy assignation. That an isolated figure whose witty speech is most often misunderstood by all around him should, as I have noted, become nearly an emblem of the century is no surprise. As a later set of tragicomic figures on that familiar eighteenth-century scene, the travel or the tour, grand or small, try to stay in touch with what should be their home, we hear, with the comic pleasure of recognition, Tabitha Bramble speaking to Quin at Bath of seeing a production of the "Ghost of Gimlet." Hamlet's situation spoke in special to those who (like Hamlet) were terrified in not having words mean what they say. Swift's distress about the imminent collapse of the vernacular produced his entirely serious *Proposal* to stabilize the English tongue, to stop the fading of the bright creation. The angry tones of that early treatise, and his longing for an ancient and pastoral world, not simply in *The Battle of the Books* but in works like the *Contests and Dissensions*, are shown in another way in the actual construction of the *Tale* or the *Tale* volume, with the three works issuing one from another, not as works usually do. To make the matter clearer, we also have signals for missing places in the text, early signs of what Smollett's Win would later, her subtext showing through, call a fit of the asterisks. In *Shandy* the asterisks are meant to conceal the actual presence on the page of obscene words, or to lure the unchaste English reader into supplying these, but precisely as "unspeakable" they contribute to that quality of the unnamable that presides over both the stylistic world of *Shandy* and the stylistic world of the Scriblerians.

In all there is always an aspiration after a world where nature of every kind might be made into a garden or a park, with a noble figure necessarily at its centre. Swift's early poetry vividly dramatizes his desire and his distress. The head-shaking observation of Dryden about what cousin Swift would never be is worth reflection, for the same observation might be made of every poet attempting Pindarics about noblemen and clergymen. The aesthetic cracks and strains in these early odes, recognized by all who write about them, given the absence of garden and park and Swift's early perception of ruined cities and their disintegrative showers, were inevitable. If poetry embodies the dialect of whatever tribe is on the scene, these poems are in their own way as poetically interesting as ones that manage to go farther than a local dialect to a language that reaches beyond its age. Swift's later poems take a middle way, a middle way reaching to a lower, flatter form, but this seems, oddly, given the author, a recognition that heroic speech is inappropriate for a state where ancient times are emphatically out of joint.

Jean Hagstrum's discussion of the Stella poems emphasizes this flatness, seeing it as Swift's real inability to speak, as it were, the language of sexual love. If there can be no familial life worked out in gardens and parks or, especially, in ruinous halls in Yorkshire at a later date, where oddity is, as it was not finally by the Scriblerians, accepted, if not actively cultivated, then language becomes necessarily as restrained as it does in the poems on Stella's birthday, or as childishly regressive as it does in parts of the *Journal to Stella*. While it can be argued that the birthday poems take a maturely detached and anti-platonic view of a woman growing old, there is little sound of any kind of passion. A little language *can* communicate exceptional closeness. In the *Journal* it seems rather to avoid human confrontation. And when a writer moves into that habitual mode of travel, he has no Ulysses as his hero, only a modern who unknowingly makes a mockery of heroism by dazzling Lilliputians or putting on a show for giants (and praising the carnage they deplore) or giving rational horses the rationale for the final solution to the Yahoo question.

War or war games are central to *Shandy*, the source of much of the comedy as Uncle Toby obsessively attempts to reconstruct the battle of Namur as a way of reconstructing and attempting to heal his wound. What is usually not said of Shandy, despite the narrator's solitary voice, is that it is not just a cock and bull story, except in so far as this phrase has its own sexual overtone. It is a long long account of anti-heroic failure to do what heroes were supposed to do: be responsible for their tribe's continuation and increase, whatever the dialect spoken. This is the traditional shape of the epic and will be of most novels, but every Scriblerian act, with the exception of serious translation, is either heroi-comical, as for *The Rape of the Lock*, or anti-heroic. Even the Homer is a document of nostalgia. Shining palaces here outlast siege, and Achilles, agent of the war, is seen as vigorous – although Gay, of course, with many others in the eighteenth century, found him ridiculous. As John Irwin Fischer observes in his study of *The Shepherd's Week*: "Gay is scarcely parodying anyone in particular, he is just thickening the soup. Of course, in doing so he laughs at all of us who want parodies to be meaningfully particular, and etymologies to be helpful, and who believe that language, religion, and civilization are stable enough never to be threatened by anything."[17] He adds later:

The pastoral breaks our sense of a humanly rational world, and it sometimes points beyond itself toward something numinous. But it does no more. Gay's "Contemplation on Night," the second of his poems on transience, ends this way: "The Stars shall drop, the Sun shall lose his flame, / But thou, O God, for ever shine the same" (89, 53–4). But these lines forecast the apocalypse. *The*

Shepherd's Week, written a few months later, ends with just a sunset over drunken Bowzybeus ... There is not a sequent sunrise ... tomorrow is Sunday, and Sunday, though mentioned, never dawns in *The Shepherd's Week*. (202)

We might add that it never dawns in the Scriblerian world. Apocalypse is hinted, only to be denied, or to be comically rendered, as for *The Rape of the Lock* in its final version, in *The Key*, and in Pope's ironic sense in his letters of Mrs Arabella Fermor.[18]

Arbuthnot is surely thinking past the locality of the immediate joke when he invents the section in *John Bull* in praise of adultery. This is the world turned upside-down. The novel of Lindamira and Indamora in the *Memoirs of Martinus Scriblerus* gets nowhere except into increasingly carnivalesque scenes. "Novels" are overtly suspect partly because they have endings, and the world of Martinus can produce nothing like an ending. Martinus is, of course, typically drawn to the sheer curiosity of the double mistress, worse by far than those women whom Pope sees, in his Second Epistle, as, at best, contradictions.

The plain fact of the matter, however, is that nothing can ensue from any union between Martinus and the ladies, or between Fossile and Townley from *Three Hours after Marriage*. Instead of building pretty rooms in sonnets, what the Scriblerians build from the best possible world they can perceive is an elaborate argument about the seat of the soul and, in terms of this seat, a problem utterly without possible result about what deeds are committed during sexual congress between a marginally normal man and a heroically abnormal woman. If she/they are obviously named to recall heroines from late seventeenth-century tragedy, the naming in itself makes an an important aesthetic as well as an anti-heroic point. The exoticism of this drama, not founded in English history but in lands far removed, signals the unreality of felt experience in the England that is. The wild comedy of the *Memoirs* is an honest dramatization of what is, and what can be if the times are out of joint.

That phrase itself suggests the grotesque, a situation where heroic form is distorted and displaced so that the reader is once again made to step aside, consider the models, and hence be engaged or amused. The most obvious example within the outer ambience of Scriblerus is the evocation of heroic forms and grotesques in *Joseph Andrews*. Adams is instantly recalled by a crabstick and a fist, Mrs Slipslop by a malapropism physically rendered into a lurching limp, and Beau Didapper by his near submersion into a hopping bird. These are not persons but objects, like Pope's conversion of Heydegger in *The Dunciad*, so that an ambiguous object can be described as something betwixt a Heydegger and an owl. The same metamorphosis, actually and stylistically, is accomplished in the portraits in the *Epistles to Several Persons*, especially in the reduction of the women in the Second Epistle to so many portraits on a wall. The near mirror-parallels between Fanny and Joseph in *Joseph Andrews* are usually seen as a way of setting up the later brief complication: they may be brother and sister. It has not usually been remarked that when Fielding gives us their portraits, he renders them in the language of history painting, as if they are noble, if not by birth, then at least in terms of virtue. The last gasps of positive Renaissance blason do not, however, usually appear in the Scriblerian ambience. The reverse comes in Swift's beautiful young nymph. The technique once more recalls or alludes to an ancient method, this time of blason, and stands it on its head. As Sean Shesgreen establishes in his study of Hogarth's reworking of the Times-of-the-Day tradition, Hogarth manages, as other Scriblerians do, to have things both ways. On the one hand the present is a miserably shrunken view of the grandeurs of the past and the images that body them forth. On the other these images themselves are overblown. In *Shandy* no one theorizes about the grotesque. A version of the grotesque has become actuality. It is possible to spend many pages of Scriblerian reflection over legal documents governing what happens to pregnant women and, to turn to another side of the same issue, to unbaptized and possibly unannealed spermatozoan. Pieces of grotesqueries like reflections on how many sperm might be baptized at once or on the effects on an emerging child's head under exceptional pressure are, at least on first encounter, very funny. They have none of the horror of, say, a diseased whore undressing and partitioning herself for the night.

Thomas Cramer argues that "the grotesque is the feeling of anxiety aroused by means of the comic pushed to the extreme ... the grotesque is the defeat, by means of the comic, of anxiety in the face of the inexplicable."[19] "Extreme types of the grotesque," Michael Steig observes, in a later gloss on this term, "... return us to childhood – the one [threatening grotesque] attempts a liberation from fear, while the other [the comic] from inhibition; but in both a state of unresolved tension is the most common result, because of the ... conflicts involved" (260). An artist under this kind of pressure does not produce what we usually call a novel. Rather he is more likely to *try* to invent a hero (not without an ancient lineage, displaced) who goes on the stock journey only to find himself perpetually and increasingly assaulted by distortion, although not in a way he can manage with the skill of an Odysseus or an Aeneas. Given the worlds into which he is propelled with increasing violence, natural storms becoming mutiny, Gulliver himself can only come home with a grotesque proposition. That we ourselves still resist the anxiety of the grotesque is shown in the nearly universal misquotation of the title of Swift's book as *Gulliver's Travels*, effectively assigning some measure of control to our anti-hero. Although Scriblerian characters like Gulliver assumed lives of their own, and the use of the ostensible hero's name as part of the title happened relatively early, Swift himself never used this title for his book. In renaming it, we domesticate its seriality into the world of the novel it preceded, the world it could not be, the world it is not. If we can self-protectively score off Lemuel, we have, in Swift's image from the *Tale*, racketed the ball of satire back into another court.

The vexatious arguments over Book 3, regarded by many readers as an embarrassment that needs explaining away, help to pinpoint central Scriblerian concerns and forms. Precisely in its disorientation, or its disorientation of the reader, this section is disturbing. The line of force, many believe, ought to go from Books 1 to 2 to 4? And does, because Swift wrote it later? The last book is about metaphysical uncertainty, while 3 establishes the grounds for this? All these hypotheses share a kind of hopefulness, that the *Travels* will turn out to be domestic after all in the best of all possible worlds. But the very disorganization of 3, with its multiple voyages and worst distortions, leaves any hypothesis hanging. Bigs and littles are bad enough for ill-fortuned seamen, but eyes up and in are another matter altogether. The voyage absolutely resists pattern. As such it is the most characteristically Scriblerian part of the work, the part that insists that travels be travels and not an account of the life of a man who often loses his character in the process of his creator's exploration of different issues in different nations. John Browning's observations on the motive of satire are instructive. In place of the usual assertions about the moral world of the satirist as one that insists, in whatever way, on forms and norms, it speaks of satire in terms of the "ecstasy of assault" (3). His description points up the destructive quality of satire most often blurred by descriptions stressing the positive quality of the satirist, his detachment from his targets so that these become generalized and no longer personal attacks.

Ecstasy is the right word, for it points up a stylistic quality especially evident in Scriblerian works like the *Memoirs* and *Three Hours* and in *The Dunciad*. There is a wild schoolboy kind of humour in the scenes envisaged in the diving contest, like those in the minor prose pieces written in assault of Curll. And in the so-called "unprintable poems" of Swift there is also a wild savagery that goes beyond ecstasy nearly into hysteria, as Swift turns blason upside-down, taking the figure of the whore to pieces, even as earlier poets had carefully itemized beauties into a whole. Swift is probably the most violent of the group, but the very fragmentary quality of the most typically Scriblerian art, or its evocation and reliance upon topicalities that inevitably provide a different kind of fragment, makes all the works of the group of a piece because they *work* in pieces.[20]

We mainly think of Gay in terms of *The Beggar's Opera* and, if past that, the cheerfully wistful world of the first set of *Fables*. As Howard Erskine-Hill has pointed out, the unread plays show an author experimenting with language, even insecure about what language could do.[21] The title of *The What D'Ye Call It* indicates a radical uncertainty about the possibility of comfortably fixing a work's genre. Its pages are more filled with literary allusion than they are with integrated action. But, as Erskine-Hill sees, there is more interesting material in Gay's rendition of *The Wife of Bath* (144–7). He invites another reader to collate the two versions. The most obvious difference is that the second version irons out the first – not to its advantage. A relatively dull play emerges from a document whose central comic subject originally was the actual process of making a play. *Three Hours After Marriage* shows the group (or part of it) working together. The motto affixed to the printed version of the play, Martial's "rumpitur, rumpatur," or let he who bursts, burst, makes only limited sense within the context of the play, as it points to the overweening pride and obsession of Fossile in his fossilizing and womanizing and to the poetical nonsense of Phoebe, with the echoes of Dennis in the background. When we contextualize the epigraph, the point becomes clearer and so does the odd and patchwork fabric of the Scriblerian house of fiction, a motley emblem stylistically of the distressed world it reflects. The motto is, as I have earlier noted, the last tag in Ben Jonson's *Poetaster*, an episode in another literary war. Using Jonson's last word as the first of *Three Hours* defines the play as a continuation of that war as much as it represents any dramatic action.

The title underlines the unities, and the unities are followed, so that the stage is crammed with a cast of characters, including a mummy and a crocodile. There is an obvious surface comedy about the human problems inherent in rigid adherence to critical canons. The most crucial point is, once again, the explicit linkage to earlier literary wars, a perception that all these battles of the books address themselves to the same issues. Literature is ultimately forced to be self-reflexive so that (however paradoxically) literature can exist with autonomy, without the improving hands of critics. The Jonsonian link in *Three Hours* is not the only look back to a hero of another generation, who was as preoccupied with the necessity of Patriot Kings as were the Scriblerians.[22] Fielding's most striking allusion to Jonson is in the preface to *Joseph Andrews*, where he declares his affinity by way of describing his own creation of characters. Like Jonson, Fielding's primary fascination was with the creation of art, so that "characters" in the usual sense, are not really part of his world, any more than the characters of *Joseph Andrews* are part of any "real" world except in so far as the real is being redefined so that the proper study of mankind is rhetoric. Fielding's anger at Richardson is in part rooted in Richardson's finding the real in actual speech; hence the deliberate vulgarizing of *Pamela* in *Shamela*. His technique in this satire vividly recalls Scriblerian stylistic techniques and concerns.

The *Peri Bathous* is the most obvious instance of this playing with rhetorical notions. As George Sherburn tells us, Pope began to collect "high flights" at a very early stage of his career, indeed around 1714, precisely the year when the Club began to meet.[23] But he had already shown this concern in his early *Pastorals*. I have earlier spoken of these neglected poems in terms of Pope's postulation of oasis, but oasis as related to the world outside, through his dedicatees and also because his shepherds inhabit no real pastoral landscape with real shepherds. The poems have probably been neglected because they are not characteristic of the official image of Pope. Apart from the dedications they exist in a world of art, carefully articulated in the context of ancient and modern pastoral and rewritten, partially through the suggestions of Walsh, with specific rhetorical effects in mind. Getting the rhetoric right, as the revisions in the text show, was central in articulating pastoral oases. Pope's quarrels with Ambrose Philips over the *Pastorals* come at a point in his career when he was associated with Scriblerus. His ironic *Guardian* 40 reveals a more familiar Popean face, one that shows his commitment to the classical canons of speech. It would be wrong to deny that Pope was angry because he had been scored off by Addison. More centrally, however, he was defending his own cold pastorals against a kind of realistic poetry that also involved the re-creation of dialect, an aspect of Spenser he did not follow, however much he wished to be included in that genealogy of pastoral poets. Pope's objections to Philips are like those of Fielding to Richardson. The point of writing was, as for Fielding in all his ancillary essays and narratorial interpolations, to call attention to the creation of structures, even to the point of making this, rather than usual dramatic action, the real "subject" of the poetic or fictional enterprise.

There was other Scriblerian involvement in the pastoral controversy. We should not forget that an important event in beginning the battle of the Ancients and the Moderns in England was Fontenelle's praise of the modern pastoral, and that that battle informs Swift's early positions. The later quarrel over the pastoral evoked the first occasion of group activity. Gay's *Shepherd's Week* was written to put down Philips by taking vulgarity a step further, and *The Beggar's Opera* emerged from a suggestion made by Swift for a Newgate pastoral. The preface to *The Shepherd's Week* locates the author's concerns squarely within the rhetorical tradition by insisting that the poems will not fit into that tradition at all. It is another *Peri Bathous*. The notes and Gay's index are also comments on the rhetorical tradition, essays in what words should do, mainly by showing them as mechanical – and then making these mechanics do something else. The scholarly gloss is rendered ridiculous in instances like the note on "queynt." By this "queynt," Gay says, he does not mean that usage that emerges in Chaucer's Miller's Tale; he merely means "quaint." The context of the passage, however, invites the obscene meaning and thus makes the scene all the more barnyard. The presence of actual footnotes lights up again a world in which learning, process, and product are central on the stage, as they are on that part of Gay's stage where we do not know what to call a play but are told all the possible choices. Once again the reader is asked to be active and is expected to see that Gay is playing, not just with ancient and modern pastoral conventions but with the form of the book itself. Gay chooses a format for *The Shepherd's Week* that was usually used for nobler brands of literature, thus building another kind of allusion into the satiric effect.[24]

This playing with format is also a central Scriblerian technique, from *A Tale of a Tub* on to the elaborate designs of the parts of *The Dunciad*. Margaret Doody's study of *The Daring Muse* documents this point in a wider way in the eighteenth century by giving many instances of the use of format to call attention to the physical fact of book.[25] Her interest in charivari and her concern from the beginning, given the grotesque bird used on the dust-jacket, with the exuberance of the Augustan mode is an issue to which I want later to return. The most famous example of this kind of Scriblerian play with the book itself is *The Dunciad*. The history of the composition of Pope's poem – a text, then a text with annotations and other pieces of scholarly apparatus – is familiar, but the notes themselves, and even the index, have been given too little attention as hallmarks of Scriblerian preoccupation and execution.

The centre of this preoccupation is in many ways the domination of the book mode itself, the way in which the fact of print, rather like the facts of annotators, is like story: an abstraction from life and from art. The first note in the poem, which highlights and absurdly dissects the title, is meant to send us for reflection to the special philosophical implications of Duns Scotus, here resurrected for the universal amusement and instruction of mankind. The notes also direct readers in a variety of ways, not least in the fourth book, where the last one, at 4.517, is an elaborate description of the entrance of the wizard with his cup, who comes to accomplish the Universal Darkness with which the book ends. If we are reading in the participatory way the Scriblerian mode demands, we should be better able to approach the shape of what happens in this last apocalyptic book. As we make our approach, we also realize that the shape or apparent shapelessness of the text prevents us from establishing any final outlines. Let me offer a suggestion about a neglected part of the apparatus to *The Dunciad* that demonstrates not only the Scriblerian delight in inventive ingenuity but also their frustration of form in conventional senses of that term.

The index to *The Dunciad* looks merely like a parody of conventional scholarship, offering to spare us work by "holding the eel of science by the tail." That warning, from the text of the poem itself, satirizes those who use indexes to avoid reading a whole work and would seem to discourage use of the index to this text. Swift, who provided an analytical table or index or key for his *Tale* (298–301), observed, anticipating eels by fish, in section 7: "we of this Age have discovered a shorter and more prudent Method, to become *Scholars* and *Wits*, without the Fatigue of *Reading* or *Thinking* ... the choic[est] ... [is] to get a thorough Insight into the *Index*, by which the whole Book is governed and turned, like *Fishes* by the *Tail*" (144–5).

Viewed in these terms, indexes could be subjects of comedy, as they are in *The Shepherd's Week*, where the notes have a way of blowing up what might look like comparatively innocent gamboling on the green. The concluding alphabetical catalogue (or index or table) begins to be comic in its title: "Names, Plants, Flowers, Fruits, Birds, Beasts, Insects, and other material things mentioned in these Pastorals" (1.123). A charivari of all such seems to come next, but it is hard not to see conscious choice behind the apparent jumble of chalk, cricket, and curd, especially in "Cow, *Colin Clout* and *Clouted Cream*," as if one sound and concept had crept up on another. If we follow Gay's line references to Monday, Tuesday, and Friday, a comically romantic sub-plot emerges. "*Deborah*, Death-Watch and *D'Urfey*" creates an elliptical critical judgment in itself (124). *Trivia* is not supposed to work in this kind of comic vein, but the index adds a different perspective. Sometimes these are simply comic touches, like "*Cheese, not loved by the author,*" or "*Tea drinkers, A necessary caution to them*" (173, 179). In others there are mini-dramas in juxtapositions: "*Father, the Happiness of a Child who knows its own,*" placed next to "*Female Walkers, what necessary for them*" (175), and, later, "*Wall, to whom to be given; Wall, to whom to be denied; Way, of whom to be inquired*" (180). In others the juxtaposition is teasing:

Author, for whom he wrote the Poem.
Asses, their Ignorance.
Ariadne's *Clue*. (172)

The last entry in the index cryptically sums up an urban danger hinted at earlier in a series on ladies, followed by a note on *Lechers, old, where they frequent* (170): "Whores, the Streets where they ply; Yeoman, a dreadful story of one" (180). These more serious entries underline the dangers of walking the streets, in every sense of that phrase.

In 1729 Pope added an index to the growing *Dunciad*. This one sounds like Gay in part of its title: "Of THINGS, (including AUTHORS)" (5.239). It begins with an entry for Addison and ends with one for whirligigs, specifically those found in 3.49. We are, in other words, near the beginning of the third book, the final one in this edition of the poem. The entry for Addison is entirely favourable. It reads:

ADDISON (Mr.) written against with vehemence, by *J. Dennis*.
    Book ii. verse 271. Railed at by *A. Philips*. iii.322.
    Abused by *J. Oldmixon*, in his Prose-Essay on Criticism, *&c.* ii.199.
    by *J. Ralph*, in a London Journal, iii.159.
    Celebrated by our Author – Upon his Discourse of Medals – in his
        Prologue to *Cato* – and in this Poem. ii.132.
    False Facts concerning him and our Author related by anonymous
        Person in *Mist's* Journals, *&c.* Test. pag. 9, 10, 11 [29ff].

Disprov'd by the Testimonies of
- The Earl of *Burlington*, 12
- Mr. *Tickel*, 10
- Mr. Addison himself, *Ibid.* and 9   (239)

We are reminded of Pope's praise for one who had been his arch-enemy, told of the rumours of inconsequential hacks writing for third-rate journals, and have these countered by a member of Addison's own circle and by an important nobleman. Addison is also represented as one attacked by three figures central to the poem – and to the index – Dennis, Oldmixon, and Ralph. The process is far from random. The entry immediately after Addison is *"Anger,* one of the Characteristics of Mr *Dennis*'s Critical Writings, i, 104" (239). This entry sends us to an important note at the beginning of the first *Dunciad.* Dennis's rage is documented; we are given his biography (son of a saddler) and a host of other uncomplimentary details. The first note on Pope's celebration of Addison takes us to the second book and to another long note. "Nothing is more remarkable than our author's love of praising good writers. He has celebrated Sir *Isaac Newton,* Mr. *Dryden,* Mr. *Congreve,* Mr. *Wycherley,* Dr. *Garth,* Mr. *Walsh,* Duke of *Buckingham,* Mr. *Addison,* Lord *Lansdown*; in a word, almost every man of his time that deserv'd it" (114). The note ends by emphasizing that "next to commending good Writers, the greatest service to learning is to expose the bad, who can only that one way be made of use to it." There is also an extract from a poem commending our author, contrasting him to Dennis.

One entry alone, then, underscores Pope's alliance with Addison, buries the quarrel, and highlights dunces. At the same time we are sent back to important notes we have probably missed *because* we read the poem as story. As these notes unfold, however, another small story is told that enlarges the major narrative, although not in a conventional narrative way. The last entry in the first index, to whirligigs (245), is preceded by Ward, Welsted, Woolston, and the infamous "*Weekly Journals,*" with the query "by whom written?" When we go to the note itself, we discover who some of these are – and that others are "persons never seen by our Author" (134). Whirligigs spin round at the beginning of Book 3, which is, as I have noted, the last in this first version of the poem. The Greater Father says to "the Greater Son: O born to see what none can see awake" (34–5). We are in the ambience of the *Tale* as the poet's bays and the owl's ivy are mixed:

> As man's maeanders to the vital spring
> Roll all their tydes, then back their circles bring;
> Or whirligigs, twirl'd round by skilful swain,
> Suck the thread in, then yield it out again:
> All nonsense thus, of old or modern date,
> Shall in thee centre, from thee circulate.
> For this, our Queen unfolds to vision true
> Thy mental eye, for thou hast much to view. (48–54)

This index, then, takes us from Addison, supporter with Pope of good poetical causes, to a trio of dunces and their ephemeral journals, to the crucial opening scene of Book 3, just before the Greater Son is given a quasi-Pisgah sight.[26]

From the beginning of the index, with Addison, we have now come to a wizard and to the universal darkness created by his Circean cup. The voice from the index prevents us from reading the simple story and forces us to make other connections, to get at other meanings – lightly comic, profoundly serious. The index is a special instance of the characteristically Scriblerian emphasis on process over product, on hard reflection over immersion in a world of romance.

It is not the only instance, as the send-up of romance in Martinus's capers with the double mistress shows. Gay's writing of a Newgate pastoral is not only a contribution to the Pope-Philips controversy. It is also, in its satiric recreation of heroism in the figure of Macheath, a dark comment on the unreal quality of heroes, as well as the improbability (here as in the implied targets of *The Shepherd's Week*) of any heroism in an unheroic age. The only true heroic was the rendering of ancient epics in translation, as for Dryden with the *Aeneid* and Pope with his Homer, although even that, as Spence justly observed, was more Ovidian than Homeric. From the time of the *Tale* onwards, heroes are invariably either actual Tom Thumbs or metaphorical secret sharers in Tom Thumb's improbable position and positions. Swift's earlier efforts at panegyric were not *meant* to represent failure in the heroic mode, but cousin Dryden, upon reading them, might well have turned Swift in the different poetic directions to which he went in the later career. The grand project of the *Memoirs*, with its hero appropriately a universal pedant, was not, of course, published until much later, but it manifests itself, in terms of the world it invokes, in the better-known productions of the Club. Lemuel Gulliver, *splendide mendax*, is a vehicle rather than a character, but in so far as Swift tries to make a person of him, he makes him, as middle son capable only of disaster, a much-diminished version of what might have been a new Odysseus, even as Pope, searching for a better hero than a piddling attorney, reached for Cibber. Even the Roubiliac bust, done in the best Roman tradition, cannot conceal the expression of folly. A theatre manager was better than an editor because an editor's powers are limited; the man of the theatre, recognized by the Crown, was a model for the audience and an image of that suspension of disbelief that is the essence of the romantic conventions against which Scriblerian style works.

As I have argued earlier, a persistent concern, even in the few theatrical works themselves, except for Gay's efforts on occasion to conform to the taste of the town, is the danger of the enchantment of the cloud-capp'd towers eventually renounced even by Prospero, that best of magicians. The stage, a final home of the delusion of story, is as dangerous as and identified *with* the pulpit in the *Tale*; it is the chief metaphor of *The Dunciad*, especially in its final form, as the index helps us to see, where theatricality is both literal theatre and the false theatre of the Greater Mysteries, practiced by the goddess. The sleep of the dunces in the lap of their Mother is comically central to the representation of the dangers of romance, inducing not simply physical but intellectual sleep, that more dangerous correlative to which all Scriblerian stylistic strategies are consistently opposed. In addition to its crazy parodies of theatrical canons, *Three Hours After Marriage* is itself a piece of nonsensical theatre, intended to be seen as such, with the exotical belonging as much to Clinket and her fragments of verse as to the mummy and the crocodile. *The Dunciad* charts the progress of the dunces from the city to the court and makes of this process in itself an experience in inverting the Word and words.

Jonas Barish sees theatre as the centre of the unreality induced by poetry. Certainly it is central to Pope's second version of *The Rape of the Lock*, whose chief additions are the sylph machinery and the Cave of Spleen, a pre-*Dunciad* representation of wild theatrical antics and mechanics – spectacle, the lowest on Aristotle's list of elements for an artistic work and one of the chief preoccupations of the stage of Pope's time. The adventure with Spleen is also, within the action of the poem, a dream, no longer regarded as a superior mode to the world of daylight experience (except in so far as we give it negative interpretation) but as an evasion of reality. Wild theatre dominates typically Scriblerian satire, as does masking and, by extension, masquerade. L.P. Goggin has reminded us of Fielding's *The Masquerade*, alleged by its author to have been the production of Lemuel Gulliver.[27] Terry Castle has most recently studied the preoccupation of the period with masking. Her view, however, is that the phenomenon should be seen more positively, so that masquerade, like satire itself, is "a kind of institutionalized disorder." "Like the world of satire," she says, "the masquerade projected an anti-nature, an intoxicating reversal of normal sexual, social, and metaphysical hierarchies" (159). In its required cross-dressing and other evasions of usual identities, the masquerade "intimated a perfected human community, free of the ravages of difference and alienation" (176). While her hypothesis has an attraction, not least in terms of current critical discussions of subversion, it would, I think, have horrified the Club, despite their evident glee at subverting usual norms when they use masks as Pope does in his fictionalized revenges against Curll, unless subversion functioned, as it *can* do, as a mode of emphasis of the object of subversion. Certainly Scriblerus envisaged a perfected human community, but in their best of all possible worlds, the ideal garden and park, there were not only no masks but no clothes. Only Pope's Hamletic costuming, worn for rather human reasons, seems to move in Castle's direction, unless the whole act of the formation of the Club was itself a version of masking. Human identity, as Christopher Fox has demonstrated, is at the centre of the *Memoirs*, or comically decentralized, as the substantial forms are hunted down in the metaphorical forest like so many wolves.

The Rape of the Lock, in its second version, begins with a comic allusion to the opening of Ovid's *Metamorphoses*. I stress again that this second version happened after the Club was formed. I have earlier considered Ovid briefly as a graphic way of pointing up the ruins in a world where park was idealized. Ovid was the group's favourite classical author, however large Homer and Virgil seem to be written in Scriblerian works, as indeed they were to some extent in the two-canto version of *The Rape*. Homer and Virgil were the heroes, but they were as scarce as real heroes in this particular age. Spence, who shrewdly observed that Pope's Homer was more Ovidian than Homeric, also records Pope's claim to have translated above a quarter of the *Metamorphoses* in his early youth. Ovid's tales fascinated the group, doubtless because his particular poetic perception and practice was like their own. As Edgar Glenn argues in *Ovid's Roman Games*, Ovid deliberately subverted the emperor, also no Patriot King, in his account of illicit loves and other dubious human practices.[28] I want to reserve a discussion of the Scriblerians and games for later; it is enough here to think of game as a mode of engagement of the reader and to see the devices of engagement I have spoken of above as quite literal playing of games. For Ovid this also involved considerable word-play and word management,[29] so that words themselves took on life and life proved insubstantial.

Central to Scriblerian style and related to its distressed world of monsters grown from gardens neglected is a preoccupation with and a representation of metamorphosis, not only in *The Rape* but also in Pope's choice of material like the *Merchant's Tale* for translation, in Gay's attraction to the Roman poet, in Swift's shifting landscapes and dissolving bodies. For those who saw the world around them in terms of flux, Ovid was a natural choice, as was his method of discontinuity, one tale borrowing another and another and ending only by way of the apotheosis that Pope echoed comically at the ending of *The Rape of the Lock*. For discontinuity, often of a radical kind, is a central and natural hallmark of the style, a feature of couplet writing, of the unexpected endings in Gay, of the fragment in Swift and Arbuthnot. Actions are never wholly completed. Stories can, quixotically, go on and on. This quality is pervasive, even in works where it may seem not to obtain. Anne McWhir argues that Gay's *Trivia*, through allusion, seems to draw "the attention of his readers to deception and concealment and role-playing, not so that we can strip away disguises, but so that we can laugh at the very existence of disguise and artificial convention."[30] In *Trivia* "Gay is teaching us how to survive in a world of experience that is sometimes frivolous and sometimes demonic, but not simply one or the other" (422). Allusion itself is a kind of index, as I have described the Scriblerian index above. It prevents readers from assuming that there can be a continuity. In her study of "Handel, Scarlatti, and Gay: Baroque Opera and *The Beggar's Opera*" Janet Wolf establishes, partially through Gay's own attempt at *opera seria* in *The Captives*, that Gay had as considerable a knowledge of the operatic tradition as Pope did of the heroic. Her conclusion, that Gay's so-called burlesque in *The Beggar* in 1728 played against the seriousness of *The Captives* in 1724, seems misdirected. Everyone in the Club had moments of participation in the more popular kinds of art, notably those who, like Gay, needed money. The more typical spirit of Gay is the sensibility McWhir describes – the learned and witty poet, the best Latinist of the lot, juggling the classics, possibly wishing that they could be realized anew, knowing that they could not. The Scriblerians went to Ovid finally as the closest of the classical brethren.[31] *The Rape* is the best known example, in its final epigraph (a change from the first) and in the crucial 1714 changes.[32] *Three Hours after Marriage* is a tissue of Ovidian allusion that underscores the breakdown of any kind of certainty in the play, for all its apparent rigid adherence to the canons of unity.

The discontinuous, fragmented, displaced, and allusive mode of Ovid, as well as the perpetual change of one person into another (more typically, or into a thing), pervades the Scriblerian mode. It *is Travels into Several Remote Nations of the World*; and, as I have suggested in another context, the discontinuity of the third voyage is more paradigmatic of the Scriblerian mode than those books that only seem, or can be made to seem to provide a more unified account of the central figure's experience. I can think of no familiar or unfamiliar Scriblerian work that does not exhibit this kind of disconnection, if only in an absence of resolution. A few of Gay's poems, like "The Mad Dog" and "The Garter," have deliberately frustrating conclusions. It is as if the Scriblerians were articulating aesthetically what others saw artistically in that favourite subject of the eighteenth-century scene, the ruin, included in gardens as a *memento mori* and as an extension of the sense that eighteenth-century man stood on the shoulders of giants. He is either a literal Tom Thumb on the edge of a precipice or simply about to expire, like Pope's rake amidst ruins, the topoi of Rome and Greece in view, but no longer viable.

The obvious visual analogue is Hogarth's *Times-of-the-Day*, a replay of an ancient tradition but with another view of it. Fielding, closer to Hogarth than his wished-for Scriblerian brothers, makes pointed use of the tradition in *Tom Jones* when he leaves the full portrait of Mrs Bridget to its Hogarthian original in the *Morning* part of Hogarth's series. While Hogarth himself worked in the high heroic tradition, he very probably, as Shesgreen has argued, had doubts not only about the ability of the present age to sustain a heroic stance but also about the heroic age itself. His mode of internal allusion, notably in the progress pieces, his acute sense of the monstrous – as in his first satiric work, *Masquerades and Operas* – and his mixture of styles help to explain why Swift wrote of him as a fellow spirit. In the penultimate stanza of *A Character, Panegyric and Description of the Legion Club*, that pile that "contains / Many a Head that holds no Brains" (3.9–10), Swift invokes the visual artist:

> How I want thee, humourous Hogart!
> Thou I hear, a pleasant rogue art,

> Were you and I acquainted,
> Every monster should be painted;
> You should try your graving tools
> On this odious group of fools;
> Draw the beasts as I describe 'em,
> Form their features, while I gibe them;
> Draw them like, for I assure you,
> You will need no caricatura.   (219–28)[33]

Margaret Doody's use of charivari in *The Daring Muse* is particularly relevant to the Scriblerian style and ethos. She observes that, "like its sociologically observable counterpart in life, the literary charivari places obstacles in the way of the *hieros gamos*, the happy marriage of order and graceful fruitfulness, or of its unselfconscious enjoyment. Yet charivari, which has self-conscious criticism of sexuality as an intellectual motive, has the sexual energy itself as a motive force" (123).[34] The examples she cites from Pope are *The Rape of the Lock* and *The Dunciad*. The misrule of the liveliest verse and prose is not quite like Castle's account of the subversion of masquerade, for while charivari can involve masking, it neither leads nor helps to lead to a kind of utopia where the distinctions of civilization are given up in favour of the goodness inherent in that discontent that torpedoes civilization. The abandon that characterizes the work of the exuberant age, notably in the Club, is at once wildly comical (and the adjective is important) and not far from being tragic in its silent assertion that a more coherent world can be neither experienced nor rendered into art. The best place to look for this particular part of Scriblerus is in the *Memoirs*, especially in the "novel" and the extended discussion of the problems encountered when a pursuer of the curious develops a passion for ladies genitally united. It even appears in the Scriblerian invitations to Club meetings, documents never really envisaged as texts for the printed canons of any one or all. To the ones we already have, Claude Rawson and F.P. Lock have recently added more as a part of their considerable augmentation of the works of Parnell, that merry melancholic who typifies both ends of the Scriblerian emotional scale. In its origins charivari involved making merry over matters sexual. The mummer's play, with its menacing hobbyhorses, is related to the charivari in origin. The Minehead Horse was led to the seashore by figures known as gullivers.

The Scriblerian invitations were invitations to play games – at the Palace of St James. It is, I think, fruitful to look at the Club in terms of game, not only as they played games with each other but also as they played with their audiences. In *Playing and Reality* D.W. Winnicott argues for the importance of play for the human psyche. Only the free or those determined so to be *can* play. In *Home Is Where We Start From* Winnicott includes an essay on the place of the monarchy. His argument is especially relevant to a group who were as nostalgic in the age of Walpole as Kramnick has made them out to be. He says: "The continued existence of the monarchy is one of the indications we have that there exist here and now the conditions in which democracy (a reflection of family affairs in a social setting) can characterize the political system, and in which a benign or a malignant dictatorship ... is for the time being unlikely to appear. Under such conditions, individuals, if they are emotionally healthy, can develop a sense of being, can realize some of their personal potential, and can play" (268). The Scriblerians work at some point in the middle of the scale one might construct from Winnicott's implied and inspired paradigm of those who play or do not or cannot. The elegant play of a world lost because turned upside-down seems mainly not within their compass, although the world of the *Pastorals* and of *The Rape of the Lock* are fleeting recollections of a flick of time when some kind of perilous balance was reached, when one could play with rhetoric and with social situations capable of being made rich with allusion. The play of their world, and probably of ours, becomes a game restricted in terrain and certainly restricted in audience. Again, a most useful comment on the Scriblerians is Sterne, who might literally as well as metaphorically have signed himself L. Scriblerus Tertius. All of *Tristram Shandy* is a game, and its aim, as Sterne says is the aim of all writing, is conversation. What he implies is that dialogic engagement that all Scriblerian works demand in a particular way of their readers, so that the text is ultimately what we half-create and half-perceive. There is evidently a central text common to us all, but nothing *absolute* can be established.

Sterne's place in this tradition of learned wit, which demands, for response, not so much a dead weight of learning as willingness to allow for the activity of wit itself, is legendary and, as for his predecessors in the century, recollects proto-Scriblerians, like Apuleius, Lucian, Rabelais, and Cervantes. I have already suggested the part Don Quixote plays in the allusive texts of the Club and its later literary cousins, stressing not so much the quality of amiable humour as the potential cruelty, the lost dreams of pastoral, the presence of ruin, and the frustration of making wholes. Lucian, translated by More and Erasmus in a kind of preparation for the *Moriae Encomium* and for some tones in the *Utopia*,[35] is found, if not so frequently as Cervantes and Rabelais or Ovid, in casual allusions throughout their work. Lucian's period parallels that of the English Augustans in many ways.[36] An anonymous writer in London in 1804 neatly represents the continuity of this world in a striking title:

Lorry Lucian and Jerry Juvenal. Assisted by the
Renowned Solomon Scriblerus. Enlivened with *serious*
Annotations and illustrated by *opaque* Biography.
British Purity: or, The World We Live in. A Poetic
Tale, of Two Centuries. Satirico-Gossippico.

On page 47 of this text we are told of "Pope's Beatitude, viz. 'Blessed are they who expect NOTHING, for they shall not be disappointed.'" The motto for the whole, uniting Lucian, Juvenal, and Scriblerus, is, wonderfully, "When shall we three meet again?"

Lucian's cynical tones in the dialogues (*dialogues*, not stories) may have given Dryden some qualms about his sceptical subject when he wrote Lucian's Life, but these spoke to the days of Erasmus and More. Pope and Swift admired these earlier satirists. They shared their love of paradox and the implied conviction that only paradox could speak to the doubleness of existence. Rabelais was a natural figure for the Scriblerians to adopt. As Raymond LaCharité observes: "In *Pantagruel*, carnivalesque recreation and humanist re-creational concerns – the acquisition, production and dissemination of learning, propagation of the text, problematics of language – go hand in hand to an unprecedented degree and appear at times to be but the reverse of the same medal."[37] He also argues that the central issues are reading as play and reader participation, noting that Rabelais has a proto-Shandean sense of the inadequacy of language – precisely the conviction of the Scriblerians. Elsewhere he describes Rabelais's presentation of "a thematic structure of opposition and corrective progression ... study of the paired episodes and characters reveals the mechanics of binary structures which contrast past and present, old and new" (93). One is tempted to add, thinking on Thélème and environs, a contrast as well of garden and ruin.[38] The binaries generated, in Rabelais, in the Scriblerians, make E.V. Telle's comment on Thélème important: "Il a ... poursuivi, parmi les Français, la vulgarisation de la *Philosophie Christi* ... L'érasmisme nous en donnera-t-il la solution? Je n'en serais pas surpris."³⁹ Even if we may not accept the solution, the parallel between Erasmus and his religious stance and Rabelais's abbey – with the added parallel to be found in their satirical procedures – is important. It is also *very* Scriblerian.

Sterne's contribution to this tradition owes much to Burton, whose *Anatomy*, for all its pretended organization, belongs in another way to the tradition of learned wit and fragment and frustration of easy solution. Efforts to solve Shandean conundrums are lines of gravity, countered by the serpentine quality of the book.⁴⁰ The moral of the next marbled page, apart from introducing folly visually into the text, is at least in part one that tells us there is no moral to be found, for every page is different – even as all readers will respond to different lines.

Full of strange sayings and allusions of every kind, the Scriblerians are immensely fond of paradox, the ultimate device in refusal to render engaged finality in meaning.⁴¹ Pope habitually works in this tradition, as the whole of *An Essay on Man*, with its insistence on the "strange sayings" made by God to man, indicates. One of the centres of the paradoxical tradition was the praise of things without honour, or apparently without honour, if honour is expanded to mean seriousness. The most famous example of this is Erasmus's *Encomium Moriae*, with its punning Latin title a tribute to the existence of that earlier circle to which the eighteenth-century Club seems to have an obvious affiliation in concern and in style. Apart from making More the only modern among the seven worthies in his *Travels*, Swift approvingly mentions More elsewhere in his work without commenting specifically on More's own paradoxical style in the *Utopia*. Utopia is a good place that is also the place that is not. It is a text filled with puns, the appreciation of whose doubleness is essential to be aware of the ambiguity of the text. *Utopia* is as inconclusive as all works written in this mode, a text that also plays with the notion of text in its teasing prefatory matter, in its insistence that it is a dialogue.⁴²

In addition to More and Erasmus, Pope at least was also drawn to another Renaissance contest of wits conducted in the paradoxical mode. In the later editions of *The Dunciad* he notes that any letters sent in commentary, and to the purpose, will be printed in forthcoming editions (he saw the process precisely as process – carrying on and on); any letters not to the purpose will be printed under the title of *Letters of Obscure Men*. He is allusive here as well, for the letters he is reviving by allusion are a comical contribution to a duncical battle in the Renaissance. Johannes Reuchlin, whose name was later tipped into Pope's correspondence (1.122n), was menaced by a zealous convert to Christianity from Judaism. The menace was in a simple form: all the books of the Jews were to be burnt. Reuchlin, the great student of these texts, got up what we should call a petition from the most distinguished scholars of his age and published it under the title of *Epistola Dignissimae Virorum*. Ulrich von Hutten's contribution to the battle was more effective. His *Epistolae Obscurorum Virorum* presents the fictional letters of dunces, easily seen as such and, as such, easily laughed out of serious contention. Clearly, in the period after the formation of the Club, Pope and his group knew of this pre-dunce activity. They could certainly have been aware of the text, for a handsome edition of it was published in 1710 in London, with its compiler, Isaac Bickerstaff, writing a dedicatory epistle that also allies it, by allusion, to More and Erasmus. The text has usually been associated with Michael Maittaire, the classicist and antiquarian whom Pope removed from *The Dunciad* at the behest of Lord Oxford. In one of the Houghton Library copies, however, an eighteenth-century hand ascribes the work to Dr Garth; if this attribution is right, then the likelihood of the Scriblerians' knowing of it at an early stage is probably considerably strengthened. Swift had a copy in his library.

The obscure are, as for later versions, in the dunces and the Tale-teller and the narrator of the *Travels*, easily condemned from their own foolish accounts of the harm they mean to wreak on the learning of Reuchlin and his crew. There are, I think, no references to the *Epistolae* in Sterne, but, creator of nonsensical documents within nonsensical documents, he is certainly part of and extender of the tradition to which von Hutten belonged. He is also aware of the text as text, even as Fielding constantly calls attention to his book as book – that is, not something real in the usual sense. His play with the text, from what was clearly actual timing of the writing of pages to the asterisks to the missing chapters, the misplaced chapters, and the dedication, all recollect Swift's play with the text in the *Tale*, although Swift's tone about the holes in his manuscript is much less comically accepting than Sterne's.

Sterne's mode also illuminates the Scriblerian in other ways. The extended play with the reader is clear only in proper eighteenth-century editions of his novel, and genuinely effective, I suppose, only *for* its original readers, who were made to wait for and respond to successive issues of the nine volumes. As we know, he waited for a response and dealt with that response in what came next, usually in satire's assaultively ecstatic mode of doing whatever had been objected to in the volumes already published. The dunces had waited too, and their anticipation became part of Pope's text. This sense of folly, as for Erasmus, as for Fielding in his essay *Upon Nothing*, as for the Scriblerians in documents like *Stradling against Stiles*, as for Pope in the poems on the *Travels*, where the work comes more literally to life as characters begin to write verse on their own, becomes real, not just in his parson Yorick but on every page. He persistently frustrates expectation about proper format and typography. Apparently careless, he controlled his whole text, even marking (as a reading aloud in a first edition will show) the page breaks themselves. Pope's anxieties about his texts (with the others in the Club) give us yet another paradox: the reader is apparently let loose, but is in reality on a leash.

In addition to formalizing this ostensibly informal book, where digressions are the sunshine of life and the line of gravity is the worst of figures, Sterne insists on his reader's participation in the process of reading. In addition to discouraging single "readings," he circumvented mass production of his book by insisting at the same time on the individual page, underlining the danger of what is mass and uniform and trumpeting the glee of the individual and his sweet sensibility. I here emphasize Sterne's warmth. By the last page of the cock and bull story all characters from Shandy Hall are officially long dead and only Tristram is left to carry the bar sinister to his projected early grave; but now they all are present and alive, even unto the Shandy bull, whatever its questionable reputation. That is the end of Book 9. Book 7 is apparently a chewed crust for the critics who complained of digression by being in itself a total digression, from the subject and from England. Its epigraph, like the others, is meant to be taken seriously. It says that this is *not* in fact a digression but the main matter itself. So it is – and the traveller is dancing across France, escaping death, or, as it were, avoiding that spleen and melancholy that can lead, in a variety of ways, to solid flesh thawing, melting, resolving into a dew. Travelling, to rather different nations of the world, is Sterne's mode too.

The Scriblerians, in their minor as well as their major works, are as zany as Sterne and as Lockean too, with all the ambiguity possible stylistically for those who live in the ambience of the philosopher who was possibly writing the new version of *An Anatomy of Melancholy*. They are, however, much less tolerant of aberration, if they are tolerant at all. Addison's unequivocal espousal of Mr Locke in the papers in the *Spectator* on wit dictates the death of the pun and establishes the test for truth as translation into another language. Sterne is not really ambiguous about Locke; rather he plays with the possibility of association and its effect on efforts to tell, say, the story of the King of Bohemia and his Seven Castles. He does not conclude gloomily that we should be better off if we believed in the possibility of a general history of mind that allows characters in fiction or elsewhere to finish smoking pipes or to continue actions until their clear and distinct conclusion. The Club, Swift in special, increasingly had little faith in either mode of apprehension. The gardens and parks were, in the end, only isolated pastoral oases, and the shining palaces of cities were finally ruined.

Scriblerian style reflects this perception or, more properly, is *created* by this perception. Nothing ends. Everything goes on. Ovidian flux is a major part of their stylistic universe. They are not exactly free to play; play can also be (and is perhaps not the less recreative for all that) a mode of preservation from what the Scriblerians perceived as that changed world in which, as nearly new Quixotes, they sought for another. Perhaps the most considerable paradox in the paradoxical mode they found real and congenial is their suspicion of language, of that very medium whose doubleness and tripleness (God's Revenge) their works constantly employ as they work to engage others, of similiar dispositions, in their perceptions of the world and their method of responding as artists to these perceptions. I am thinking not only of Swift's attempt to stop the changing of the language but also of phrases like Pope's about "wit oblique" in *An Essay on Man* and how this wit breaks the steady light of Nature that obtained in that Golden Age represented in the poem (in cities even more than in rural scenes). The third voyage in the *Travels*, in the section on the Grand Academy, can be read as a critique only of the useless science that builds houses from the roof down. And there is, of course, a quite direct comment on the virtues of those who can make another grain of corn grow where only one has grown before.

But in general a fear of innovation (and this is hardly a new perception) dominates the group; innovation is most dangerous in the tongue. Their suspicion is not restricted to attacks on the vulgarities of Philips or to the world apparently supported by the Little Senate; it seems to apply to the insubstantiality of all language, so that the speech of the Houyhnhnms is closer to that primeval world to which Swift, whatever his learning, whatever his wit, finally belonged. It is, after all, in the episode of the gypsies in *Tom Jones*, that impossible oasis where all is literal and the tongue is different in being as unsophisticated as Fielding can make it, that Fielding gives his disquisition on and praise of an absolute monarchy that is also impossible. His premise is that this depends upon a king like the gypsy ruler, a man of no external distinction, a version in the secular world of the unadorned will of the *Tale*, whose action, in both the religious and critical sections is a concern with words, a concern that works consistently to keep all simple and plain. The confusions of *Three Hours* are inherent in mistaken words, like the assumption that Phoebe's "offspring" are children, not names for her poetical works.

The existence of the Club is a testimonial not only to the merriment one assumes went on at the meetings, to the merriment of the works we have, but also to Swift's notion that one could not talk to everyone, that only a very few understood what was happening, in the past and in the present, so that the future, of the realm and of the tongue, looked very gloomy. In terms of Arbuthnot's initial plea for a manner of correspondence, one that would preserve their company and continue to articulate their games, one might well ask who corresponds, and with what? Their chief appeal, like the appeal of modern writers who resemble them in their mode (Nabokov, Barth, Barthelme, Coover, Pynchon, and so on) is to those who are not put off but rather drawn on by the diverting puzzles they often present, those who wish to belong to this circle. Joyce, frequent quoter of Swift and Sterne and inventor of that nice pun "zeroic couplet," talked of his Work in Progress, implying that literature, at least of his sort, should do that, so as to vex and divert in the best traditions of very learned play, an activity that asks for players, a reading community, so that books do not make us solitary, and hacks and victims of a mass culture, but sociable, if only with what is perceived as a fit audience though few. Funferall at a funeral for a wake. The letter about correspondence is a sad one, written at a sad time, but it is a preamble to many years of correspondence (in both senses) that might not have been possible had the whole group remained together. As writers they necessarily have a limited appeal, not simply because their work is so often topical but because not all are prepared to trail their topoi or to accept the mode David Vieth has aptly described in his "Toward an Anti-Aristotelian Poetic." His principal text is Rochester, but he comments on the *Tale* and on the *Travels* in a way that can be extended to Scriblerus as a whole:

Anti-Aristotelian literature ... dramatizes with amusement the absurdity inherent in the assumption that any work of art could be altogether autonomous –

that it could, for example, be isolated from the audience which responds to it, the author who created it, the time of its writing and other circumstances surrounding its composition, the traditions it may embody, and the accumulated characteristics of the language it uses ... It may deliberately cultivate internal discontinuities: in chronology, in questions of cause and effect, in tone, in meanings and values.[43]

Perhaps the paradox of the Club's merry and melancholy universe and style is best caught by another modern Scriblerian. Beckett's *Happy Days* introduces us to a world where things seem hardly to be happy at all. The heroine sits in the rising sand, waiting to sing her song, counting out the contents of her purse as her spouse creeps menacingly behind her. Even the final song of the merry widow was meant, as we know from Beckett's own directions (and like Sterne he distrusted his audience enough to want to control the whole production), to be played as a running-down record. Still, and the French is better, it is "O les beaux jours." What else can one do, if escape from sand is impossible, and even if the grass widow has only a postponed song whose notes, growing ever slower, will vanish, after the audience has gone home? In Phillip Fehl's "Farewell to Jokes," an essay on Tiepolo, he says: "Rain ... does not only make us wet. Without it there would be no umbrellas, and, perhaps, not even harlequins to accompany us on a lonely road and to lead the way."[44]

Notes

CHAPTER ONE

1 MacLean's phrase for the period, "The age of passion" (48), shapes the title of Steven Shankman's *Pope's Iliad: Homer in the Age of Passion* (1983). See also Margaret A. Doody, *The Daring Muse: Augustan Poetry Reconsidered* (1985), and Terry J. Castle, *Masquerade and Civilization: The Carnivalesque in Eighteenth-Century English Culture and Fiction* (1986).
2 Swift adds, after Opera, "but not till it hath fully done its Jobb." 3.278.
3 See the discussion in Parnell, *Poems*, ed. Lock and Rawson, intro., 18–23.
4 See *Memoirs*, ed. Kerby-Miller, 2–10.
5 These were children in the Lincoln's Inn Fields production. See Gay, *The Beggar's Opera As it is Acted at the Theatre-Royal in Lincoln's Inn Fields* (London 1728). The "Names of the Lilliputians" appear on p. 7. Two girls play Peachum and Macheath.
6 *Gulliver Decypher'd* or REMARKS on a late BOOK, intitled TRAVELS Into Several Remote Nations of the World. By Capt. LEMUEL GULLIVER. Vindicating the Reverend Dean on whom it is Maliciously Father'd. With Some probable Conjectures concerning the Real AUTHOR (London 1728).
7 Irving, *John Gay: Favourite of the Wits*, 303.
8 "Pope's *An Essay on Man*, IV, 195–6," 308–9.
9 "Satiric Allusions in John Gay's Welcome to Mr. Pope," 427–32. See also Weinbrot, *Augustus Caesar in "Augustan" England*.
10 See *Collected in Himself*, 424, 434, 412, 397, 411.

11 "Addison," 1.
12 *The Early Career of Alexander Pope*, 170.
13 Rawson, *Henry Fielding*, 173–7.
14 Quennell, *Four Portraits*, 148.
15 "Of the Hazards of Game," trans. of Huygens, *De rationciniis in ludoaleae*, 260. The first edition of Huygens' original appeared in 1692, and there was a second edition in 1714.
16 Poggioli, *The Oaten Flute*; Lerner, *The Uses of Nostalgia: Studies in Pastoral Poetry*; Alpers, "What is Pastoral?"

CHAPTER TWO

1 See Hunt and Willis, *The Genius of the Place*; Jarrett, *The English Landscape Garden*.
2 See Baridon, "Ruins as Mental Construct"; Stafford, "Illiterate Monuments."
3 For the other side of this ostensibly ideal landscape, see the second half of chapter 4, especially the representation of Allworthy. See my discussion of the ambiguities of Allworthy.
4 See Addison on the imagination, *Spectator* 3.411–21.535–82. For the sublime, see especially 3.412.540–1.
5 This was called "Paradise." See Swift, *Corr.* 4.414n 1. For references to Milton in the text of the novel, see the Wesleyan Edition, 2.1072. The episode concerning the Man of the Hill and his gloomy prospect seems to glance back to Milton and the panorama offered to Adam (*Paradise Lost*, 11, 12) as well as Satan's offer to Christ in *Paradise Regained*. The possible link between Allworthy's retirement, despite his occasional (and ill-timed) forays into the city, and the Man of the Hill's extreme seclusion has not, I think, been noted. See below, n 8.
6 See below, chap. 3, on the metropolis.
7 Tom's spiritual relation to his uncle is not usually remarked (2.2.78), nor is the implication of his Christian name. "Thomas" means "twin."
8 See my "An Early Hint of Miss Bridget's Affairs, with a Parallel Note on Mr. Allworthy," 73–9, and David Oakleaf, "'Sliding down Together': Fielding, Addison and the Pleasures of the Imagination."
9 "Architecture as Virtue: The Luminous Palace from Homeric Dream to Stuart Propaganda," espec. 428–9.
10 Arbuthnot, *An Essay concerning the Effects of Air on Human Bodies* (London 1733).

11 See my discussion below of Bolingbroke's treatise, and writers on the country house like Summerson, "The Classical Country House in Eighteenth-Century England," and Hibbard, "The Country House Poem of the Seventeenth Century." See also Mack, *The Garden and the City*; Kenny, *The Country-house Ethos in English Literature, 1688–1750*; O'Loughlin, *The Garlands of Repose*; Martin, *Pursuing Innocent Pleasures*; Kelsall, *The Great Good Place*; Congleton, *Theories of Pastoral Poetry in England, 1684–1798*; Patterson, *Pastoral and Ideology*; Weinbrot, *Britannia's Issue*.

12 Alpers, "What is Pastoral?" See also Rosenmeyer, *The Green Cabinet: Theocritus and the European Pastoral Lyric*.

13 Fielding, *Joseph Andrews*, 1.6.32.

14 See, for correction, Folkenflik, "Tom Jones, the Gypsies and the Masquerade." See also Greene, "Fielding's Gypsy Episode and Sancho Panza's Governorship"; Battestin, "Tom Jones and 'His Egyptian Majesty'"; and Schonhorn, "Fielding's Digressive-Parodic Artistry."

15 Matthew Bramble's idyllic Welsh estate lacks this warmth, and his progress is in large part a rediscovery of former friends. The revelation of his relationship to Clinker takes place at the re-created country estate of Charles Dennis, who is one such friend. Dennison, unlike Bramble, is not a snob. His reclamation of ruin has been accomplished by the whole community. See my account below of Bolingbroke's ideal estate. For other discussions of the country estate, see above, n 11.

16 See n 15 above and the discussion of Bolingbroke below.

17 The extent of Pope's indebtedness to and, especially, differences from his sources is not always clear in the notes to the Twickenham edition. The editors cite the passages closest to Pope's text, a procedure that is economical and apparently sound. This method does not, however, do justice to Pope as reader and reviser. A more elaborate discussion of Pope's rendering of his sources would have answered to the issues.

18 Rapin, *Discourse of Pastorals*, in Creech's *Idylliums of Theocritus*, 19.

19 "The Life of Pope," in *The Lives of the Poets*, 3.224–5. See also Congleton, *Theories of Pastoral Poetry*, and Patterson, *Pastoral Ideology*.

20 See the Twickenham edition and the parallels Wakefield suggests.

21 In Pope, *Prose Works*, 1.97–106.

22 "The Place of Thomas Nashe in the Learning of His Time," PhD, Cambridge University 1943. See McLuhan's manuscript note on p. 32. In his *Pope's Dunciad* Aubrey Williams acknowledges his "special debt to McLuhan" (viii) and cites him later on *translatio studii* (46, n 2). In his

chapter on wisdom and dullness, Williams cites the thesis once more, especially for McLuhan's contribution to the background of the chapter (105, n 1). Later (134, n 1) he cites McLuhan again, this time principally through his "An Ancient Quarrel in Modern America." The arguments of McLuhan's thesis, never published but often lent, made him a significant influence on later students of the eighteenth century. The dissertation begins with a study of Newton on language, and McLuhan's notes on the manuscript extend his reflections on the eighteenth century, not least on Swift and Pope. There is a manuscript note after vi in the introduction to the thesis: "Swift devotee of translatio studii." This note comes from the late sixties, when McLuhan was revising the dissertation for a publication that has never appeared, although the text was read approvingly by members of the Pontifical Institute, who were particularly impressed by McLuhan's study of the ancient and medieval background for Nashe.

23 "A Sermom [sic] Preach'd to the People at the Mercat Cross of Edinburgh; on the Subject of the Union," 3.
24 *An Essay Concerning the Effects of Air*, 205. See also 210: "The Country Air in Spring and Summer has a considerable Influence upon Mankind by the Steams of Vegetables, which variously stimulate, and perhaps exhilerate the Spirits and upon the same Account the Air of a planted and inclos'd Garden is different from that of an Open, and in some Cases less refreshing." There is a steamy oxmoor in front of Shandy Hall.
25 Gay, *Poetry and Prose*, 1.493–500.157.
26 See also 5.926–34; 6.304–11 (the "stately Courts" of Priam); and especially the account of the "shining Palace" of Nepture, 13.34–9, an "Eternal Frame! not rais'd by mortal Hands."
27 See Wasserman on *Windsor-Forest* in *The Subtler Language*.
28 Poggioli, *The Oaten Flute*, 1–3.
29 See DePorte, "Swift's Horses of Instruction."
30 *Prose Works*, 8, *Political Tracts 1713–1719*, 134–5.
31 See his letter to Mrs Caesar, 30 July 1733 (4.184), to Gay and to the Duchess of Queensberry, 10 July 1732 (4.40). He had the same kind of reservations about Pope. See his observations on *An Essay on Man* to Pope, 1 May 1733 (4.153).
32 Jefferson, *Family Letters*, 437–8. Bolingbroke's interest in Erasmus was also important. See my discussion in this chapter.
33 See L.K. Born's discussion in the introduction to his translation of Erasmus's *Education of a Christian Prince*, 44–93, and Ernst Kantorowicz, *The King's Two Bodies*.

34 See 3.134-5.
35 See *Viscount Bolingbroke: Tory Humanist*, 85-6.
36 The poem is meant to be affirmative and to suggest an age of gold. Its tones are hollow, in the manner of Swift's early odes. See my discussion in chapter 4.
37 *Historical Writings*, 291-340.
38 This device is particularly striking in Swift, notably in the fourth voyage of the *Travels*, as Gulliver angrily scores off England. We may regret the tone and perhaps his despair, but nothing he says of England is false.
39 "Knickerbocker, Bolingbroke and the Fiction of History," 327. See also Alexander Pettit, "Anxiety, Political Rhetoric and Historical Drama under Walpole," 109-36.
40 See J.R. Jones, *Charles II: Royal Politician*, for the most recent study.
41 As the indexes to the Twickenham edition show, Miltonic allusion is everywhere present. It is especially striking in *An Essay on Man*, where it underlines the biblical.
42 "'The Care of Heav'n': Biblical Echo in *An Essay on Man*."
43 "Of the Hazards of the Game," preface, 7-8.
44 "Empson on Pastoral," 102.
45 Empson, *Some Versions of Pastoral*.
46 "The 1720 Version of *Rural Sports* and the Georgic Tradition."
47 As in Armens, *John Gay: Social Critic*. See, for example, 3-4.
48 "Thomas D'Urfey, The Pope-Philips Quarrel and *The Shepherd's Week*."
49 Poggioli, *The Oaten Flute*, 36.
50 Ames, "Gay's *Trivia* and the Art of Allusion," 207. See also Sherbo, "Virgil, Dryden, Gay, and Matters Trivial," PMLA 85 (1970): 1063-7.
51 For women in retirement, see, for example, the poems of Anne Finch, Countess of Winchilsea (nos. 10, 12, 16), in Lonsdale, ed., *Eighteenth-Century Women Poets*.
52 See Mack, *The Garden and the City*, and O'Loughlin, *Garlands of Repose*.
53 Hughes, *Dryden's Heroic Plays*, 68-9, n 3. See also Canfield, "Royalism's Last Dramatic Stand," "The Significance of the Restoration Rhymed Heroic Plays," and "The Jewel of Great Price."
54 "'Awed by Reason': Pope on Achilles," 196.
55 "John Gay's 'Achilles': The Burlesque Element," 23-4.
56 *Tables of Ancient Coins, Weights and Measures, Explain'd and Exemplify'd in Several Dissertations*, 1-3.
57 Rees, "'A Great Man in Distress': Macheath as Hercules," and Owen, "Polly and the Choice of Virtue"; Hagstrum, *The Sister Arts*, 193.
58 "The Sin of Pride," 24-5.

59 See my "'The Care of Heav'n.'"
60 "Gulliver: *Cum Grano Salis*," 9.
61 Arbuthnot, "Stradling vs. Stiles."
62 "Landscape Gardening by Jonathan Swift and His Friends in Ireland," 72.
63 See Swift, *Corr.*, 3.14 and n, 21 and n, 43 and n, 59 and n, 60 and n, 74n, 91, 129n, 199 and n, 286 and n, 373 and n, 383 and n; 4.154 and n, 159, 170 and n, 200, 252; 3.91.298.
64 "Pope's Wasteland: Reflections on Mock-Heroic," 53.
65 Ariès, *Centuries of Childhood*.
66 "Sense and Sensibility: The Child and the Man in 'The Rape of the Lock,'" 277.
67 "'Virgins Visited by Angel Pow'rs': *The Rape of the Lock*, Platonicks, Mysticks and Sylphs."
68 *Utopia*, 121.
69 "Gardens and Parks," *New Yorker*, 17 June 1950, 28–33; and *Speak Memory: An Autobiography Revisited*, 15.295–310. Nabokov begins and ends his narrative of himself with a vision of the child and a child's game, appropriately "Find What the Sailor Has Hidden."

CHAPTER THREE

1 See Webber, *The Eloquent I*.
2 See Sitter, *Literary Loneliness in Mid-Eighteenth-Century England*; Carnochan, *Gibbon's Solitude*; Oakleaf, "Solitary Voices."
3 See Baker, "Henry Fielding's Comic Romances," 411–19.
4 See Hunter, *Occasional Form*, and Rawson, *Henry Fielding*.
5 "Chastity and Interpolation: Two Aspects of *Joseph Andrews*."
6 *Anatomy of Melancholy*, 1.1.2.5. p 208.
7 See Klibansky, Panofsky, and Saxl, *Saturn and Melancholy*, 284ff.
8 I am indebted in my discussion of Shandy Hall to Martha F. Bowden, "Nature is Nature," PhD, University of Toronto 1980. See also my "Mr Shandy's Hip."
9 "Sterne, Burton, and Ferriar: Allusion to the *Anatomy of Melancholy* in Volumes Five to Nine of *Tristram Shandy*." Jackson's dissertation, "The Anatomy of Melancholy in England, 1750–1800," PhD, University of Toronto 1973, shows the mid-century interest in Burton, so much that a new edition was wanted in 1800. Many of the epigraphs come from "Democritus Junior to the Reader," Burton's Utopia.
10 See Barish, *The Anti-Theatrical Prejudice*.

11 Fussell, *The Rhetorical World of Augustan Humanism*, 283. Tom Jones and Mr Partridge go to see a production of *Hamlet*. In *Humphry Clinker* Tabitha speaks, memorably, of the "ghost of Gimlet," 51. Walpole's *Castle* is haunted by Shakespearean ghosts. Boswell's first meeting with Johnson is marked by "Look, my Lord, it comes" (*Life of Johnson*, 1.392).
12 *Reflexivity in "Tristram Shandy,"* 196–257.
13 "Holland and Britain in the Age of Observation." For the authoritative study of Locke and English literature of the eighteenth century, see MacLean, *John Locke*.
14 *Locke and the Scriblerians*.
15 Wimsatt, *The Portraits of Alexander Pope*, xv.
16 *An Essay on Man*, 3.311–16.
17 This is related to his ambivalence about his friends as it is expressed in his verses on his own death, beginning with the maxim from La Rochefoucault that is their epigraph. See Nokes's portrait of him, "Dean and Drapier," espec. chap. 4.
18 See the letters to Pope (Aug. 1726, 3.159); to Lady Worsley (Nov. 1732, 4.79) – "fighting with Beasts like St. Paul, not at Ephesus, but in Ireland"; and to the Duke of Dorset (Dec. 1735, 4.450).
19 Goldsmith, "The Life of Dr. Parnell," in *Collected Works of Oliver Goldsmith*, 3.415.
20 See my "'Religious Hope and Resignation': The Process of 'Eloisa to Abelard,'" *English Studies in Canada* 3 (1977): 153–63.
21 "The Significance of Gay's Drama," 161.
22 This is the fable Catherine Morland knows by heart in *Northanger Abbey*. Austen uses this allusion early in the novel to hint at the action to come, as she does with the other quotations in Catherine's repertoire.
23 "The Reach and Wit of the Inventor," 4.
24 "Situations of Identity in the *Memoirs of Martinus Scriblerus*," 388–9.
25 *Pope's Epistle to Bathurst*, 11–55.
26 Hagstrum, *Sex and Sensibility*, 50–71.
27 *Dryden: The Poetics of Translation*.
28 See Hagstrum's discussion of Swift, Vanessa, and Stella, *Sex and Sensibility*, 145–69.
29 Doody's "Swift among the Women" admirably delineates Swift's friendships with women and his way of not enclosing them in the usual conventions. To argue that he wants emotional distance is not to deny his refusal to make women into echoes of literary conventionality.
30 For a recent study of Pope and women, see Rumbold, *Women's Place in Pope's World*.

31 Ferriar, *Illustrations of Sterne*, 1.95. For an account of other instances of Sterne and Martinus, see the Florida edition, 3.40, 49, 152–3, 165, 195–6, 250, 328, 364, 397, 400–1, 417, 430, 469–70, 480–1, 486.
32 See *OED*, 1.131, "adust" 2, and Klibansky, Panofsky, and Saxl, *Saturn and Melancholy*, 52. Melancholy, or excess wit, can burn out the intellects. This is what Hamlet here implies.
33 See my "'*In familiari colloquio*': An Intervention in *Utopia*," 9 and 13 n 5.
34 More is the only modern among the six virtuous persons listed in the *Travels* (3.196). There are no references in the correspondence, but see "Of Mean and Great Figures: Sir Tho More during his Imprisonment, and at his Execution" (5.84), and, in the *Marginalia*: "The only Man of true Virtue that(t) ever Engld produced" (5.247). On More's death: "(H)ere the detestable (Ty)rant murdered (Vir)tue herself" (5.248). "Concerning that Universal Hatred, which Prevails against the Clergy," in an attack on Henry VII, who "cut off the head of Sir Thomas More, a person of the greatest virtue this kingdom ever produced" (13.125). There is also a reference in the *Travels* in Gulliver's letter to Sympson: it has been alleged "that the *Houyhnhnms* and *Yahoos* have no more Existence than the Inhabitants of *Utopia*" (11.8).
35 *Memoirs*, ed. Kerby-Miller, 249.
36 See Rothstein, *Restoration Tragedy*.
37 *A Treatise of Human Nature*, 1.4.264–5.
38 In a long letter to Caryll written on 25 June 1711, Pope comments on Dennis's criticism of *An Essay on Criticism* in a moderate spirit, noting the justice of some of Dennis's observations, declining, at least then, to take more vigorous action because Dennis has indicated in his preface "that he is at this time persecuted by fortune" (1.121). He says that "whoever sets up for wit in these days ought to have the constancy of a primitive Christian, and be prepared to suffer even martyrdom in the cause of it. But sure this is the first time that a wit was attacked for his religion, as you'll find I'm most zealously in this treatise" (121–2). He goes on to commend Thomas Southcote's candour and to address his evaluation of the monks: "The only difference between us in relation to the monks is, that he thinks most sorts of learning *flourish'd* among 'em, and I am of opinion that only some sort of learning was barely *kept alive* by 'em." Just after his insistence that learning in the *Essay* meant only polite learning and not, as Southcote argued, learning in general, Sherburn notes that "at this point in his printed texts Pope inserted, from no known letter, the following sentence: 'It is true, that the *Monks* did preserve what learning there was, about *Nicholas* the *Fifth*'s time; but those who

succeeded fell into the depth of *Barbarism*, or at least stood at a stay while others rose from thence, insomuch that even *Erasmus* and *Reuchlin* could hardly laugh them out of it.'"

39 See DePorte, "Swift and the Licence of Satire," 57–62.
40 I am indebted for this observation to the unpublished essay of G.H. Hopson, written for my graduate seminar, as I am in general for his argument in that essay about the importance of *Three Hours* in the Scriblerian canon. The play is much more than a local effort to strike out at Woodward and other favourite butts and enemies.
41 Pope suggested that Gay leave out the crocodile. See Gay, *Letters*, 32 (Gay to Pope, Jan. 1716/17).
42 See Vieth, "Toward an Anti-Aristotelian Poetic," 123–45.
43 *The Orphic Voice*, 135.
44 Shearer, "Ovid and Scriblerus," PhD, University of Toronto 1980.
45 Spence, *Anecdotes of Books and Men*, 1.188.
46 "Virgins Visited by Angel Pow'rs."
47 "*The Rape of the Lock* as a Comedy of Continuity." Quintana relates Pope's Ovidian technique in the poem to Swift's in his "Verses wrote in a Lady's Ivory Table-Book" and notes the closeness of Pope and Swift in 1714. He also illuminates his argument about the comedy of continuity by suggesting the ways in which certain figures of rhetoric accomplish this changing pattern (12–16).
48 See Halsband, "*The Rape of the Lock*" *and Its Illustrations, 1714–1896*.
49 Quoted by Halsband, *Illustrations*, 20, from Tillotson, *On the Poetry of Pope*, 157.
50 See "Füseli, Pope and the Nightmare," and Schiff, *Johann Heinrich Füssli, 1741–1825*.
51 See above, n 48.
52 See Goldberg, "The Interpolated Stories in *Joseph Andrews*."
53 See Carretta, *The Snarling Muse*, and Doody, *The Daring Muse*.
54 See the print in Paulson, *Hogarth*, 1, plate 181, p 474.
55 See Kayser, *The Grotesque in Art and Literature*, and Steig, "Defining the Grotesque."
56 *An Essay on Human Understanding*, 1.2.55.
57 See Richardson, *Sir Charles Grandison*, 1.115f; Burney, *Camilla, Cecilia*. See Castle, *Masquerade and Civilization*.
58 See Novak, ed., *English Literature in the Age of Disguise*.
59 Blewett, "Roxana and the Masquerades."
60 Fielding continued to love theatre as an art form. He also makes brilliant use of theatre when he sends Tom to see *Hamlet*, a wholly appropriate

play for a man so close to his mother. There is a difference, however, between this kind of technique and his reading of those for whom life is only a stage.
61 See Battestin, "Menalcas' Song: The Meaning of Art and Artifice in Gay's Poetry."
62 See Yoch, "Architecture as Virtue," 141–2.
63 This was pointed out to me by Patricia Köster.
64 Miller, "Regal Hunting: Dryden's Influence on *Windsor-Forest.*"
65 *Reflections*, 171.
66 "'The Wolf in the Fold': John Gay in *The Shepherd's Week* and *Trivia.*"
67 "The *Dunciad* as Mock-Book."
68 *Essay on the Different Styles of Poetry*. The full couplet reads: "And where a *Friendship's* generously strong, / They celebrate the Knot of Souls in Song" (413–14).
69 *Jubilate Agno*, B84. Smart's other tribute to Pope is in B568: "*For Flowers can see, and Pope's Carnations knew him.*"
70 See Manning, "Mirth and Melancholy."

CHAPTER FOUR

1 Rochester, "A Satyr against Reason and Mankind," in Wilmot, *Complete Poems*, 94–101. Pope imitated Rochester in his "Upon Silence."
2 See Winnicott, *Playing and Reality* and *Home Is Where We Start From*. See also Huizinga, *Homo Ludens*. For other studies of play, see the *Yale French Studies* special issue on *Game, Play and Literature* 41 (1968), espec. Ehrmann's introduction, his "Homo Ludens Revisited" (31–57), and Beaujour, "The Game of Poetics" (58–67), Wimsatt, "How To Compose Chess Problems" (68–85), Holquist, "How To Play Utopia" (106–23), and Bakhtin, "The Role of Games in Rabelais" (124–32).
3 *Arguments of Augustan Wit*, 186.
4 I am indebted to Corinne McLuhan for allowing me to read and to cite from the dissertation and from the manuscript notes McLuhan made in the late sixties. McLuhan's interest at every state of his career was in the canons and tropes of rhetoric. Ben Jonson, an important figure for the Scriblerians, says, "*Language* most shews a man: speak, that I may see thee" (*Oratio Imago Animi*, *Works*, 8.625). Jonson's statement is itself paradoxical.
5 *Swift's Rhetorical Art*. See the *Peri Bathous*.
6 "Letters on the Study and Use of History," *Works*, 2.212. Bolingbroke's enmity to historical romance is a recurrent theme, one that accompanies his scoffing at credulity and easy belief.

7 I owe this observation to Martha F. Bowden's "'Night Overtook Them or Met Them': Darkness in *Joseph Andrews*."
8 "The Interpolated Stories in *Joseph Andrews*."
9 Forcione, *Cervantes and the Humanist Vision*, 170–1.
10 *New York Times* Book Review, 6 Mar. 1986, 15. I owe this reference to Jill L. Levenson.
11 *The Order of Things*, 46–9.
12 See, for examples of efforts to domesticate the wildness of the *Tale*, Paulson, *Theme and Structure*; Clark, *Form and Frenzy* (where form prevails over frenzy); Smith, *Language and Reality*. Contrast DePorte, *Nightmares and Hobby-horses* and "Teaching the Third Voyage."
13 For some samples of Fielding on Jonson, see *Tom Jones*, 2.525, 1.327n; *Miscellanies*, 85n, 95n; *Covent Garden Journal* 55, 18 July 1752, 209. Fielding quotes here at length from *Every Man out of His Humour* to illustrate the conception of humour; *Miscellanies*, 89n (an allusion in a note to *Volpone*); *Covent Garden Journal* 21, 21 Mar. 1752, 152, on the "literary Government" in the reign of James; *Covent Garden Journal* 26, 31 Mar. 1752, 168 – on the assumption that *The Alchemist* is a classic. In his note to *Tom Jones* 12.5.638 Battestin observes that, in his preface to *Plutus, the God of Riches*, Fielding contrasts "the comic genius of an Aristophanes or a Wycherley to the dullness of the modern stage." Perhaps most importantly, in the *Covent Garden Journal* 15, 22 Feb. 1752, 110–11, he places Jonson among the subjects of "the kingdom of Wit" who had been forced to pander to Grub Street and "plainly writ some of his Plays, with no other View than that of offering a Tribute to the Republic." Pope hesitated to give Bounce the epitaph O RARE BOUNCE! for fear of having it read as "a ridicule upon Ben Jonson" (Mrs. Rackett in Spence, *Anecdotes* 1.118).
14 See Allentuck, "In Defense of an Unfinished *Tristram Shandy*," 145–55.
15 *Sterne's Fiction and the Double Principle*, 2.
16 A splendid modern instance of this kind of deliberate frustration is Nabokov, *passim*. Every novel creates this effect, but it is central to *The Real Life of Sebastian Knight*. Mr Goodman, a Boswell in search of Sebastian's "real life" (never, of course, to be found) is perpetually teased by Sebastian's brother, who feeds him the plots of novels Sebastian never published. The first one is obvious. A student returns from his university to find that his father has been poisoned and his mother married to an uncle. The uncle is an ear specialist, an updated Claudius. Nobody would miss this. Then the next. Not for the English reader. The narratorial voice intervenes, in Scriblerian tones: "harder one, this time reader, short story by Chekhov" (65). Being able to produce learned glosses is

hardly contemptible. But we are not supposed to rest in this, but to accept the uncertainty, the delight of not being able to pluck out the heart of anyone's mystery.
17 "Never on Sunday: John Gay's *The Shepherd's Week*," 196.
18 See Pope, *Corr.*, 1.269 (to Martha Blount, 24 Nov. 1714): "it was but tother day I heard of Mrs Fermor's being Actually, directly, and consummatively married."
19 Quoted in Steig, "Defining the Grotesque," 26.
20 See Harries, "Sterne's Novels."
21 See "The Significance of Gay's Drama."
22 See Wolf, *The Reform of the Fallen World*.
23 *The Early Career of Alexander Pope*, 81–3.
24 I am indebted for this observation to Diana Patterson.
25 *The Daring Muse*, 59–62.
26 Collation of the indexes to the two versions of the poem show that Pope was as painstaking about revising here as he was elsewhere. Poor Tibbald, cast out by proclamation, is also reduced in the second entry. The first gave an elaborate account of why he was made hero, his relations to Pope, and his shady associations. The main entry in the second version shrinks to "TIBBALD, not the Hero of this poem, i. *init.* Publish'd an edition of Shakespear, i.133. Author, secretly, and abettor of Scurrilities against Mr. P." (5.425) Shakespeare is edited down from a very long entry in the first version to "Shakespeare, to be spell'd always with an *e* at the end … but not with an *e* in the middle [this *e* is in the middle] … An Edition of him in Marble … mangled, altered and cut by the prayers and Critics … very sore still of Tibbald" (425).

Many of the changes in the second version have to do with the conversion of the progression of Books and the Man to the new account of the Mighty Mother and her Son. The index reflects the change. Forty-six lines on Dulness become sixty-eight. Each section gives a plot, and the second, of course, is vastly expanded. *Nous* is added and highlighted, in a long note pointed up by the index. The addition (and the index) makes of Dulness a much more serious business than the boredom of hacks and their friends.

The last entry in the second index is crucial. It is "Wizard, his Cup, and the strange Effects of it, iv.516 *&c.*" (426). Since Book 4 does not close until line 656, we are still far from the end. But we are being told that these last lines, marked in the index, are the climax. The very long note signed by Scriblerus to which we are sent reinforces this: "Here beginneth the celebration of the *greater Mysteries* of the Goddess, which the Poet in his Invocation ... promised to sing" (393n). The Twickenham editor's suggestion that the Wizard is Walpole is politically right, but the theological context Pope adumbrates in his account of the mysteries provides a much grander gesture, and a seriousness larger than the topicality of the prime minister.

27 "Fielding's *The Masquerade.*"
28 *The Metamorphoses: Ovid's Roman Games*, 225.
29 See Ahl, *Metaformations*; Otis, *Ovid as an Epic Poet*; Galinsky, *Ovid's Metamorphoses.*
30 "The Wolf in the Fold," 417–18.
31 To list every allusion in the poems, plays, prose works, and correspondence would be an exercise in overdocumentation. The indexes to the works of the Club will supply an immediate confirmation. For the most complete study, see Shearer, *The Ovidian Scriblerus.*
32 See Quintana's important essay "*The Rape of the Lock* as a Comedy of Continuity." The paper is brief, but it offers interesting speculations about Scriblerian preferences in rhetorical modes.
33 See Wagner, "Hogarth's Graphic Palimpsests," and Elkins, "On the Impossibility of Stories."
34 See also her note for charivari, 273 n 2. In n 4 Doody declines to use Bakhtinian carnival for the Augustan phenomenon she describes as charivari, but the effect seems the same.
35 See Thompson, *The Translations of Lucian by Erasmus and St. Thomas More*, 44.
36 Robinson. *Lucian and His Influence in Europe*, 2.
37 *Recreation, Reflection and Re-creation*, 72
38 See also Screech's studies of Rabelais, *Rabelais* and *The Rabelaisian Marriage*, and, for another context, his *Montaigne and Melancholy.*
39 Telle, *Erasme de Rotterdam et le Septième Sacrement*, 119.
40 See above, chap. 3, n 31, for the parallels drawn between the *Memoirs* and *Tristram Shandy.*
41 See Colie, *Paradoxia Epidemica*, espec. her discussions of Rabelais (43–71) and Burton (430–60).
42 See Ong, *Ramus, Method and the Decay of Dialogue*, *The Barbarian Within*, *Interfaces of the Word*, and, as a particular Scriblerian gloss, notably on Scriblerian concern with book and text, "Swift on the Mind," in *Rhetoric, Romance and Technology*, 190–212.
43 *Language and Style* 5 (1972): 123–4.
44 "Farewell to Jokes," 791.

Bibliography

ABBREVIATIONS

- AN&Q American Notes and Queries
- ECS Eighteenth-Century Studies
- ELH English Literary History
- ES English Studies
- HLQ Huntington Library Quarterly
- JEGP Journal of English and Germanic Philology
- JHI Journal of the History of Ideas
- JWCI Journal of the Warburg and Courtauld Institutes
- MLN Modern Language Notes
- MLQ Modern Language Quarterly
- MLR Modern Language Review
- MP Modern Philology
- N&Q Notes and Queries
- PLL Papers in Language and Literature
- PQ Philological Quarterly
- PMLA Publications of the Modern Language Association
- RES Review of English Studies
- SECC Studies in Eighteenth-Century Culture
- SEL Studies in English Literature
- SP Studies in Philology
- UTQ University of Toronto Quarterly
- YES Yearbook of English Studies

Bibliography

PRIMARY WORKS

Anonymous. *The Scribleriad.* Intro. A.J. Sambrook. Los Angeles: Augustan Reprint Society 1967.

Anonymous. *Swiftiana. Travels into Several Remote Nations of the World.* New York 1974.

Apuleius, Lucius. *The Golden Asse: Adlington's Translation 1556.* T. Petronius Arbiter. *The Satyricon: Burnaby's Translation,* 1694. Longus, *Daphnis and Chloe: Thornley's Translation, 1657.* Complete in 1 vol. London: Simpkin Marshall 1933.

Arbuthnot, John. *An Essay on the Usefulness of Mathematical Learning.* Oxford 1701.

– *An Argument for Divine Providence.* In *Philosophical Transactions* 27, no. 325. London 1701.

– *Tables of Ancient Coins, Weights and Measures, explain'd and Exemplify'd in Several Dissertations.* London 1705, 1727.

– *A Sermom [sic] Preach'd to the People, at the Mercat-Cross of Edinburgh; on the Subject of the Union.* London 1707.

– *A Brief Account of Mr. John Ginglicutt's Treatise concerning the Altercation of Scolding of the Ancients.* London 1731.

– *An Essay concerning the Nature of Aliments.* London 1731.

– *An Essay concerning the Effects of Air on Human Bodies.* London 1733.

– "An Account of the Sickness and Death of Dr. W—d W—d." In *Miscellaneous Works.* London 1770.

– "An Examination of Dr. Woodward's Account of the Deluge, &c." In *Miscellaneous Works* 2. London 1770.

– "Of the Hazards of Game." Huygens, *De Ratiociniis in Ludo Aleae.* In *Miscellaneous Works* 2. London 1770.

– "The Life and Adventures of Don Bilioso de L'Estomac." In *Miscellaneous Works* 2. London 1770.

– *The History of John Bull.* Ed. A.W. Bower and R.E. Erickson. Oxford: Clarendon Press 1976.

Arbuthnotiana. Intro. Patricia Köster. Los Angeles: Augustan Reprint Society 1972.

[Aston, Anthony.] *The Authors of the Town: A Satire: Inscribed to the Author of The Universal Passion.* London 1725.

– *The Fool's Opera; or the Taste of the Age Written by Mat. Medley, And Performed by His Company in Oxford.* London 1731.

Bolingbroke, Henry St John, Viscount. *Historical Writings.* Ed. Isaac Kramnick. Chicago: University of Chicago Press 1972.

Bibliography

– *The Works of Lord Bolingbroke*. 4 vols. Philadelphia: Carey and Hart 1841.

Bunbury, Henry William. *City Fowlers*. London 1806.

Burke, Edmund. *Reflections on the French Revolution*. Ed. Conor Cruise O'Brien. Harmondsworth: Penguin 1970.

Burney, Frances. *Camilla*. Ed. Edward A. Bloom and Lillian D. Bloom. Oxford: Oxford University Press 1983.

– *Cecilia*. Ed. Peter Sabor and Margaret Anne Doody. Oxford: Oxford University Press 1988.

Burton, Robert. *The Anatomy of Melancholy*. Ed. Floyd Dell and Paul Jordan Smith. London: Routledge & Kegan Paul 1931.

Cervantes Saavedra, Miguel de. *The Adventures of Don Quixote*. Trans. J.M. Cohen. Harmondsworth: Penguin 1950.

Chaucer, Geoffrey. *The Works of Geoffrey Chaucer*. Ed. F.N. Robinson. Boston: Houghton Mifflin 1957.

Cibber, Colley. *The Refusal: or, The Ladies Philosophy*. 4th ed. London 1777.

D'Anvers, Caleb. *A Selection of Poems on Several Occasions, Publish'd in The Craftsman*. London 1731.

Donne, John. *The Complete English Poems of John Donne*. Ed. C.A. Patrides. London: J.M. Dent 1985.

The Dramatic Poetaster: A Vision. London 1732.

Dryden, John. *Works*. Ed. Walter Scott and the Rev. George Saintsbury. 18 vols. Edinburgh 1882–93.

– *The Poems of John Dryden*. Ed. James Kinsley. 4 vols. Oxford: Clarendon Press 1958.

Epistolae Obscurorum Virorum. London 1710.

– *The Latin Text with an English Rendering, Notes and an Historical Introduction*. Ed. Francis Griffin Stokes. London: Chatto & Windus 1909.

Erasmus, Desiderius. *The Education of a Christian Prince*. Ed. L.K. Born. New York: Columbia University Press 1936.

– *The Praise of Folly, Translated by John Wilson, 1668*. Ann Arbor: University of Michigan Press 1958.

– *Twenty Select Colloquies of Erasmus, Translated out of the Latin by Sir Roger L'Estrange, 1680*. London: Chapman & Dodd 1923.

Essay on the New Species of Writing Founded by Mr. Fielding. 1751. Los Angeles: Augustan Reprint Society 1962.

Fielding, Henry. *The Grub-Street opera ... By Scriblerus Secundus. To which is added, The Masquerade, a poem. Pr. in 1728*. With a separate title page, reading "The Masquerade, a poem, By Lemuel Gulliver." London 1731.

– *The Welsh opera: or, The grey mare the better horse ... Written by Scriblerus secundus*. London 1731.

- *The Author's Farce*. Ed. Charles B. Woods. Lincoln: University of Nebraska Press 1966.
- *The Historical Register for the Year 1736* and *Eurydice Hissed*. Ed. William Appleton. Lincoln: University of Nebraska Press 1967.
- *Joseph Andrews*. Ed. Martin C. Battestin. Oxford: Clarendon Press 1967.
- *The Grub-Street Opera*. Ed. Edgar V. Roberts. Lincoln: University of Nebraska Press 1968.
- *The Criticism of Henry Fielding*. Ed. Ioan Williams. London: Routledge & Kegan Paul 1970.
- *Tom Thumb* and *The Tragedy of Tragedies*. Ed. L.J. Morrissey. Edinburgh: Oliver & Boyd 1970.
- *Miscellanies by Henry Fielding, Esq.* 1. Ed. Henry Knight Miller. Oxford: Clarendon Press 1972.
- *Jonathan Wild* and *The Journey of a Voyage to Lisbon*. Intro. A.R. Humphreys, notes by Douglas Brooks. Rev. ed. London: Dent 1973.
- *A Journey from this World to the Next*. Intro. Claude J. Rawson. London: Dent 1973.
- *The History of Tom Jones, A Foundling*. Ed. Fredson Bowers, with intro. and commentary by Martin C. Battestin. The Wesleyan Edition. 2 vols. Oxford: Clarendon Press 1974.
- *The Covent-Garden Journal and A Plan of the Universal Register Office*. Ed. Bertrand A. Goldgar. Oxford: Clarendon Press 1988.

Garth, Samuel. *Works*. Dublin 1769.

Gay, John. *The Wife of Bath*. London 1713.
- *Trivia: Or, the Art of Walking the Streets of London*. London 1716.
- *Three Hours after Marriage. A Comedy*. London 1717.
- *An Epistle To the most Learned Doctor W—d—d; From a Prude That was unfortunately Metamorphos'd on Saturday December 29, 1722*. London 1723.
- *The Beggar's Opera*. London 1728.
- *Acis and Galatea, A Serenata*. London 1732.
- *The Songs and Symphonys in the Masque of Acis and Galatea made and perform'd for his Grace the Duke of Chandos. Compos'd by Mr. Handel with the Additional Songs*. London 1733–36?
- *Plays*. London 1760.
- *Fables*. Edinburgh 1792; London 1793.
- *The Letters*. Ed. C.F. Burgess. Oxford: Oxford University Press 1966.
- *John Gay, Poetry and Prose*. Ed. Vinton A. Dearing, with Charles E. Beckwith. 2 vols. Oxford: Clarendon Press 1974.
- *Dramatic Works*. 2 vols. Ed. John Fuller. Oxford: Oxford University Press 1983.

Goldsmith, Oliver. *Collected Works of Oliver Goldsmith*. Ed. Arthur Friedman. 5 vols. Oxford: Clarendon Press 1956–66.

Gravelot, H.F. *Fables by the late Mr. Gay*. London 1717.

[Griffin, ?]. *A Complete Key to the last new* FARCE, THE WHAT D'YE CALL IT. London 1715.

– *Gulliver Decypher'd: Or Remarks on a late Book, intitled, Travels into Several Remote Nations of the World, by Captain Lemuel Gulliver*. 2nd ed. London 1727.

Hogarth, William. *Graphic Works*. Ed. Ronald Paulson. Rev. and enl. ed. 2 vols. New Haven: Yale University Press 1970.

Horace. *Odes and Epodes*. With a trans. by C.E. Bennett. Cambridge: Heinemann 1960.

– *Satires, Epistles and Ars Poetica*. With a trans. by H. Rushton Fairclough. Cambridge: Heinemann 1961.

Hume, David. *Enquiries: Concerning Human Understanding and Concerning the Principles of Morals*. Ed. L.A. Selby-Bigge. 3rd ed., rev. P.H. Nidditch. Oxford: Clarendon Press 1975.

– *A Treatise of Human Nature*. Ed. L.A. Selby-Bigge. 2nd ed. rev. P.H. Nidditch. Oxford: Clarendon Press 1980.

[Huygens, Christiaan]. *Of the Laws of Change, or, a Method of Calculation of the Hazards of the Game*. 4th ed. rev. John Ham. London 1738.

Jefferson, Thomas. *The Complete Jefferson*. Ed. Saul K. Padover. 1943. Rpt Freeport, NY: Books for Libraries Press 1969.

– *The Family Letters of Thomas Jefferson*. Ed. Edwin Morris Betts and James Adam Bear, Jr. Columbia: University of Missouri Press 1966.

Johnson, Samuel. *Lives of the English Poets*. Ed. George Birkbeck Hill. 3 vols. Oxford 1905. Rpt New York 1967.

Jonson, Ben. *Works*. Ed. C.H. Herford and P. Simpson. 11 vols. Oxford: Clarendon Press 1925–52.

– *Literary Criticism*. Ed. J.D. Redwine, Jr. Lincoln: University of Nebraska Press 1970.

Locke, John. *An Essay Concerning Human Understanding*. Ed. P.H. Nidditch. Oxford: Clarendon Press 1975.

Lucian. *Works*. Trans. A.M. Harmon *et al*. 8 vols. London: Heinemann, and Cambridge, Mass.: Harvard University Press 1913–67.

– *The Metamorphosis of the Town. Or a View of the Present Fashions. A Tale After the Manner of Fontaine*. London 1730.

Marvell, Andrew. *The Poems and Letters of Andrew Marvell*. 2 vols, Ed. H.M. Margoliouth. Oxford: Clarendon Press 1927.

The Memoirs of the Extraordinary Life, Works, and Discoveries of Martinus Scriblerus. Ed. Charles Kerby-Miller. New Haven, Conn.: Yale University Press 1950, 1966.

Milton, John. *The Poems of John Milton*. Ed. John Carey and Alastair Fowler. 2nd ed. London: Longmans 1968.

Montaigne, Michel de. *Oeuvres complètes*. Ed. Albert Thibaudet and Maurice Rat. Paris 1962.

More, St Thomas. *Utopia*. Ed. Edward Surtz, S.J., and J.H. Hexter. New Haven: Yale University Press 1964.

Nabokov, Vladimir. *The Real Life of Sebastian Knight*. Norfolk, Conn.: New Directions 1959.

– *Pale Fire*. New York: Putnam 1962.

– *Eugene Onegin: A Novel in Verse*. Trans. with a commentary. New York: Bollingen 1964.

– *Speak Memory: An Autobiography Revisited*. New York: Putnam 1966.

– *Lectures on Literature*. New York: Harcourt Brace Jovanovich 1980.

– *Lectures on Don Quixote*. Ed. Fredson Bowers. New York: Harcourt Brace Jovanovich 1983.

Ovid. *Metamorphoses*. With a trans. by F.J. Miller. 2 vols. Cambridge: Heinemann 1964.

Parker, E. *A Complete Key To the New Farce, call'd Three Hours after Marriage*. London 1717.

Parnell, Thomas. *Collected Poems of Thomas Parnell*. Ed. Claude J. Rawson and F.P. Lock. Newark: University of Delaware Press 1989.

– *An Essay on the Different Stiles of Poetry*. London 1713.

– *The Hermit. A Poem*. np, nd.

– *Homer's Battle of the Frogs and Mice*. London 1717.

– *Poems on Several Occasions*. London 1722.

– *Posthumous Works*. Dublin 1758.

– *The Poetical Works*. Glasgow 1786.

Petronius. *Satyricon*. With a trans. by Michael Heseltine. Cambridge: Heinemann 1961.

Pope, Alexander. *The Correspondence of Alexander Pope*. Ed. George Sherburn. 5 vols. Oxford: Clarendon Press 1956.

– *The Prose Works of Alexander Pope*. 1. *The Earlier Works, 1711–1720*. Ed. Norman Ault. Oxford: Blackwell 1936. 2. *The Major Works, 1725–1744*. Ed. Rosemary Cowler. Hamden, Conn.: Archon 1986.

– *The Twickenham Edition of the Poems of Alexander Pope*. Ed. John Butt *et al*. 11 vols. in 12. London: Methuen, and New Haven: Yale University Press 1939–69.

Rabelais, Francis. *The Works of Francis Rabelais*. Trans. John Ozell. 4 vols. Dublin 1738.

Rapin, René. *Discourse of Pastorals*. In Thomas Creech's *The Idylliums of Theocritus*. Oxford 1684.

Richardson, Samuel. *Sir Charles Grandison*. Ed. Jocelyn Harris. 3 vols. Oxford: Oxford University Press 1972.

Scriblerus Maximus. *The Art of Scribling*. London 1733.
Seneca. *Apokolocyntosis*. With a trans. by W.H.D. Rouse. Cambridge: Heinemann 1961.
– *Letters from a Stoic*. Sel. and trans. Robin Campbell. Harmondsworth: Penguin 1969.
Shakespeare, William. *Works*. Ed. Alexander Pope. 6 vols. 1723.
Smart, Christopher. *Poetical Works of Christopher Smart*. 1. Ed. Karina Williamson. Oxford: Clarendon Press 1980.
Smollett, Tobias. *The Expedition of Humphry Clinker*. Intro. and notes by Thomas R. Preston, text by O.M. Brack, Jr. Athens: University of Georgia Press 1990.
Spectator. Ed. Donald F. Bond. 5 vols. Oxford: Clarendon Press 1965.
Spence, Joseph. *Observations, Anecdotes and Characters of Books and Men*. Ed. James M. Osborn. 2 vols. Oxford: Clarendon Press 1966.
Sterne, Laurence. *The Life and Opinions of Tristram Shandy, Gentleman*. Ed. Melvyn New and Joan New. 3 vols. Gainesville: University Presses of Florida 1978–84.
Swift, Jonathan. *The Correspondence of Jonathan Swift*. Ed. Harold Williams. 5 vols. Oxford: Clarendon Press 1963–65.
– *A Discourse of the Contests and Dissentions Between the Nobles and Commons in Athens and Rome*. Ed. Frank H. Ellis. Oxford: Clarendon Press 1967.
– *A Journal to Stella*. Ed. Harold Williams. 2 vols. Oxford: Clarendon Press 1948.
– *The Poems*. Ed. Harold Williams. 3 vols. Oxford: Clarendon Press 1958.
– *Prose Writings*. Ed. Herbert Davis. 14 vols. Oxford: Blackwell, 1939–68.
– *A Tale of a Tub, to which is added The Battle of the Books and The Mechanical Operation of the Spirit*. Ed. A.C. Guthkelch and D. Nichol Smith. 2nd ed. Oxford: Clarendon Press 1958.
Virgil. *Eclogues, Georgics, Aeneid*. With a trans. by H. Rushton Fairclough. 2 vols. Cambridge: Heinemann 1960.
Welsted, Leonard. *Palaemon To Caelia, at Bath; Or, The Triumvirate*. London 1717.
– *An Epistle to the Late Dr. Garth*. London 1722.
Whistoneutes: Or, Remarks on Mr. Whiston's Historical Memoirs of the Life of Dr Samuel Clarke, &c. By a Person of Retirement and Obscurity; But of the Antique Family of the Scriblerians. London 1731. Signed by Simon Scriblerus.
Wilmot, John, Earl of Rochester. *The Complete Poems of John Wilmot, Earl of Rochester*. Ed. David M. Vieth. New Haven and London: Yale University Press 1968.
Wordsworth, William. *The Prelude*. Ed. Ernest de Selincourt. 2nd ed. rev. Helen Darbishire. Oxford: Clarendon Press 1959.

SECONDARY SOURCES

Aden, John M. "The 1720 Version of *Rural Sports* and the Georgic Tradition." *MLQ* 20 (1959): 228–32.
— "Corinna and the Sterner Muse of Swift." *English Language Notes* 4 (1966): 23–31.
— *Pope's Once and Future Kings: Satire and Politics in the Early Career.* Knoxville: University of Tennessee Press 1978.
Ahl, Frederick. *Metaformations: Soundplay and Wordplay in Ovid and Other Classical Poets.* Ithaca, NY: Cornell University Press 1985.
Aitken, George A. *The Life and Works of John Arbuthnot.* Oxford 1892. Rpt New York: Russell and Russell 1968.
Allentuck, Marcia. "In Defense of an Unfinished *Tristram Shandy:* Laurence Sterne and the *Non-Finito.*" In *The Winged Skull: Papers from the Laurence Sterne Bicentenary Conference,* ed. Arthur Cash and John Stedmond. London: Methuen 1971. 145–55.
Alpers, Paul. "Empson on Pastoral." *New Literary History* 10 (1978–79): 101–23.
— "What Is Pastoral?" *Critical Inquiry* 8 (1982): 437–60.
Alter, Robert. *Fielding and the Nature of the Novel.* Cambridge, Mass.: Harvard University Press 1968.
— "Fielding and the Uses of Style." In *Twentieth Century Interpretations of Tom Jones,* ed. Martin C. Battestin. Englewood Cliffs, NJ: Prentice-Hall 1968. 97–109.
— *Partial Magic: The Novel as a Self-Conscious Genre.* Berkeley: University of California Press 1978.
Ames, Dianne S. "Gay's *Trivia* and the Art of Allusion." *SP* 75 (1978): 199–222.
Amory, Hugh. "The Evidence of Things Not Seen: Concealed Proofs of Fielding's Juvenal." *Papers of the Bibliographical Society of America* 80 (1986): 15–53.
Anderson, Graham. *Studies in Lucian's Comic Fiction.* Leiden: E.J. Brill 1976.
Antal, Frederick. *Hogarth and His Place in European Art.* London: Routledge & Kegan Paul 1962.
Ariès, Philippe. *Centuries of Childhood.* New York: Knopf 1962.
Armens, Sven. *John Gay: Social Critic.* Rpt New York: Octagon Books 1966.
Aston, Margaret. "English Ruins and English History: The Dissolution and the Sense of the Past." *JWCI* 36 (1973): 231–55.
Auerbach, Erich. "The World in Pantagruel's Mouth." In *Mimesis.* Trans. Willard Trask. Princeton: Princeton University Press 1957. 229–49.
Axton, Marie, and Raymond Williams. *English Drama: Forms and Development: Essays in Honour of Muriel Clara Bradbrook.* Cambridge: Cambridge University Press 1977.

Bachrach, A.G.H. "Henry Fielding's Comic Romances." *Papers of the Michigan Academy of Science, Arts and Letters* 45 (1960): 411–19.

- "Holland and Britain in the Age of Observation." In *The Orange and the Rose: Holland and Britain in the Age of Observation*. Catalogue of an Exhibition, Victoria and Albert Museum, 22 Oct. to 13 Dec. 1964: 10–18.

Baker, Sheridan. "Fielding's Comic Epic-in-Prose Romances Again." *PQ* 58 (1979): 63–81.

Bakhtin, Mikhail. "The Role of Games in Rabelais." *Yale French Studies* 41 (1968): 124–32.

- *Rabelais and His World*. 1965. Trans. Hélène Iswolsky. Bloomington: Indiana University Press 1984.

Baltrusaihs, Jurgis. "Gardens and Lands of Illusion: An Essay on the Legend of Forms." *Lotus International* 31 (1981): 51–69.

Barasch, Frances K. *The Grotesque: A Study in Meanings*. The Hague: Mouton 1971.

Baridon, Michel. "Ruins as Mental Construct." *Journal of Garden History* 5 (1985): 84–96.

Barish, Jonas A. *Ben Jonson and the Language of Prose Comedy*. Cambridge, Mass.: Harvard University Press 1960.

- *The Anti-Theatrical Prejudice*. Berkeley: University of California Press 1980.

Barnett, G.L. "Gay, Swift, and 'Tristram Shandy.'" *N&Q* 185 (1943): 346–47.

Barthelsen, Lance. *The Nonsense Club: Literature and Popular Culture, 1749–1764*. Oxford: Oxford University Press 1986.

Battestin, Martin. *The Moral Basis of Fielding's Art: A Study of Joseph Andrews*. Middletown, Conn.: Wesleyan University Press 1959.

- "Menalcas' Song: The Meaning of Art and Artifice in Gay's Poetry." *JEGP* 65 (1966): 662–79.

- "Tom Jones and 'His *Egyptian* Majesty': Fielding's Parable of Government." *PMLA* 82 (1967): 68–77.

- "Fielding's Definition of Wisdom: Some Functions of Ambiguity and Emblem in *Tom Jones*." *ELH* 35 (1968): 188–217.

- *The Providence of Wit: Aspects of Form in Augustan Literature and the Arts*. Oxford: Clarendon Press 1974.

Beam, Marjorie. "'The Reach and Wit of the Inventor': Swift's *Tale of a Tub* and *Hamlet*." *UTQ* 46 (1976): 1–13.

Beattie, Lester M. *John Arbuthnot: Mathematician and Satirist*. Cambridge, Mass.: Harvard University Press 1935. Rpt New York 1967.

Beaujour, Michel. *Le Jeu de Rabelais*. Paris: L'Herne 1969.

- Introduction to "In Memory of Jacques Ehrmann: Inside Play Outside Game." *Yale French Studies* 58 (1979): 5–14.

Behrendt, Stephen C. "Art as Deceptive Intruder: Audience Entrapment in Eighteenth-Century Verbal and Visual Art." *PLL* 19 (1983): 37–52.

Bender, John. *Imagining the Penitentiary: Fiction and the Architecture of Mind in Eighteenth-Century England.* Chicago: University of Chicago Press 1987.

Bentley, J.H. "Erasmus, Jean Le Clerc, and the Principle of the Harder Reading." *Renaissance Quarterly* 31 (1978): 309–21.

Beranger, Jean. Review of Bruneteau (see below) in *ECS* 8 (1974- 75): 369–71.

Berry, Alice Fiola. *Rabelais: Homo Logos.* Chapel Hill: University of North Carolina Press 1979.

Berry, Reginald. "Chaucer Transformed, 1700–1721." PhD, University of Toronto 1978.

Black, Jeremy, ed. *Britain in the Age of Walpole.* New York: St Martin's Press 1984.

Blair, R.L. "The Classical and Mythographic Sources of Pope's Dulness." *HLQ* 43 (1980): 213–46.

Blewett, David. "'Roxana' and the Masquerades." *MLR* 65 (1970): 499–502.

Bogorad, Samuel N. "Milton's 'Paradise Lost' and Gay's 'Trivia': A Borrowing." *N&Q* 195 (1950): 98–9.

Booth, Wayne. "Did Sterne Complete *Tristram Shandy*?" *MP* 48 (1951): 172–83.

– "The Self-Conscious Narrator in Comic Fiction before *Tristram Shandy*." *PMLA* 67 (1952): 163–85.

Boucé, P.-G., ed. *Sexuality in Eighteenth-Century Britain.* Manchester: Manchester University Press 1982.

Bowden, Martha F. "Nature is Nature: The Several Societies of Shandy Hall". PhD, University of Toronto 1980.

– "'Night Overtook Them or Met Them': Darkness in *Joseph Andrews*." Paper presented at the North East American Society for Eighteenth-Century Studies, Allentown, Pa. 1988.

Bowen, Barbara. "Rabelais and the Comedy of the Spoken Word." *MLR* 63 (1968): 575–80.

– *The Art of Bluff: Paradox and Ambiguity in Rabelais and Montaigne.* Urbana: University of Illinois Press 1972.

Brady, Frank. "*Tristram Shandy*: Sexuality, Morality and Sensibility." *ECS* 4 (1970): 41–56.

Braudy, Leo. *Narrative Form in History and Fiction: Hume, Fielding, and Gibbon.* Princeton: Princeton University Press 1970.

Bredvold, Louis. "The Gloom of the Tory Satirists." In *Pope and His Contemporaries: Essays Presented to George Sherburn*, ed. James L. Clifford and Louis A. Landa. Oxford: Clarendon Press 1949. 1–19.

Briggs, Peter. "Locke's *Essay* and the Tentativeness of *Tristram Shandy*." SP 82 (1985): 493–520.

Brissenden, R.F. "'Trusting to Almighty God': Another Look at the Composition of *Tristram Shandy*." In *The Winged Skull: Papers from the Laurence Sterne Bicentenary Conference*, ed. Arthur Cash and John M. Stedmond. London: Methuen 1971. 258–69.

Bronson, B.H. "The Beggar's Opera." *University of California Publications in English* 8 (1941): 197–231.

– "The True Proportions of Gay's *Acis and Galatea*." PMLA 80 (1965): 325–31.

Brooks-Davies, Douglas. *The Mercurian Monarch: Magical Politics from Spenser to Pope*. Manchester: Manchester University Press 1983.

Brown, Huntington. "Ben Jonson and Rabelais." MLN 44 (1929): 6–13.

– *Rabelais in English Literature*. New York: Octagon Books 1967.

Brown, Laura and Felicity Nussbaum, eds. *The New 18th Century: Theory, Politics, English Literature*. New York: Methuen 1987.

Brownell, Morris R. *Alexander Pope and the Arts of Georgian England*. Oxford: Clarendon Press 1978.

Browning, J.D., ed. *Satire in the 18th Century*. New York: Garland 1983.

Brückmann, Patricia C. "Gulliver: *Cum Grano Salis*." *Satire Newsletter* 1 (1963): 5–11.

– "'Religious Hope and Resignation': The Process of 'Eloisa to Abelard.'" ECS 3 (1977): 153–63.

– "*In familiari colloquio*: An Intervention in *Utopia*." In *Familiar Colloquy: Essays Presented to Arthur Edward Barker*, ed. Patricia Brückmann. Ottawa: Oberon Press 1978. 1–10.

– "Am'rous Causes." UTQ 51 (1982): 298–303.

– "Mr. Shandy's Hip." *American Notes and Queries* 23 (1985): 138–9.

– "An Early Hint of Miss Bridget's Affairs, with a Parallel Note on Mr. Allworthy." In *Man and Nature*, ed. Kenneth W. Graham and Neal Johnson. Edmonton, Alta.: Academic Printing and Publishing 1987. 73–9.

– "'The Care of Heav'n': Biblical Echo in *An Essay on Man*." YES, 18 (1988): 171–80.

– "Matter and Manner of Correspondences: Scriblerus His Life and His Style." *Eighteenth-Century Life* 12 (1988): 86–100.

– "'Virgins Visited by Angel Pow'rs: *The Rape of the Lock*, Platonicks, Mysticks and Sylphs." In *The Enduring Legacy*, ed. Pat Rogers and G.S. Rousseau. Cambridge: Cambridge University Press 1988. 1–20.

Bruneteau, Claude. *John Arbuthnot (1667–1735) et les idées au début du dix-huitième siècle*. 2 vols. Lille 1974.

- "John Arbuthnot: The History of John Bull (1712): Bibliographie sélective et commentée." *Bulletin de la Société d'Études Anglo-Américaines des XVIIe et XVIIIe siècles* 15 (1982): 35–42.
- and Georges Lamoine. "Le Langage de Chicane dans John Bull." *Bulletin de la Société d'Études Anglo-Américaines des XVIIe et XVIIIe siècles* 15 (1982): 87–100.

Bruns, Gerald L. "Allegory and Satire: A Rhetorical Meditation." *New Literary History* 11 (1979): 121–32.

Bruss, Elizabeth. "The Game of Literature and Some Literary Games." *New Literary History* 9 (1977): 153–72.

Burgess, C.F. "Scriblerian Influence in 'The Shepherd's Week.'" *N&Q* 208 (1963): 218.
- "The Ambivalent Point of View in John Gay's Trivia." *Cithara* 4 (1964): 53–65.

Burgess, Theodore. "Epideictic Literature." *University of Chicago Studies in Classical Philology* 3 (1902): 89–248.

Burke, Joseph. "Hogarth, Handel and Roubiliac: A Note on the Interrelationships of the Arts in England, c. 1730–1760." *ECS* 3 (1969): 157–74.

Burton, A.P. "Cervantes the Man Seen through English Eyes in the Seventeenth and Eighteenth Centuries." *Bulletin of Hispanic Studies* 45 (1968): 1–15.

Calderwood, James L. "Structural Parody in Swift's 'Fragment.'" *MLQ* 23 (1962): 243–53.

Cameron, Kenneth M. "Duffett's New Poems and Vacation Plays." *Theatre Survey* 5 (1964): 64–70.

Canfield, J. Douglas. "The Jewel of Great Price: Mutability and Constancy in Dryden's *All for Love*." *ELH* 42 (1975): 38–61.
- "The Significance of the Restoration Rhymed Heroic Play." *ECS* 13 (1979): 49–62.
- "Royalism's Last Dramatic Stand: English Political Tragedy, 1679–89." *SP* 82 (1985): 234–63.

Carnochan, W.B. *Confinement and Flight: An Essay on English Literature of the Eighteenth Century*. Berkeley: University of California Press 1977.
- *Gibbon's Solitude: The Inward World of the Historian*. Stanford: Stanford University Press 1987.

Carretta, Vincent. "John Gay in a Riddle Print." *The Scriblerian* 14 (1982): 73–7.
- *The Snarling Muse: Verbal and Visual Political Satire from Pope to Churchill*. Philadelphia: University of Pennsylvania Press 1983.

Cash, Arthur H., and John M. Stedmond, eds. *The Winged Skull: Papers from the Laurence Sterne Bicentenary Conference*. London: Methuen 1971.

Castle, Terry. "Why the Houyhnhnms Don't Write: Swift, Satire and the Fear of the Text." *Essays in Literature* 7 (1980): 31–44.
– *Masquerade and Civilization: The Carnivalesque in Eighteenth-Century English Culture and Fiction.* Stanford: Stanford University Press 1986.
Chalker, John. *Violence in Augustan Literature.* London: Westfield College 1975.
Champion, Larry S. "Gulliver's Voyages: The Framing Events as a Guide to Interpretation." *Texas Studies in Literature and Language* 10 (1969): 529–36.
Clark, H.F. "Eighteenth-Century Elysiums: The Role of 'Association' in the Landscape Movement." *JWCI* 6 (1943): 165–89.
Clark, John R. *Form and Frenzy in Swift's "Tale of a Tub".* Ithaca, NY: Cornell University Press 1970.
Clayborough, Arthur. *The Grotesque in English Literature.* Oxford: Clarendon Press 1965.
Close, Anthony. *The Romantic Approach to "Don Quixote": A Critical History of the Romantic Tradition of "Quixote" Criticism.* Cambridge: Cambridge University Press 1978.
Cody, Richard. *The Landscape of the Mind: Pastoralism and Platonic Theory in Tasso's "Aminta" and Shakespeare's Early Comedies.* Oxford: Clarendon Press 1969.
Colie, Rosalie L. *Paradoxia Epidemica.* Princeton: Princeton University Press 1966.
Congleton, James E. *Theories of Pastoral Poetry in England, 1684–1798.* Rpt New York: Haskell House 1968.
Conolly, L.W. "Anna Margaretta Larpent, The Duchess of Queensberry and Gay's *Polly* in 1777." *PQ* 51 (1972): 955–7.
Craig, H. "Dryden's Lucian." *Classical Philology* 16 (1921): 141–63.
Crane, R.S. "The Houyhnhnms, the Yahoos, and the History of Ideas." In *Reason and Imagination*, ed. J.A. Mazzeo. New York: Columbia University Press 1962. 231–53.
Cruickshanks, Eveline. *Political Untouchables: The Tories and the '45.* New York: Holmes & Meier 1979.
Damrosch, Leopold Jr. *The Imaginative World of Alexander Pope.* Berkeley: University of California Press 1987.
Defaux, Gérard. "Rhétorique humaniste et sceptique chrétienne dans la première moitié du XVIe siècle: Empédocle, Panurge, et la 'vana gloria.'" *Revue d'histoire littéraire de la France* 82 (1982): 3–22.
Demetz, Peter, Thomas Green, and Lowry Nelson, Jr., eds. *The Disciplines of Criticism: Essays in Literary Theory, Interpretation and History.* New Haven: Yale University Press 1968.

DePorte, Michael V. *Nightmares and Hobby-horses*. San Marino, Calif.: Huntington Library 1974.
- "Swift and the License of Satire." In *Satire in the 18th Century*, ed. J.D. Browning. New York: Garland 1983. 57–62.
- "From the Womb of Things to Their Grave: Madness and Memory in Swift." *UTQ* 58 (1989): 376–90.
- "Swift's Horses of Instruction." Paper read to the Second Münster Symposium on Jonathan Swift, 1989.
- "The Road to St. Patrick's: Swift and the Problem of Belief." *Swift Studies* 8 (1993): 5–17.

Derrida, Jacques. "Scribble (writing power)." 1978. Trans. Cary Plotkin, *Yale French Studies* 58 (1979): 117–49.

Devereux, E.J. *A Checklist of English Translations of Erasmus to 1700*. Oxford: Oxford Bibliographical Society 1968.
- *Renaissance English Translations of Erasmus: A Bibliography to 1700*. Toronto: University of Toronto Press 1983.

Dickinson, H.T. *Bolingbroke*. London: Constable 1970.

Donaldson, Ian. "The Clockwork Novel: Three Notes on an Eighteenth-Century Analogy." *RES* 21 (1970): 14–22.
- *The World Upside Down: Comedy from Jonson to Fielding*. Oxford: Clarendon Press 1970.
- "Concealing and Revealing: Pope's *Epistle to Dr. Arbuthnot*." *YES* 18 (1988): 181–99.

Doody, Margaret Anne. *The Daring Muse: Augustan Poetry Reconsidered*. Cambridge: Cambridge University Press 1985.
- "Swift among the Women." *YES* 18 (1988): 68–92.

Downie, J.A. *Jonathan Swift, Political Writer*. London: Routledge & Kegan Paul 1984.

Duckworth, Alistair. *Landscapes in the Gardens and Literature of Eighteenth-Century England*. Los Angeles: University of California 1981.
- "'Whig' Landscapes in Defoe's *Tour*." *PQ* 61 (1982): 453–65.

Due, Otto Steen. *Changing Forms: Studies in the Metamorphoses of Ovid*. Copenhagen: Glydendal 1974.

Dugaw, Dianne. "Folklore and John Gay's Satire." *SEL* 31 (1991): 515–33.

Duncan, Jeffrey. "The Rural Ideal in Eighteenth-Century Fiction." *SEL* 8 (1968): 517–35.

Duval, Edwin M. "Pantagruel's Genealogy and the Redemptive Design of Rabelais's *Pantagruel*." *PMLA* 99 (1984): 162–78.

Ehrenpreis, Irvin. *Swift: The Man, His Works and the Age*. 3 vols. Cambridge, Mass.: Harvard University Press 1962–83.
- "The Scriblerian Imagination." *Swift Studies* 6 (1991): 49–57.

Ehrmann, Jacques. *Un Paradis désespéré: l'amour et l'illusion dans "L'Astrée."* Preface Jean Starobinski. New Haven: Yale University Press, and Paris: Presses Universitaires de France 1963.
- "La Temporalité dans l'oeuvre de Rabelais." *French Review* 37 (1963): 188–99.

Eisenberg, Daniel. *"Don Quixote": A study of Narrative Technique.* Chapel Hill: University of North Carolina Press 1975.

Elkins, James. "On the Impossibility of Stories: The Anti-narrative and Non-narrative Impulse in Modern Painting." *Word and Image* 7 (1991): 348–64.

Ellis, William D., Jr. "Thomas D'Urfey, The Pope-Philips Quarrel and *The Shepherd's Week.*" *PMLA* 74 (1959): 203–12.

El Saffar, Ruth. *Novel to Romance: A Study of Cervantes's Novelas Ejemplares.* Baltimore: Johns Hopkins University Press 1974.

Empson, William. *Some Versions of Pastoral.* Norfolk, Conn.: New Directions, 1950.

England, A.B. "World Without Order: Some Thoughts on the Poetry of Swift." *Essays in Criticism* 16 (1966): 32–43.
- "Swift's 'An Elegy on Mr. Patrige' and Cowley's 'On the Death of Mr. Crashaw.'" *N&Q* 218 (1973): 412–13.
- "The Subversion of Logic in Some Poems by Swift." *SEL* 14 (1974): 343–56.

Erickson, R.A. "Situations of Identity in the *Memoirs of Martinus Scriblerus.*" *MLQ* 26 (1965): 388–400.

Erskine-Hill, Howard. *The Dunciad.* London: Edward Arnold 1972.
- *The Social Milieu of Alexander Pope: Lives, Example, and the Poetic Response.* New Haven: Yale University 1975.
- "The Significance of Gay's Drama." In *English Drama: Forms and Development,* ed. Marie Axton and Raymond Williams. Cambridge: Cambridge University Press 1977. 142–63.
- *The Art of Alexander Pope.* London: Vision 1979.
- "Alexander Pope: The Political Poet in His Time." *ECS* 15 (1981–2): 123–48.
- *The Augustan Idea in English Literature.* London: Edward Arnold 1983.

Eskin, Stanley G. "Mythic Unity in Rabelais." *PMLA* 79 (1964): 548–53.

Ettinghausen, Henry. *Francisco de Quevedo and the Neo Stoic Movement.* London: Oxford University Press 1972.

Fabricant, Carole. *Swift's Landscape.* Baltimore: Johns Hopkins University Press 1982.

Faulkner, Thomas C., and Harold Bloom, eds. *Modern Critical Interpretations. John Gay's Beggar's Opera.* New York: Chelsea 1988.

Fehl, Philipp P. "Farewell to Jokes: The Last *Capricci* of Giovanni Domenico Tiepolo and the Tradition of Irony in Venetian Painting." *Critical Inquiry* 5 (1979): 761–91.

Ferriar, John. *Illustrations of Sterne.* 2 vols. 2nd ed. London 1812.

Fischer, John Irwin. "How to Die: 'Verses on the Death of Dr. Swift.'" *RES* 21 (1970): 422–41.
- *On Swift's Poetry*. Gainesville: University Presses of Florida 1978.
- and Donald C. Mell, Jr., eds. *Contemporary Studies of Swift's Poetry*. Newark, Del.: Associated University Presses 1981.
- "Never on Sunday: John Gay's *The Shepherd's Week*." In *SECC*, ed. Harry C. Payne, 10 (1981): 191–203.
- et al., eds. *Swift and His Contexts*. New York: AMS Press 1989.
Fisher, Alan S. "An End to the Renaissance: Erasmus, Hobbes, and *A Tale of a Tub*." *HLQ* 38 (1974): 1–20.
- "Swift's Verse Portraits: A Study of His Originality as an Augustan Satirist." *SEL* 14 (1974): 343–56.
Fitzgerald, Robert P. "Swift's Immortals: The Satiric Point." *SEL* 24 (1984): 483–95.
Folkenflik, Robert. "Tom Jones, the Gypsies, and the Masquerade." *UTQ* 44 (1975): 224–37.
- "'The Author's Farce' and 'Othello.'" *N&Q* 221 (1976): 163–4.
- "'Homo Alludens' in the Eighteenth Century." *Criticism* 24 (1982): 218–32.
Forcione, Alban K. *Cervantes and the Humanist Vision: A Study of Four "Exemplary Novels."* Princeton: Princeton University Press 1982.
Forsgren, A. *Gay: A Poet of a Lower Order*. Stockholm: Natur och Kultur 1971.
Foucault, Michel. *Madness and Civilization: A History of Insanity in the Age of Reason*. Trans. Richard Howard. New York: Pantheon Books 1965.
- *The Order of Things*. Trans. anon. New York: Vintage Books 1970.
- "What Is an Author?" in *Textual Strategies*, ed. J.V. Harari. Ithaca: Cornell University Press 1979. 141–60.
Fox, Christopher. "Locke and the Scriblerians: The Discussion of Identity in Early Eighteenth-Century England." *ECS* 16 (1982): 1–25.
- *Locke and the Scriblerians: Identity and Consciousness in Early Eighteenth-Century Britain*. Berkeley: University of California Press 1988.
Foxon, David. *Pope and the Early Eighteenth-Century Book Trade*. Oxford: Clarendon Press 1991.
Fuchs, Jacob. *Reading Pope's Imitations of Horace*. Lewisburg, Pa.: Bucknell University Press 1989.
Fuentes, Carlos. "When Don Quixote Left His Village, The Modern World Began." *New York Times* Book Review Section, 6 Mar. 1986, 15.
Fussell, Paul. *The Rhetorical World of Augustan Humanism: Ethics and Imagery from Swift to Burke*. Oxford: Clarendon Press 1965.
Galinsky, G.K. *Ovid's Metamorphoses: An Introduction to the Basic Aspects*. Oxford: Blackwell 1975.

"Game, Play and Literature." *Yale French Studies* 41 (1968).

Gendre, André. *Humanisme et Folie chez Sebastien Brant, Erasme et Rabelais.* Basel: Helbing & Lichtenhahn 1978.

Gibbon, Edward. *Memoirs of My Life.* London: Nelson 1966.

Glenn, Edgar M. *The Metamorphoses: Ovid's Roman Games.* Lanham, Md.: University Press of America 1986.

Goggin, L.P. "Fielding's *The Masquerade.*" *PQ* 36 (1957): 475–87.

Goldberg, Homer. "The Interpolated Stories in *Joseph Andrews*, or 'The History of the World in General' Satirically Revised." *MP* 63 (1966): 295–310.

Goldstein, Laurence. *Ruins and Empire: The Evolution of a Theme in Augustan and Romantic Literature.* Pittsburgh: University of Pittsburgh Press 1977.

Gordon, D.J. "The Imagery of Ben Jonson's *The Masque of Blacknesse* and *The Masque of Beautie.*" *JWCI* 6 (1943): 122–41.

– "Poet and Architect: The Intellectual Setting of the Quarrel between Ben Jonson and Inigo Jones." *JWCI* 12 (1949): 152–78.

Greene, Donald. "The Sin of Pride: A Sketch for a Literary Exploration." *New Mexico Quarterly* 34 (1964): 9–30.

– *The Age of Exuberance: Backgrounds to Eighteenth-Century English Literature.* New York: Random House 1970.

Greene, J. Lee. "Fielding's Gypsy Episode and Sancho Panza's Governorship." *South Atlantic Bulletin* 39 (1974): 117–21.

Guérinot, J.V., and Rodney D. Jilg, eds. *The Beggar's Opera.* Hamden, Conn.: Archon 1976.

Hagstrum, Jean H. *The Sister Arts.* Chicago: University of Chicago Press 1948.

– *Sex and Sensibility: Ideal and Erotic Love from Milton to Mozart.* Chicago: University of Chicago Press 1980.

Halsband, Robert. *The Rape of the Lock and Its Illustrations: 1714–1896.* Oxford: Oxford University Press 1980.

Hammond, Brean S. *Pope and Bolingbroke: A Study of Friendship and Influence.* Columbia: University of Missouri Press 1984.

– "Scriblerian Self-Fashioning." *YES* 18 (1988): 108–24.

Hammond, Eugene R. "In Praise of Wisdom and the Will of God: Erasmus' *Praise of Folly* and Swift's *A Tale of a Tub.*" *SP* 80 (1983): 253–76.

Harpham, Geoffrey G. *On the Grotesque: Strategies of Contradiction in Art and Literature.* Princeton: Princeton University Press 1982.

Harries, Elizabeth W. "Sterne's Novels: Gathering Up the Fragments." *ELH* 49 (1982): 35–49.

Harris, Kathryn M. "'Occasions so Few': Satire as a Strategy of Praise in Swift's Early Odes." *MLQ* 31 (1970): 22–37.

Hart, Jeffrey. *Viscount Bolingbroke: Tory Humanist*. London: Routledge & Kegan Paul 1965.

Hayley, R.L. "The Scriblerians and the South Sea Bubble: A Hit by Cibber." *RES* 24 (1973): 452–8.

Hedges, William. "Knickerbocker, Bolingbroke and the Fiction of History." *JHI* 20 (1959): 317–28.

Hibbard, George. "The Country House Poem of the Seventeenth Century." *JWCI* 19 (1956): 159–74.

Higgins, Ian. "Swift and Sparta: The Nostalgia of 'Gulliver's Travels.'" *MLR* 78 (1983): 513–31.

Hind, George. "Mandeville's *Fable of the Bees* as Menippean Satire." *Genre* 1 (1968): 307–15.

Hoilman, Dennis R. "Pope's *An Essay on Man*, IV, 195–6." *PQ* 50 (1971): 308–9.

Holquist, Michael. "How To Play Utopia: Some Brief Notes on the Distinctiveness of Utopian Fiction." *Yale French Studies* 41 (1968): 106–23.

Householder, F.W. *Literary Quotation and Allusion in Lucian*. New York: King's Crown Press 1941.

Howard, William J. "The Mystery of the Cibberian *Dunciad*." *SEL* 8 (1968): 463–74.

Howes, Alan B. "Laurence Sterne, Rabelais and Cervantes: the Two Kinds of Laughter in *Tristram Shandy*." In *Laurence Sterne: Riddles and Mysteries*, ed. Valerie Grosvenor Myer. London: Vision Press 1984. 39–56.

Hughes, Derek. *Dryden's Heroic Plays*. London: Macmillan 1981.

Huizinga, Johan. *Homo Ludens: A Study of the Play Element in Culture*. Beacon Press 1962.

Hume, Robert D. *Henry Fielding and the London Theatre, 1728–1737*. Oxford: Clarendon Press 1988.

Hunt, John Dixon and Peter Willis, eds. *The Genius of the Place: The English Landscape Garden, 1620–1820*. New York: Harper & Row 1975.

– "Theatres, Gardens, and Garden-theatres." *Essays and Studies* 33 (1980): 95–118.

Hunter, J. Paul. "Response as Reformation: *Tristram Shandy* and the Art of Interruption." *Novel* 4 (1971): 132–46.

– *Occasional Form: Henry Fielding and the Chains of Circumstance*. Baltimore: Johns Hopkins University Press 1975.

– *Before Novels: The Cultural Contexts of Eighteenth-Century English Fiction*. New York: Norton, 1990.

Impey, Oliver, and Arthur MacGregor. *The Origins of Museums: The Cabinet of Curiosities in Sixteenth- and Seventeenth-Century Europe*. Oxford: Clarendon Press 1985.

Irving, W.H. *John Gay: Favourite of the Wits*. 1940. New York: Russell & Russell 1962.
Irwin, W.R. "Swift the Verse Man." *PQ* 54 (1975): 222–38.
Jackson, Heather J. "The Anatomy of Melancholy in England, 1750–1800." PhD, University of Toronto 1973.
– "Sterne, Burton, and Ferriar: Allusions to the *Anatomy of Melancholy* in Volumes Five to Nine of *Tristram Shandy*." *PQ* 54 (1975): 457–470.
Jacques, David. "The Art and Sense of the Scribblerus Club in England, 1715–35." *Garden History* 4 (1976): 30–53.
Jarrett, David. *The English Landscape Garden*. New York: Rizzoli International Publications 1978.
Jones, J.R. *Charles II: Royal Politician*. London: Allen & Unwin 1987.
Josipovici, Gabriel. *The World and the Book: A Study of Modern Fiction*. London: Macmillan 1971.
Kaiser, Walter. *Praisers of Folly: Erasmus, Rabelais, Shakes-peare*. Cambridge, Mass.: Harvard University Press 1963.
Kalman, H.D. "Füssli, Pope and the Nightmare." *Pantheon* 29 (1971): 226–36.
Kantorowicz, Ernst. *The King's Two Bodies: A Study in Mediaeval Political Theology*. Princeton: Princeton University Press 1957.
Kayser, W.J. *The Grotesque in Art and Literature*. Trans. Ulrich Weisstein. New York: Columbia University Press 1981.
Keller, Abraham C. *The Telling of Tales in Rabelais: Aspects of His Narrative Art*. Frankfurt-am-Main: V. Klostermann 1963.
– "Stage and Theater in Rabelais." *French Review* 41 (1968): 479–84.
Kelsall, M.M. *The Great Good Place: The Country House and English Literature*. New York: Harvester Wheatsheaf 1993.
Kenny, Virginia C. *The Country-house Ethos in English Literature, 1688–1750*. Sussex: Harvester Press 1984.
Kinahan, Frank. "The Melancholy of Anatomy: Voice and Theme in *A Tale of a Tub*." *JEGP* 69 (1970): 278–91.
Kinsley, William. "The *Dunciad* as Mock-Book." *HLQ* 35 (1971): 29–47.
Kirk, Eugene. "Gay's 'Roving Muse': Problems of Genre and Intention in *Trivia*." *ES* 62 (1981): 259–70.
Klibansky, Raymond, Erwin Panofsky and Fritz Saxl. *Saturn and Melancholy: Studies in the History of Natural Philosophy, Religion and Art*. London: Nelson 1964.
Korkowski, Eugene. "Menippus and His Imitators: A Conspectus up to Sterne for a Misunderstood Genre." PhD, University of California 1973.
Köster, Patricia. "The Political Satire of John Arbuthnot." PhD, University of London 1958.

- "Arbuthnot's Use of Quotation and Parody in His Account of the Sacheverell Affair." *PQ* 48 (1969): 201–11.
- ed. *Arbuthnotiana*. Augustan Reprint Society no. 154. Los Angeles 1972.

Kramnick, Isaac. *Bolingbroke and His Circle: The Politics of Nostalgia in the Age of Walpole*. Cambridge: Harvard University Press 1968.

Kupersmith, William. "Asses, Adages, and the Illustrations in Pope's *Dunciad*." *ECS* 8 (1974–75): 206–11.

LaCharité, Raymond C. *Recreation, Reflection and Re-creation: Perspectives on Rabelais's Pantagruel*. Lexington: University of Kentucky Press 1980.

Lamb, Jonathan. *Sterne's Fiction and the Double Principle*. Cambridge: Cambridge University Press 1989.

Lanham, Richard A. *Tristram Shandy: The Games of Pleasure*. Berkeley: University of California Press 1973.

Lerner, Laurence. *The Uses of Nostalgia: Studies in Pastoral Poetry*. London: Chatto & Windus 1972.

Levine, Joseph. *Dr. Woodward's Shield: History, Science and Satire in Augustan England*. Berkeley: University of California Press 1977.

- *The Battle of the Books: History and Literature in the Augustan Age*. Ithaca, NY: Cornell University Press 1991.

Lewis, C.S. "Addison." In *Essays on the Eighteenth Century Presented to David Nichol Smith in Honour of His Seventieth Birthday*. Oxford: Clarendon Press 1945. 1–14.

Lewis. Peter. "The Three Dramatic Burlesques of Thomas Duffett." *Durham University Journal* 27 (1966): 149–56.

- "Gay's Burlesque Method in *The What D'ye Call It*." *Durham University Journal* 29 (1967): 13–25.
- "Another Look at John Gay's 'The Mohocks.'" *MLR* 63 (1968): 790–3.
- "Dramatic Burlesque in *Three Hours after Marriage*." *Durham University Journal* 33 (1972): 232–9.
- "John Gay's 'Achilles': The Burlesque Element." *Ariel* 3 (1972): 17–28.
- *John Gay: The Beggar's Opera*. London: Edward Arnold 1976.
- "'An Irregular Dog': Gay's Alternative Theatre." *YES* 18 (1988): 231–46.
- ed., with Nigel Wood. *John Gay and the Scriblerians*. London: Vision Press 1988.

Lock, F.P. *The Politics of Gulliver's Travels*. Oxford: Clarendon Press 1980.

- *Swift's Tory Politics*. Newark: University of Delaware Press 1983.

Loftis, John, ed. *Restoration Drama: Modern Essays in Criticism*. New York: Oxford University Press 1966.

Lonsdale, Roger, ed. *Eighteenth-Century Women Poets: An Oxford Anthology*. Oxford: Oxford University Press 1989.

Losse, Deborah. *Rhetoric at Play: Rabelais and Satirical Eulogy.* Bern: Peter Lang 1980.

Lund, Roger. "Martinus Scriblerus and the Search for the Soul." *PLL* 25 (1989): 135–50.

McCue, Daniel L. "Samuel Garth, Physician and Man of Letters." *Bulletin of the New York Academy of Medicine* 53 (1977): 368–402.

McFarland, Thomas. *Romanticism and the Forms of Ruin: Wordsworth, Coleridge and Modalities of Fragmentation.* Princeton: Princeton University Press 1981.

McIntosh, W.A. "Handel, Walpole and Gay: The Aims of *The Beggar's Opera.*" *ECS* 7 (1974): 415–33.

Mack, Maynard. "The Muse of Satire." *Yale Review* 41 (1951): 80–92.

– *The Garden and the City: Retirement and Politics in the Later Poetry of Pope, 1731–1743.* Toronto: University of Toronto Press 1969.

– "Pope's Books: A Biographical Survey with a Finding List." In *English Literature in the Age of Disguise*, ed. Maximilian E. Novak. Berkeley: University of California Press 1977. 209–305.

– and J. Winn, eds. *Pope: Recent Essays by Several Hands.* Hamden, Conn.: Harvester/Shoestring 1980.

– *Collected in Himself: Essays Critical, Biographical and Bibliographical on Pope and Some of His Contemporaries.* Newark: University of Delaware Press 1982.

– *The Last and Greatest Art: Some Unpublished Poetical Manuscripts of Alexander Pope.* Newark: University of Delaware Press 1984.

– *Alexander Pope: A Life.* New York: Norton 1985.

MacLean, Kenneth. *John Locke and English Literature of the Eighteenth Century.* 1936. Rpt New York: Russell & Russell 1962.

McLuhan, H. Marshall. "Thomas Nashe and the Learning of His Time." PhD, Cambridge 1943.

McMaster, Juliet. "Walter Shandy, Sterne, and Gender: A Feminist Foray." *English Studies in Canada* 15 (1989): 441–58.

McWhir, Anne. "The Wolf in the Fold: John Gay in *The Shepherd's Week* and *Trivia.*" *SEL* 23 (1983): 413–23.

Malins, Edward, and the Knight of Glin. "Landscape Gardening by Jonathan Swift and His Friends in Ireland." *Garden History* 2 (1973):

Mancing, Howard. "Cide Hamete Benengali vs. Miguel de Cervantes: The Metafictional Dialectic of *Don Quijote.*" *Cervantes* 1 (1981): 63–81.

– *The Chivalric World of "Don Quijote": Style, Structure and Narrative Technique.* Columbia: University of Missouri Press 1982.

Manning, Susan L. "Mirth and Melancholy: The Generative Language of Fantasy in Swift and Smart." *Swift Studies* 7 (1992): 54–68.

Martin, Peter E. *Pursuing Innocent Pleasures: The Gardening World of Alexander Pope*. Hamden, Conn.: Archon 1984.

Martindale, Charles. "Sense and Sensibility: The Child and the Man in 'The Rape of the Lock.'" MLR 78 (1983): 273–84.

Mecziems, Jenny. "The Unity of Swift's *Voyage to Laputa*: Structure as Meaning in Utopian Fiction." MLR 72 (1977): 1–21.

Mell, Donald C., Jr. "Irony, Poetry and Swift: Entrapment in 'On Poetry: A Rapsody.'" PLL 18 (1982): 310–24.

Mengel, Elias F. "The *Dunciad* Illustrations." ECS 7 (1973): 45, 161–78.

Miller, Henry Knight. "The Paradoxical Encomium with Special Reference to Its Vogue in England, 1600–1800." MP 53 (1956): 145–78.

– *Essays on Fielding's Miscellanies: A Commentary on Volume One*. Princeton: Princeton University Press 1961.

Miller, R.A. "Regal Hunting: Dryden's Influence on *Windsor-Forest*." ECS 13 (1979): 169–88.

Mortier, Roland. *La Poétique des ruines en France: ses origines, ses variations de la Renaissance à Victor Hugo*. Geneva: Librairie Droz 1974.

Needler, Howard I. "Of Truly Gargantuan Proportions: From the Abbey of Thélème to the Androgynous Self." UTQ 51 (1982): 221–47.

Neill, Michael. "Monuments and Ruins as Symbols in *The Duchess of Malfi*." *Themes in Drama* 4 (1982): 71–87.

Nelson, Lowry Jr. *Cervantes: A Collection of Critical Essays*. Englewood Cliffs, NJ: Prentice-Hall 1969.

New, Melvyn. "Sterne's Rabelaisian Fragment: A Text from the Holograph Manuscript." PMLA 87 (1972): 1083–92.

Nichols, Frederick Doveton, and Ralph E. Griswold. *Thomas Jefferson: Landscape Architect*. Charlottesville: University Press of Virginia 1978.

Noble, Yvonne. "Sex and Gender in Gay's *Achilles*." In *John Gay and the Scriblerians*, ed. Peter Lewis and Nigel Wood. London: Vision Press 1988. 184–215.

Nokes, David. *Jonathan Swift: A Hypocrite Revers'd*. Oxford: Oxford University Press 1985.

– *Raillery and Rage: A Study of Eighteenth-Century Satire*. New York: St Martin's Press 1987.

Novak, Maximilian, ed. *English Literature in the Age of Disguise*. Berkeley: University of California Press 1977.

Oakleaf, David. "Solitary Voices." PhD, University of Toronto 1977.

– "'Sliding Down Together': Fielding, Addison, and the Pleasures of the Imagination." *English Studies in Canada*, 9 (1983): 402–17.

– "*Trompe l'Oeil*: Gulliver and the Distortions of the Observing Eye." *UTQ* 53 (1983): 166–80.
O'Loughlin, Michael. *The Garlands of Repose: The Literary Celebration of Civic and Retired Leisure.* Chicago: University of Chicago Press 1978.
Ong, Walter J. *Ramus, Method and the Decay of Dialogue: From the Art of Discourse to the Art of Reason.* Cambridge, Mass.: Harvard University Press 1958.
– *The Barbarian Within, and Other Fugitive Essays and Studies.* New York: Macmillan 1962.
– "Swift on the Mind: Satire in a Closed Field." In *Rhetoric, Romance, and Technology: Studies in the Interaction of Expression and Culture.* Ithaca, NY: Cornell University Press 1971. 190–212.
– *Interfaces of the Word: Studies in the Evolution of Consciousness and Culture.* Ithaca, NY: Cornell University Press 1977.
O'Shaughnessy, Toni-Lynn. "A Single Capacity in *The Beggar's Opera*." *ECS* 21 (1987): 212–27.
Ostovich, Helen. "Reader as Hobby-horse in *Tristram Shandy*." *PQ* 68 (1989): 325–42.
Otis, Brooks. *Ovid as an Epic Poet.* Cambridge: Cambridge University Press 1966.
Owen, Joan H. "*Polly* and the Choice of Virtue." *Bulletin of the New York Public Library* 77 (1974): 393–406.
Panofsky, Erwin. "*Et in Arcadia Ego*: Poussin and the Elegiac Tradition." In *Meaning in the Visual Arts: Papers in and on Art History.* New York: Doubleday 1955. 295–320.
Parr, James A. *Don Quixote: An Anatomy of Subversive Discourse.* Newark, Del.: Juan de la Cuestra 1988.
Patterson, Annabel M. *Pastoral and Ideology: Virgil to Valery.* Oxford: Clarendon Press 1988.
Paulson, Ronald. *Theme and Structure in Swift's Tale of a Tub.* New Haven: Yale University Press 1960.
– *Hogarth: His Life, Art and Times.* 2 vols. New Haven: Yale University Press 1971.
Pease, A.S. "Things without Honour." *Classical Philology* 21 (1926): 27–42.
Pettit, Alexander. "Anxiety, Political Rhetoric, and Historical Drama under Walpole." In *1650–1850: Ideas, Aesthetics, and Inquiries in the Early Modern Era*, ed. Kevin L. Cope, 1 (1994): 109–36.
Poggioli, Renato. *The Oaten Flute: Essays on Pastoral and the Pastoral Ideal.* Cambridge, Mass.: Harvard University Press, 1975.

Pollak, Ellen. *The Poetics of Sexual Myth: Gender and Ideology in the Verse of Swift and Pope.* Chicago: University of Chicago Press 1985.
Pons, Emile. "Les Langues imaginaires dans le voyage utopique. Un précurseur: Thomas Morus." *Revue de Littérature Comparée* 10 (1930): 589–607.
Porter, Roy, ed. *The Enlightenment in National Context.* Cambridge: Cambridge University Press 1981.
Poulet, Georges. *Les Métamorphoses du Cercle.* Paris: Plon 1961.
Price, Martin. *Swift's Rhetorical Art.* New Haven: Yale University Press 1953.
Quintana, Ricardo. "*The Rape of the Lock* as a Comedy of Continuity." *Review of English Literature* 7 (1966): 9–19.
Rawson, C.J. "Parnell's Night-piece on Death." *N&Q* 206 (1961): 50–1.
– *Henry Fielding and the Augustan Ideal under Stress: 'Nature's Dance of Death' and Other Studies.* London: Routledge & Kegan Paul 1972.
– *Gulliver and the Gentle Reader: Studies in Swift and Our Time.* London: Routledge & Kegan Paul 1973.
– "Order and Misrule: Eighteenth-Century Literature in the 1970's." *ELH* 42 (1975), 471–505.
– "Pope's Wasteland: Reflections on Mock-Heroic." *Essays and Studies* 35 (1982): 45–65.
– ed. *The Character of Swift's Satire: A Revised Focus.* Newark: University of Delaware Press 1983.
– *Order from Confusion Sprung: Studies in Eighteenth-Century Literature from Swift to Cowper.* London: Allen & Unwin 1985.
Rees, John O. Jr. "'A Great Man in Distress': Macheath as Hercules." *Univ. of Colorado Studies in Language and Literature* 10 (1966): 73–7.
Riley, E.C. "Cervantes and the Cynics." *Bulletin of Hispanic Studies* 53 (1976): 189–99.
Rivero, Albert. *The Plays of Henry Fielding: A Critical Study of His Dramatic Career.* Charlottesville: University Press of Virginia 1989.
Robert, Marthe. *The Old and the New: From "Don Quixote" to Kafka.* Trans. Carol Cosman. Foreword Robert Alter. Berkeley: University of California Press 1977.
Robinson, Christopher. *Lucian and His Influence in Europe.* Chapel Hill: University of North Carolina Press 1979.
Rogers, Pat. "Satiric Allusions in John Gay's Welcome to Mr. Pope." *PLL* 10 (1974): 427–32.
Rogers, Patrick. "Dating 'Acis and Galatea.'" *Musical Times* 114 (1973): 792.
Rosenmeyer, Thomas G. *The Green Cabinet: Theocritus and the European Pastoral Lyric.* Berkeley: University of California Press 1969.

Ross, Angus M. "The Correspondence of Dr. John Arbuthnot." PhD, Cambridge 1956.
Rosslyn, Felicity. "'Awed by Reason': Pope on Achilles." *Cambridge Quarterly* 9 (1980): 189–202.
Rothstein, Eric. *Restoration Tragedy: Form and the Process of Change*. Madison: University of Wisconsin Press 1967.
– "The Framework of Shamela." *ELH* 35 (1968): 381–402.
– *Systems of Order and Inquiry in Later Eighteenth-Century Fiction*. Berkeley: University of California Press 1975.
– "'Ideal Presence' and the '*Non-Finito*' in Eighteenth-Century Aesthetics." *ECS* 9 (1976): 307–32.
Rudolph, Valerie C. "People and Puppets: Fielding's Burlesque of the 'Recognition Scene' in *The Author's Farce*." *PLL* 11 (1975): 31–8.
Rumbold, Valerie. *Women's Place in Pope's World*. Cambridge: Cambridge University Press 1989.
Said, Edward W. "Swift's Tory Anarchy." *ECS* 3 (1969): 48–66.
– "Molestation and Authority in Narrative Fiction." In *Aspects of Narrative*, ed. J. Hillis Miller. New York: Columbia University Press 1971. 47–88.
Sambrook, A.J. "The English Lord and the Happy Husbandman." *Studies in Voltaire and the Eighteenth Century* 57 (1967): 1357–75.
Sams, H.W. "Anti-Stoicism in Seventeenth- and Early Eighteenth-Century England." *SP* 41 (1944): 65–78.
Schiff, Gert. *Johann Heinrich Füssli, 1741–1825*. Zurich: Verlag Berichthaus 1973.
Schonhorn, Manuel. "Fielding's Digressive-Parodic Artistry: *Tom Jones* and the Man of the Hill." *Texas Studies in Language and Literature* 10 (1968): 207–14.
Scott, K. "Humour at the Expense of the Ruler Cult." *Classical Philology* 27 (1932): 317–28.
Screech, M.A. *The Rabelaisian Marriage: Aspects of Rabelais's Religion, Ethics and Comic Philosophy*. London: Edward Arnold 1958.
– "Some Reflexions on the *Abbey of Thelema*." *Études Rabelaisiennes* 8 (1969): 109–14.
– *Rabelais*. London: Duckworth 1979.
– *Ecstasy and the Praise of Folly*. London: Duckworth 1980.
– *Montaigne and Melancholy: The Wisdom of the Essays*. London: Duckworth 1983.
Seidel, Michael. *Satiric Inheritance: Rabelais to Sterne*. Princeton: Princeton University Press 1979.
– "Satire and Metaphoric Collapse: The Bottom of the Sublime." In *Satire in the Eighteenth Century*, ed. J.D. Browning. New York: Garland Press 1983. 16–23.

Sessoms, Henry M. "The Art of Scriblerian Satire." PhD, Vanderbilt 1968.

Sewell, Elizabeth. *The Orphic Voice: Poetry and Natural History.* London: Routledge & Kegan Paul 1961.

Shankman, Steven. *Pope's Iliad: Homer in the Age of Passion.* Princeton: Princeton University Press 1983.

Shearer, Ellen B. "Ovid and Scriblerus: An Exploration of Techniques and Themes from the Metamorphoses of Ovid in the Works of Pope, Swift, Gay, Arbuthnot, and Parnell." PhD, University of Toronto 1980.

Sherbo, Arthur. "Virgil, Dryden, Gay, and Matters Trivial." *PMLA* 85 (1970): 1063–71.

Sherburn, George. "Errors Concerning the Houyhnhnms." *MP* 56 (1958): 92–7.

– *The Early Career of Alexander Pope.* 1934. Rpt New York: Russell & Russell 1963.

Shesgreen, Sean. *Hogarth and the Times-of-the-Day Tradition.* Ithaca, NY: Cornell University Press 1983.

Sillars, S.J. "Musical Iconography in *The Beggar's Opera.*" *British Journal for Eighteenth-Century Studies* 1 (1978): 182–5.

Sitter, John. *Literary Loneliness in Mid-Eighteenth-Century England.* Ithaca, NY: Cornell University Press 1982.

– *Arguments of Augustan Wit.* Cambridge: Cambridge University Press 1991.

Sloman, Judith. *Dryden: The Poetics of Translation.* Toronto: University of Toronto Press 1985.

Smith, D.F., and M.L. Lawlor. *Plays about the Theatre in England, 1737–1800.* London, 1979.

Smith, Frederik N. *Language and Reality in Swift's "Tale of a Tub."* Columbus: Ohio State University Press 1979.

– *The Genres of Gulliver's Travels.* Newark: University of Delaware Press 1990.

Spacks, Patricia. *John Gay.* New York: Twayne 1965.

Stack, Frank. *Pope and Horace: Studies in Imitation.* Cambridge: Cambridge University Press 1985.

Stafford, Barbara Maria. "'Illiterate Monuments': The Ruin as Dialect or Broken Classic." In *The Age of Johnson*, ed. Paul Korshin. New York: AMS Press 1987. 1–34.

Steensma, Robert C. *Dr. John Arbuthnot.* Boston: Twayne 1979.

Steeves, Edna L., ed. *The Art of Sinking in Poetry: Martinus Scriblerus' Peri Bathous.* New York: King's Crown Press, 1952.

Steig, Michael. "Defining the Grotesque: An Attempt at Synthesis." *Journal of Aesthetics and Art Criticism* 29 (1970): 253–60.

Stroup, T.B. "Gay's *Mohocks* and Milton." *JEGP* 46 (1947): 164–7.

Summerson, Sir John. "The Classical Country House in Eighteenth-Century England." *Journal of the Royal Society of Arts* 107 (1959): 539–87.

Swearingen, James. *Reflexivity in "Tristram Shandy": An Essay in Phenomenological Criticism.* New Haven: Yale University Press 1977.

Telle, E.V. *Erasme de Rotterdam et le Septième Sacrement: Étude d'évangélisme matrimonial au XVIᵉ siècle et contribution à la biographie intellectuelle d'Erasme.* Genève: Libraire E. Droz 1954.

Thompson, Craig. *The Translations of Lucian by Erasmus and St. Thomas More.* Ithaca, NY: Cornell University Press 1940.

Thompson, James. "Reading and Acting in *Love for Love*." *Essays in Literature* 7 (1980): 21–30.

Thomson, Philip. *The Grotesque.* London: Methuen 1972.

Traugott, John. "A Voyage to Nowhere with Thomas More and Jonathan Swift: *Utopia* and *The Voyage to the Houyhnhnms*." *Sewanee Review* 69 (1961): 534–65.

Trowbridge, H. "Pope, Gay and *The Shepherd's Week*." *MLQ* 5 (1944): 79–88.

Ullman, Pierre L. "Romanticism and Irony in *Don Quixote*: A Continuing Controversy." *PLL* 17 (1981): 320–33.

Varey, Simon. "John Gay: A Contribution to *The Craftsman*." *Etudes anglaises* 29 (1976): 579–82.

Vieth, David M. "Toward an Anti-Aristotelian Poetic: Rochester's *Satyr Against Mankind* and *Artemisia to Chloe*, with Notes on Swift's *Tale of a Tub* and *Gulliver's Travels*." *Language and Style* 5 (1972): 123–45.

Wagner, Peter. "Hogarth's Graphic Palimpsests: Intermedial Adaptation of Popular Literature." *Word and Image* 7 (1991): 329–47.

Walsh, P.G. *The Roman Novel: The 'Satyricon' of Petronius and the 'Metamorphoses' of Apuleius.* Cambridge: Cambridge University Press 1970.

Wasserman, Earl. *Pope's Epistle to Bathurst: A Critical Reading, with An Edition of the Manuscripts.* Baltimore: Johns Hopkins University Press 1960.

– "The Limits of Allusion in *The Rape of the Lock*." *JEGP* 65 (1966): 425–44.

– *The Subtler Language.* Baltimore: Johns Hopkins University Press 1968.

Watson, Sheila. "Swift and Ovid: The Development of Metasatire." *Open Letter*, 3rd. ser., 1 (1974–75): 139–50.

Webber, Joan. *The Eloquent I: Style and Self in Seventeenth-Century Prose.* Madison: University of Wisconsin Press 1968.

Weinbrot, Howard D. "Chastity and Interpolation: Two Aspects of *Joseph Andrews*." *JEGP* 69 (1970): 14–31.

– *Augustus Caesar in 'Augustan' England.* Princeton: Princeton University Press 1978.

- "'An Ambition to Excell': The Aesthetics of Emulation in the Seventeenth and Eighteenth Centuries." *HLQ* 48 (1985): 121–39.
- *18th Century Satire: Essays on Text and Context from Dryden to Peter Pindar.* Cambridge: Cambridge University Press 1988.
- *Britannia's Issue: The Rise of British Literature from Dryden to Ossian.* New York: Cambridge University Press 1993.

Wellek, René, ed. *William Warburton, 1698–1799.* New York: Garland 1978.

Wicks, Ulrich. "Metafiction in *Don Quixote*: What is the Author Up To?" In *Approaches to Teaching Cervantes' "Don Quixote,"* ed. Richard Bjornson. New York: MLA 1984. 69–76.

Williams, Aubrey. *Pope's Dunciad: A Study of Its Meaning.* Baton Rouge: Louisiana State University Press 1955.

Wills, Garry. *Inventing America: Jefferson's Declaration of Independence.* New York: Random House 1979.

Wimsatt, W.K. Jr. *The Portraits of Alexander Pope.* New Haven: Yale University Press 1965.
- "Rhetoric and Poems: The Example of Pope." In *The Author and His Works*, ed. Louis L. Martz and Aubrey Williams. New Haven: Yale University Press 1978. 229–44.

Wind, Edgar. "Two Notes on the Cult of Ruins: (i) Ruins and Echoes; (ii) Utopian Ruins." *JWCI* 1 (1937–38): 259–60.

Winnicott, D.W. *Playing and Reality.* New York: Basic Books 1971.
- *Home Is Where We Start From.* New York: Norton 1986.

Winton, Calhoun. *John Gay and the London Theatre.* Lexington: University Press of Kentucky 1993.

Wolf, William D. *The Reform of the Fallen World: The "Virtuous Prince" in Jonsonian Tragedy and Comedy.* Salzburg: Institut für Englische Sprache und Literatur 1973.

Woodbridge, Kenneth. "Bolingbroke's Chateau de La Source." *Garden History* 4 (1976): 88–109.
- "Iconographic Variations: Classical and Gothic Themes in the English Landscape Garden in the 18th Century." *Lotus International* 30 (1981): 11–27.

Woodman, Thomas. "Parnell, Politeness and Pre-Romanticism." *Essays in Criticism* 33 (1983): 205–19.

Yoch, James J. "Architecture as Virtue: The Luminous Palace from Homeric Dream to Stuart Propaganda." *SP* 75 (1978): 403–29.

Zimmerman, Everett. "Swift's Scatological Poetry: A Praise of Folly." *MLQ* 48 (1987): 124–44.

Index

Addison, Joseph, 9, 63, 118; in the *Dunciad* index, 121–3; on Locke, 133–4; on Ovid and Virgil, 83, 85; *Spectator*, 83–4, 87
Allusion, 111, 127
Allworthy, Thomas, 20, 59–61, 99; to be succeeded by Thomas Jones, 89
Alpers, Paul, 20, 24, 26, 41
Anne, Queen, 3, 28
Apuleius, 4, 80, 85, 100, 129
Arbuthnot, John, 3; *Argument for Providence*, 7; *Art of Political Lying*, 56; *Essay concerning the Effects of Air on Human Bodies*, 7, 20; *Gnothi Seauton*, 69; "Of the Hazards of the Game," 15, 41; *The History of John Bull*, 12, 23, 40–1, 50, 56, 61, 110, 114; *Mercat Cross Sermon*, 28–9; *Stradling versus Stiles*, 51, 133; *Tables and Measures*, 45–6, 49
– his children and his papers, 71; need for reissue of less well-known works, 7; pastoral, 41; proposes a manner of correspondence, 16; a slouch in his walk, 10; Swift on, 10

Barker, Arthur E., 7–136
Barth, John, 106, 135
Barthelme, Donald, 135
Bathurst, Allen, Lord, 28, 30, 46, 59, 70
Beam, Marjorie, 69, 143n23
Beckett, Samuel: *Happy Days*, 136; *Waiting for Godot*, 103
Bedlam, 8
Bolingbroke, Henry St John, 3, 9, 30–9, 51; on Cervantes, 105; *Idea of a Patriot King*, 31–9, 44, 91, 92, 93; *Letters on History*, 38; *Remarks on the History of England*, 32; sets Pope to imitate Horace, 9
Bounce, 50, 85, 97; *see also* Harley
Bowden, Martha F., 61, 105, 142n8, 147n7
Boyd, Brian, 57
Bredvold, Louis, 63
Brothers Club, 3
Brückmann, Elisabeth, *passim*
Bunyan, John, 60, 70, 96
Burke, Edmund, 93
Burlington, Richard Boyle, 21–2, 59; shining palace, 90
Burton, Robert, 61–4, 131

Carr, Patrick L., 16
Castle, Terry, on Houyhnhnms, 109
Cervantes, 4, 68, 72, 100, 103–7, 129

Chambers, Douglas, 57
Chaucer, Geoffrey, 17
Children, 14, 55, 61, 142n69
Cibber, Colley, 13, 88, 124; *The Refusal*, 11
Cobham, Sir Richard Temple, 28, 30, 59, 70
Colie, Rosalie L., 102, 149n41
Congreve, William, 9
Coover, Robert, 135
Corman, Brian, 7–17, 47
Curll, Edmund, 14, 56, 77

Davidson, Susan Kent, xi-xii
Defoe, Daniel, 93; *Journal of the Plague Year*, 59, 90; *Moll Flanders*, 59, 87–8; *Robinson Crusoe*, 59; *Roxana*, 87–8
Dennis, John, 81
Deporte, Michael, 140n29, 147n12
Derrida, Jacques, "Scribble," 8
Dog, 49, 60, 85; see also Bounce and Harley
Donne, John, 70; *Metempsychosis*, 81; *Of Religion*, 37–8
Doody, Margaret A., on charivari, 128
Double Mistress, a Novel, 102
Dryden, John, 38, 45, 81, 97; *Absalom and Achitophel* and Pope's *Odyssey*, 92; *Examen Poeticum*, *Fables*, *Sylvae*, 70; plays, 45
DuGuernier, Louis, illustrations for *The Rape of the Lock*, 82

Dürer, Albrecht: drawing for the Prodigal Son, 96; *Melencolia I*, 61, 84

Elizabeth I, 34
Empson, William, on *The Beggar's Opera*, 45, 46–7
Epistolae Obscurorum Virorum, 77; given by Pope to Swift, 13, 78
Erasmus, Desiderius, 4, 133, 145n38; *Enchiridion Militis Christiani*, 31; Pope leaves his set of the Basel edition to Bolingbroke, 16, 98; Pope's project for a life, 16; *Praise of Folly*, 4, 31, 102, 131; translator of Lucian, 129
Erskine-Hill, Howard, 66, 117

Fabricant, Carole, 51
Families, happy, 16; see also Carr, Patrick
Ferriar, John, 17, 71–2
Fielding, Henry, 93; *Grub-Street Opera*, 100; *Historical Register*, 108; *Jonathan Wild*, 110; *Joseph Andrews*, 23, 60, 84, 86, 88, 101, 103–4, 105–6, 107, 114–15; *Masquerade*, 125; plays, 99–100; praise of absolute monarchy, 135; as Scriblerus Secondus, 14, 23; *Shamela*, 23, 100–1, 118; and theatre, 88; *Tom Jones*, 16, 19–23, 27, 31, 54, 59–61, 87, 88, 99, 108; *Tom Thumb*, 23, 100; "Upon Nothing," 100, 133

Fontenelle, Bernard de, 24–5, 81
Foucault, Michel, on Cervantes, 107
Fox, Christopher, 63, 87, 125
Friendship, 7–17
Füseli, Henry, *The Dream of Belinda*, 82
Fussell, Paul, on Hamlet, 62

Games, 125, 128–9
Garth, Samuel, 6, 26, 81, 132
Gay, John, 3; *Achilles*, 45; *Acis and Galatea*, 65, 83; "Araminta," 65; *Beggar's Opera*, 9, 41, 44, 46–7, 117; *The Captives*, 126; "A Contemplation on *Night*," 65; *Dione*, 42, 65; *The Distress'd Wife*, 13, 43, 66; "Elegiac Epistle," 65; "Epistle to Her Grace Henrietta Dutchess of MARLBOROUGH," 45; "Epistle to Paul Methuen," 43–4; *Fables*, 43, 45, 49, 56, 66, 85, 93, 117; "The Garter," 127; "The Lady's Lamentation," 43; "The Mad Dog," 67–8; *The Mohocks*, 89, dedicated to Dennis, 13; *Newgate's Garland*, 12; "Panthea," 65; *Polly*, 38, 47–8; "Mr. Pope's Welcome from Greece," 12; *The Rehearsal at Goatham*, 12, 68; *Rural Sports*, dedicated to Pope, 9, 51, revised, 42; *The Shepherd's Week*,

dedicated to Bolingbroke, 9, 30, 42, 66, 89, 93, 101, 111, 113–14; format, 119; "A Thought on Eternity," 65; translation of Ovid, 9, 45, 81; *Trivia*, 10–11, 13, 29, 43, 90, 126; "A True Story of an Apparition," 66–7, 70; *The What D'Ye Call It*, 11, 42, 62, 65–6, 117; *Wife of Bath*, 43, 47; *Zerbin and Isabella*, 12
Goldsmith, Oliver, on Parnell's melancholy, 65
Greene, Donald, 8, 48
Greuze, Jean Baptiste, *The Lady with the Dog*, 67
Grotesque, 76, 85–6, 114–16
Grotto, 63–4
Gulliver Decipher'd, 11–12
Gullivers, 128
Gypsies, 21–3, 31, 34, 36, 40, 50, 94, 104, 132

Hagstrum, Jean, 8, 70
Hall-Stevenson, John, *Crazy Castle*, 14
Hamlet, 62, 63, 72, 80; and the *Tale*, 68, 79, 145n60
Harcourt, Simon, 3
Harlequins, 136
Harley, Robert, Earl of Oxford and Mortimer, 3, 10, 97; *see also* Bounce
Harris, Diane, 80
Harris, Jocelyn M., 7–17
Hedges, William, 38
Heroic drama, 74–5
Heroism, in an unheroic age, 123

Hogarth, William, 86, 107–8, 110; *Characters and Caricaturas*, 85–6, 98; *Characters who frequented Button's coffee-house*, 6; *Masquerades and Operas*, 127; *Royal Masquerade*, 58; *Times-of-the-Day*, 115, 127
Hopson, G.H., 145n40
Horses, Swift names one for Bolingbroke, 30, 48, 50
Hospitality, in the *Iliad*, 44
Howard, W.J., 70, 78
Hume, David, 75–6
Hunter, J. Paul, 99
Hyde, Edward, Earl of Clarendon, 92

Indexes: apparently gratuitous, 5; collation, 148–9n26; to *Dunciad* and *Shepherd's Week*, 120–3
Irving, Washington, 38

Jackson, Heather J., on Burton and Sterne, 61
James I, Bolingbroke's dark view of him, 34
Jefferson, Thomas, 31, 38, 92
Job, Swift's birthday reading, 65
Johnson, Samuel, 81; on pastoral, 4; on Pope's *Pastorals*, 26, 89
Jokes, farewell, 149n44
Jonson, Ben, 80, 107, 118, 146n4, 147n13; *Poetaster*, 16, 61, 117
Joyce, James, 135
Juvenal, Jerry, 130

Kantorowicz, Ernst, 31
Kerby-Miller, Charles, 3, 74

Kinsley, William, on *Dunciad* as mock-book, 94
Köster, Patricia, 7, 146n63
Kramnick, Isaac, 9, 34, 37–8

Labyrinth, 56, 57, 59, 89–90, 91, 93
Lamb, Jonathan, 110–11
Lamb, Susan, 111
Landscape, 19, 83
Lansdown, George, 27, 59
Letters of Obscure Men, 131
Levenson, Jill L., 147n10
Lewis, C.S., on Addison, 14
Locke, John, 62–3, 74, 86–7; a new anatomist, 133; *Treatises of Government*, 92
Locus amoenus, 16, 21, 26, 39, 43, 91
London: attraction of Scriblerus to, 89; a bad place, 88
Lucian, 100; *True History*, 4, translated by More and Erasmus, 129–30
Lucian, Lorry, 130

Maccubbin, Robert, 7–17
Machiavelli, Nicolo, 31
Mack, Maynard, 13, 63, 69, 91
MacLean, Kenneth, 8, 137n1, 143n13
McLuhan, Corinne, 146n4
McLuhan, Marshall, 94; doctoral dissertation, 103; manuscript notes on, 139–40n22; on *translatio studii*, 27
McWhir, Anne, 93, 126
Maittaire, Michael, 13; not the editor of the 1710 *Epistolae*, 132

Martial, 16, 80, 117
Marvell, Andrew, 46
Masquerade, 58, 87–9, 109
Medley, 108
Melancholy, 20, 61, 64, 72–3, 144n32
Memoirs of Martinus Scriblerus, 4, 8, 51, 72–6, 87, 101, 114; more important than thought for the Club, 13; Ovidian additions to 81
Metamorphosis, 35, 102, 126, 138n5
Milton, John, 30, 38, 39, 94, 95; in Pope, 141n41; in *Rural Sports*, 42; echoed in *Tom Jones*, 20
Monkeys, 55, 64, 76
Monsters, 76, 78, 91, 128
Monstrosity, and ruin, 75
Montagu, Lady Mary Wortley, 82
More, Thomas, 4, 131, 144n34; only modern among persons of virtue in Swift's *Travels*, 16; translator with Erasmus of Lucian, 129; *Utopia*, 22, 25, 48, 72–3, 104, 130–1; Utopian gardens, 57

Nabokov, Vladimir, 135, 142n69; *Ada*, 57; *Invitation to a Beheading*, 57; *Lolita*, 57; *The Real Life of Sebastian Knight*, 147–8n16; *Speak Memory*, 57
Naboth's Vineyard, 53–5, 96
Nicolson, Marjorie Hope, 79
Novak, Maximilian, 87
Nova Zembla, 78
Novels, not written by Scriblerians, 101

Oakleaf, David, 59, 138n8
Ovid, 80–5, 87, 125–7, 134; allusions in *Three Hours After Marriage*, 80
Owen, Joan, 47

Paine, Thomas, 31
Paradise Hall, 30, 38, 59
Paradox, 102, 130, 131
Parnell, Thomas, 3, 65, 71, 128; "The Book-Worm," 12–13; *Essay on Different Stiles of Poetry*, 96; dedicated to Bolingbroke, 30; "To Mr. Pope," 10, 82; Pope's edition of his *Poems on Several Occasions 1722*, 9; "On Queen Anne's Peace," 31
Pastoral, 39; described, 4; a state of mind, 16; in *Tom Jones*, 20, 89
Patterson, Diana, 148n24
Pepys, Samuel, 90
Philip, James A., 44
Philips, Ambrose, 9, 56, 118
Play, 100, 129, 132, 146n2
Poggioli, Renato, 16, 29, 43, 53–7, 97
Pope, Alexander, 3, 6; *To Bathurst*, 46; echo of Chaucer in lines on Bounce, 97; *Elegy to the Memory of an Unfortunate Lady*, 44, 65; *An Essay on Criticism*, 27, 77, 94; his grotto, 29, 63–4; *Guardian*, 40, 27; his *Homer*, 113; "Lines on Bounce," 97; *Merchant's Tale*, 126; *Pastorals*, 24–7, 32, 36; *Peri Bathous*, 79, 118; poems on Swift's *Travels*, 10, 48, 133; edition of Shakespeare, 63; "To A Lady," 71, 88; Twickenham house and garden, 29; *Works of the Unlearned*, 3
– *The Dunciad*, 8, 64, 66, 70, 87, 89, 93; Advertisement to, 77; dedicated to Swift, 9; Notes Variorum, 11; as theatre, 88; title, 77
– *Eloisa to Abelard*, 44, 70; and melancholy, 65
– *Epistles to Several Persons*, 21–2, 27, 31, 70, 88; Lockean in psychology, 63
– *An Essay on Man*, 9, 49, 64, 69, 95; biblical presence in, 34, 40; echoes from Swift's *Tale*, 12; illustrations for, 96; Lockean, 62; as pastoral, 23, 27, 29, 30, 39, 44, 49
– *Iliad*, 44; on Achilles, 45; city pastoral, 29; on friendship, 14
– *Odyssey*, 44–5, animals in, 49–50
– *The Rape of the Lock*, 28, 55, 67–8, 70, 84, 85, 114, 126; as Ovidian, 81, 125
– *Windsor-Forest*, 36, 60; as pastoral, 27–9, 93
Pope, Alexander, John Arbuthnot, and John Gay, *Three Hours after Marriage*, 11, 75, 79–81,

114, 117–8; motto from Martial, 16
Print, suspected, 109
Prior, Tim, 86
Proto-Scriblerians, 129
Pynchon, Thomas, 135

Quintana, Ricardo, 81–2

Rabelais, Francois, 4, 100, 129, 130–1
Rapin, René, 24–6
Rawson, Claude J., 7, 14, 55, 99
Reuchlin, Johannes, 77, 131–2, 145n38
Richardson, Samuel, 43; *Pamela*, 59, 87–8
Rogers, Pat, 12
Rothstein, Eric, 101
Ruins, 61, 63, 69, 75, 78, 88, 91, 96, 127, 138n2

Salt, not among the horses, 50
Screech, Michael, 149n38
Scriblerians: and allusion, 108, 111, 126–7; children, 55–7, 61; creators of paradox, 102; denial of story, 108, 123; discontinuity, 126–7; dislocation of the reader, 107; displacement, 101; fragment, 110, 124; and format, 119–20; grotesque, 114–16, invoking pastoral, 119; involvement of the reader, 100; linearity of, 106; metamorphosis in, 101, 126m; misogyny of, 70; necessary perception of linkages, 101, 117; as Ovidian, 127; perceived as a group, 10–

13; play with readers, 132; schoolboy humour in, 116–17; sensibilities as secular, 4; silence as the ideal, 51; suspicion of language, 134
Scriblerus, Martinus, 4, 51, 91
Seneca, 34; *Apokolyntosis*, 4, 32
Sewell, Elizabeth, on Ovid, 80, 85
Shearer, Ellen, 145n44, 149n31
Sherburn, George, troubled by Pope, 14
Shining palace, 20, 57
Simplicity, 56
Sloman, Judith, 70
Smart, Christopher, 97, 146n69
Smollett, Tobias, *Humphry Clinker*, 44, 76, 112
Sneddon, Scott, 86
Solitude, 20, 75–6
Spence, Joseph, 83
Spenser, Edmund, 118; *Shepherd's Calendar*, 26
Sterne, Laurence, 17, 23; at Crazy Castle, 14; *Political Romance*, 110; *Tristram Shandy*, 38, 56, 59, 60, 60–3, 71, 79, 80, 82, 89, 110–13, 131–3
Stowe, 30, 38; plan of house and gardens, 18
Sublime, 20; in *Windsor-Forest* and *The Rape of the Lock*, 28
Swift, Jonathan, founder of the Scriblerus Club: his gardens, 51–5; on love and women, 70; his sense of the Club, 10; on Thomas More,

131; on violent friendship, 14
– "An Apology to the Lady C—R—T," 52; "A Beautiful Young Nymph Going to Bed," 70, 77, 88; "A Character, Panegyric and Description of the Legion Club," 127; *Contests and Dissensions*, 112; early poetry, 112; *Enquiry into the Behaviour of the Queen's Last Ministry*, 30; "An Epistle upon an Epistle," 52. *Four Last Years of the Queen*, 30, 46, 89; *Journal to Stella*, 56, 71, 113; "My Lady's Lamentation," 52; poems to Stella, 71, 95, 112; *Proposal for the English Tongue*, 112; *Sermons*, 96; *A Tale of a Tub*, 3, 15, 66, 73, 76, 78, 79, 89, 101, 107, 109; Tale-teller as theatrical, 88; *Verses on the Death of Dr. Swift*, 97
– *Travels into Several Remote Nations of the World*, 48–9, 51, 71, 73, 76, 78; fourth book as pastoral, 23; as Ovidian, 84; title, 116, 127

Temple, Richard, Viscount Cobham, plan of house and gardens at Stowe, 18
Terence, 33
Text as text, 132
Theatricality, 62, 64, 80, 85, 88, 90, 109, 124;

Hamlet, 125, 136
  related to masquerades, 124
Theobald, Lewis, 27, 148n26
Thomson, James, 92
Tiger, Virginia, 15, 44
Tillotson, Geoffrey, 82
Translatio studii, 27, 103
Trumbull, Sir William, 26, 59

Umbrellas, 136
Uncertainty, 117

Vieth, David, 135–6
Virgil, 27, 32, 36, 53;
  Aeneid, Georgics, 37
von Hutten, Ulrich, 77–8, 102, 132

Walmsley, Peter, 7–17
Walpole, Sir Robert, 92
Walsh, William, 24, 26, 118
Warburton, William, 74;
  Divine Legation of Moses, 8
Watson, Sheila, 83–4

Weinbrot, Howard, 7–17, 60
Williams, Aubrey, 70, 103
Wilson, Milton, 7–17
Wimsatt, W.K., Jr., 8, 63
Wizard, last item in *Dunciad* index, 123
Wordsworth, William, *The Prelude*, 40, 90–1
Wycherley, William, 24, 26

Yoch, James: no cities in masque machinery, 90; on shining palaces, 20